Cultural Orientation
An Approach to Understanding
Intercultural Communication

George A. Borden
Fulbright Scholar to
Panamá and Central America

Prentice Hall
Englewood Cliffs, New Jersey 07632

Library of Congress Cataloging-in-Publication Data

Borden, George A.
    Cultural orientation : an approach to understanding intercultural
  communication / George A. Borden.
        p.   cm.
    Includes bibliographical references.
    ISBN 0-13-946104-3
    1. Intercultural communication.   I. Title.
  GN345.6.B67 1991
  303.48'2--dc20   90-6974
                                                                    CIP

Editorial/production supervision: Betti T. Knapp
Cover design: Wanda Lubelska
Manufacturing Buyer: Ed O'Dougherty

© 1991 by Prentice-Hall, Inc.
A Division of Simon & Schuster
Englewood Cliffs, New Jersey 07632

Printed in the United States of America
10 9 8 7 6 5 4 3 2 1

ISBN 0-13-946104-3

Prentice-Hall International (UK) Limited, *London*
Prentice-Hall of Australia Pty. Limited, *Sydney*
Prentice-Hall Canada, *Toronto*
Prentice-Hall Hispanamericana, S.A., *Mexico*
Prentice-Hall of India Private Limited, *New Delhi*
Prentice-Hall of Japan, Inc., *Tokyo*
Simon & Schuster Asia Pte. Ltd., *Singapore*
Editora Prentice-Hall do Brasil, Ltda., *Rio de Janeiro*

Text Credits

Pp. 26, 149, and 150—Tables 1, 9, and 10, and p. 33, Figure 3, Borden, G. A. 1985. *Human Communication Systems*. Boston: American Press. Reprinted by permission of the publisher. ; pp. 54, 84–93, 157, 158, 163–168, 192—Glenn, E. S. *Man and Mankind*, Norwood, N.J.: ABLEX Publishing Corp., 1981. Reprinted by permission of the publisher.; pp. 62, 63—from "Social Cognition and Social Perception," reproduced with permission from the *Annual Review of Psychology*, Volume 38, © 1987 by Annual Reviews, Inc., R. R. Rosenzweig and L. W. Porter, eds.; pp. 179, 180—Table 13 and excerpts, from *Cultural Literacy: What Every American Needs to Know* by E. D. Hirsch. Copyright © 1987 by Houghton Mifflin Company. Reprinted by permission of Houghton Mifflin Company.; pp. 78, 79, 81, and 203—from *Cultural Materialism*.

Marvin Harris, author. © 1979 Random House, Inc., N.Y.; pp. 68–73 and excerpts—from Goldstein, K. M., & Blackman, S. *Cognitive Style: Five Approaches and Relevant Research*. Copyright © 1978 by John Wiley & Sons, Inc., New York. Reprinted by permission of John Wiley & Sons, Inc.; pp. 200–201—excerpts from *Language* by Edward Sapir, copyright 1921 by Harcourt Brace Jovanovich, Inc., and renewed 1949 by Jean V. Sapir, reprinted by permission of Harcourt Brace Jovanovich, Inc.; pp. 47, 145–148, excerpts and Table 8—J. E. Williams and D. L. Best, *Measuring Sex Stereotypes: A Thirty-Nation Study*, pp. 272, 274–275, 277, 278. Copyright © 1982 by

*credits continued on page 240, which constitutes
an extension of the copyright page.*

"What is true is that which appears clearly and distinctly to the mind—not that which is confirmed by observation or by experimental testing of hypotheses."

In memory of

Professor Edmund S. Glenn

friend, gentleman, scholar,
and the epitome of an effective
intercultural communicator.

Contents

Preface   xi

Introduction   xiii

Chapter One   Human Communication: By Definition   1

A Systems Approach   2
     General Systems Theory   3
     Levels of Systems Complexity   5
     Human Communication Systems   6

Defining Human Communication   7

The Human Cybernetic   10
     The Bodily Self   11
     Self-Identity   12
     Self-Extension   12
     Self-Esteem   13
     Self-Image   13

Applications   14

Transition   15

Independent Study   16

Chapter Two   Human Communication Codes   17

Ritualism   18

The Basics   19

Verbal Codes   21
   Information Management   22
   General Semantics   23

Semantics   24
   Semantic Space   24
   Coding Meaning   26

The Nature of Nonverbal Communication   27

The Nonverbal Codes   28
   Artifacts   28
   Personal Appearance   29
   Chromatics   30
   Facial Expression   30
   Oculemics   30
   Kinesics   31
   Haptics   31
   Proxemics   32
   Chronemics   33
   Olfactics   33
   Gustics   34
   Vocalics   34
   Acoustics   35
   Silence   35

Nonverbal Behavior   35

Transition   36

Independent Study   37

Chapter Three   Human Communication: Dimensions and Constraints   38

Dimensions of Human Communication   39

Constraints on Human Communication Systems   40
   The Situational Dimension   41
   The Personal Dimension   43
   The Cultural Dimension   45

Transition   48

Independent Study   49

Chapter Four   Situational Orientations   50

Defining the Situation   51
    Stereotyping   52
    Making Sense   54
    Some Examples   55

Perspective Taking   58

Perception   62

Transition   63

Independent Study   64

Chapter Five   Personal Orientations   65

Cognition   66

Personal Constructs   66

Defining Cognitive Styles   68
    Authoritarianism   69
    Dogmatism   70
    Cognitive Complexity   71
    Integrative Complexity   72
    Field Dependence   73

Cognitive Structure   74

Transition   75

Independent Study   76

Chapter Six   Cultural Orientations   77

Perspectives on Culture   78
    Cultural Materialism   78
    The Evolutionary Perspective   80
    The Cognitive Perspective   81
    Cultural Interpretation   81
    A Taxonomic Perspective   82

Cultural Images   83

Defining the Cultural Orientation Model   84
    Closed-Minded/Open-Minded   87
    Associative-Abstractive   88
    Particularism-Universalism   90

Applications   92

Transition   92

Independent Study   94

Chapter Seven   Cultural Belief Systems   95

Belief Structures   96
Value Structures   98
Values and Ethics   101
Values and Communication   102
A System of Values   103
Transition   106
Independent Study   107

Chapter Eight   Power Distance   108

On Defining Power Distance   109
   Cultural Inequalities   110
   Conflict Management   111
   Environmental Concerns   112
   Types of Power   113
   High and Low Power Distance   114
Cultural Characteristics   115
Transition   117
Independent Study   118
Tentative Questions   118

Chapter Nine   Uncertainty Avoidance   119

Defining Uncertainty Avoidance   120
   Sources of Anxiety   122
   Communication and Uncertainty   125
   High and Low Uncertainty Avoidance   128
Cultural Characteristics   128
Transition   130
Independent Study   130
Tentative Questions   131

Chapter Ten   Individualism/Collectivism   132

Defining Individualism/Collectivism   133
   Locus of Control   136
   Lifestyles   137
   High and Low Individualism   138
Cultural Characteristics   139
Transition   140
Independent Study   140

Chapter Eleven   Masculine/Feminine 142

Defining Masculine/Feminine 143
   Sex-Role Stereotypes 145
   Sex-Trait Stereotypes 146
   Stereotypical Communicative Behavior 149
   Changing Stereotypes 151
   High and Low Masculinity 152
Cultural Characteristics 153
Transition 154
Independent Study 154

Chapter Twelve   Culture and Enculturation 156

An Enculturation Model 156
First Culture Enculturation 159
   Language 160
   Enculturation 163
Transition 168
Independent Study 169

Chapter Thirteen   Cultural Literacy 170

Definitions 170
Language Competence 173
   Verbal 173
   Nonverbal 173
Knowledge 174
   Cultural Symbols 176
   Cultural Knowledge 178
   Cultural Processes 180
Symbolic Interaction 181
Transition 183
Independent Study 183

Chapter Fourteen   Second Culture Acculturation 185

Second Culture Communication 186
Second Culture Learning 187
   Language 187
   Culture 188
A Second Culture Acculturation Model 192
   Cognitive Processes 192
   Visualizing Acculturation 194
Transition 196
Independent Study 197

Chapter Fifteen   Developing Intercultural Understanding   198
Creating Culture   199
The Sapir-Whorf Hypothesis   200
Subjective Culture   204
Communicating Culture   205
Transition   208
Independent Study   209

Chapter Sixteen   Constructs for Understanding
    Intercultural Communication   210
Recapitulation   211
Intercultural Communication Competence   214
Communication Style   216
    Open Style   217
    Dramatic Style   217
    Attentive Style   218
Communication Strategies   219
Independent Study   221

References   222

Author Index   232

Subject Index   235

Preface

Most intercultural communication texts either tell you *about* a culture or cultures, or give you explicit instructions on how to adapt to a specific culture. The readers may go to the culture thinking that they know how to behave because they have learned some of the verbal and/or nonverbal languages used there. This surface knowledge will give them the erroneous feeling of being able to communicate (understand and be understood) with their hosts. Not knowing that similar behaviors may stem from different beliefs (or different behaviors from similar beliefs) causes many intercultural problems. How the beliefs of one culture differ from those of another, and, more importantly, how these belief systems are translated into communicative behaviors are essential to understanding intercultural communication.

Understanding the languages of a culture, both verbal and nonverbal, is extremely important to effective intercultural communication. However, the ease with which one grasps a surface knowledge of a verbal code, and the tendencies we all have for interpreting nonverbal codes according to our own cultural dictionary, make it essential that we understand the interplay between culture and language. Certainly we are interested in knowing the communication codes of a culture so we can communicate fluently. However, of greater importance is an understanding of the cognitive structures which generate the communicative behaviors of a culture. Two cultures may appear to be "saying" the same thing, but because of the differences in their cognitive orientations they may be saying something very different.

The cognitive orientation of a culture is reflected in the interaction between the cognitive structures of its members and their belief and disbelief systems. Thus, a basic question to be answered in this text is: How can we know what a culture's cognitive structures and processes are and what the belief systems are upon which they act? The reader should not expect to be given an equation or algorithm by which he or she can translate beliefs into behaviors. Communication is much too complex for that. What they will be given is an awareness of, and a way of viewing, the differences in the cognitive structures of different cultures. This is the purpose of the Cultural Orientation Model, and it will help one understand intercultural communication. To become a competent intercultural communicator, one must develop one's own communication strategies.

This text does not concentrate on the obvious differences between cultures; rather, it probes for the reasons behind both the obvious and the hidden differences. These reasons are found in the cognitive orientation of a culture and its belief and disbelief systems. Being able to understand these cultural differences and their implications for effective communication gives one an opportunity to communicate more effectively with other cultures. If one can determine the underlying cultural perspective of the communicator from the host culture (and knows one's own), then strategies can be developed to effect authentic communication by understanding each other's communicative behavior and value structures.

A schema is developed that integrates theory with practicality to form a series of constructs that will aid a person in the understanding of another culture and enable him or her to communicate in that culture more effectively. The approach is culture-general with sufficient applications to non-U.S. cultures to make it applicable to the study of any specific culture. Conceptually, it is based on the work of Edmund Glenn, with help from Geert Hofstede, Milton Rokeach, and George Kelly, all within the framework of the author's own systems theory.

This book is biased in favor of theory. It is based on the author's 25 years of university teaching of all aspects of human communication, and his work in the last ten years in Costa Rica, Panamá, Mexico, and Puerto Rico. This has etched on his mind the futility of ethnocentrism and the need to inject some communication theory into the study of intercultural communication. It is hoped that this book will do the same to you.

Many of the quotes in this book are from pre-feminist times. They have not been changed so you can see the cultural change that has taken place in the U.S. in the last 20 years.

There are many people who must be thanked for their help in conceptualizing this book. Foremost are Drs. E. Payson Hall of Radford University, Francisco Escobar of the University of Costa Rica, Greville Rumble of the Open University of England, and Luis González of the University of Panamá. Others include the author's Costa Rican family, the Sanchez: papa Sanchez, mama Rosa, Willie, and Mario; and the Jiménez family, especially Ginnette Sibaja and Cynthia Espinoza.

G.A.B.

Introduction

Do not plan to read this book and be "filled" with its knowledge. The only truths you will find herein are the ones you find by challenging its perspective in light of your own experiences. Unless you become involved with the ideas presented here, they will have no meaning and will leave you poorer than when you came, for you will have spent your time searching for the tree of knowledge rather than cultivating the seeds of truth you have gleaned from your own human experiences. To extend the metaphor, this book should be used as fertilizer to help you grow a better harvest of experiences in intercultural communication.

James Downs (1971) highlighted one of the premises of this book when he said, "one of the greatest stumbling blocks to understanding other peoples within or without a particular culture is the tendency to judge others' behavior by our own standards" (p. 15). As you progress through this book, you will see how many things point to the difficulty of breaking out of our ethnocentric chains. But you cannot do this by just reading and accepting or rejecting what the author has said. You must challenge each point, dialogue about it with your professor, classmates, friends, and acquaintances from cultures other than your own. For this reason the exercises at the end of each chapter are extremely important. They will help you begin to understand other cultures. You will be given some basic human communication constructs with which you can analyze intercultural communication events. This is not an easy task, especially if you are not aware of the cultural constraints within which you must work. You will be given several ways of looking at culture to help you determine how those cultural constraints work and why a cultural orientation is necessary for understanding intercultural communication.

Smith (1979) presents a basic problem of intercultural communication when he writes, "Again and again intercultural communication runs into that hornet's nest, the classification of cultures. When people of one group communicate with people of another group, they need to know what those others are like. To describe and characterize them is to classify them" (p. 1). Stereotypes! Some are good, but most are bad, because we seldom get beyond them in our communication with the stereotyped.

If, however, we know "the relevant features of different groups, and . . . how such features generally relate to one another, (we) may be able to predict the results when the groups interact" (p. 1). The key here is "relevant features." For example, if we take color of skin, social status, or type of sex organ as the relevant features and accept no others, then we have created a stereotype that can interfere with effective communication. On the other hand, each of these may be used as a feature that will allow us to engage in communication processes that will help us develop the knowledge about the other person required for effective human bonding.

The features we will focus on in this text are cognitive as opposed to anatomical or physical. If we can develop a system by which we can understand how the other person approaches life, and we accept the differences and similarities between us, perhaps we can improve our intercultural communication. This should hold true on all levels of communication, from that between individuals to that between nations. But alas, what are the relevant features of a culture, and how shall we expose them once we have discovered what they are?

A structure has been developed for social science research which differentiates between external and internal analyses of systems. These two perspectives are referred to as the *etic* and *emic* approach to cultural analysis. Hall (1986) says that, "each perspective embraces a separate epistemological view point. . . . It is this recognition—of the scientist as an external observer and universal (in intent) sense-maker, and of the behaving human as an internal observer and particular sense-maker—that is the source of Pike's etic-emic distinction" (p. 129). Pike (1966) had first developed this schema in 1954, and it has found its way into nearly all aspects of social science research today.

The etic approach describes cultures from outside and is concerned with cultural comparisons. It is an objective approach with preconceived categories of behaviors (Jones, 1979). The emic approach describes cultures from within and is concerned with descriptions of individual cultures. It is also an objective approach wherein the categories of behavior are allowed to emerge from the collected data (Harris, 1979). In both approaches the objectivity of the observation is the ideal scenario. In reality, both approaches are just as likely to be subjective. Using both the etic and the emic approaches will help us develop a model to understand similarities and differences among cultures.

It is assumed that the reader has a grasp of the basic concepts of human communication. In the first three chapters of the book, we will detail the specific systems constructs that will be used to build an understanding of intercultural communication throughout this book. These constructs should be looked upon as building blocks for the theory being presented in the rest of the text. The assumptions about human communication should prepare the reader psychologically to understand the nature of human communication as the author does and so make similar abstractions as the information is presented.

Chapter 1 defines what is meant by human communication in terms of the systems perspective and builds the systems theoretic structures within which we will consider intercultural communication. Chapter 2 presents basic information on verbal and nonverbal codes and shows how they interact with culture. Chapter 3 presents the three dimensions within which human communication is constrained (the environment and boundaries of the human communication system).* All communication takes place somewhere in space and time; thus, the situation puts major constraints on the communication that can take place. These constraints are discussed in Chapter 4. Chapter 5 details the personal constructs one brings to any communication event, i.e., one's cognitive orientation, including its structure and processes along with its belief and disbelief systems.

In Chapter 6 the concept of culture is reviewed and the Cultural Orientation Model is presented, showing the constraints that one's culture puts on understanding intercultural communication. We then build in Chapter 7 the basis for the beliefs and value structures that underlie our communicative behavior. This is followed by chapters on each of the four universal belief systems developed by Hofstede: Chapter 8 considers the communicative implications of Power Distance, Chapter 9 does the same for Uncertainty Avoidance, Chapter 10 for Individualism, and Chapter 11 for Masculinity.

Chapter 12 presents a model for first culture enculturation and speaks to the importance of being culturally literate. Chapter 13 looks at U.S. culture to see what one must know to be culturally literate, and it develops the constructs one can use to become literate in any culture. Chapter 14 presents a model for second culture acculturation and developing literacy in that culture. In Chapter 15 we look at the processes by which one can develop an understanding of another culture. Finally, in Chapter 16 we sum up the constructs we need to understand intercultural communication and present some ideas on the types of communication strategies that are applicable to intercultural communication.

Each chapter begins with an intercultural experience that is pertinent to the subject matter of that chapter. Most of these examples come from the author's experiences in Costa Rica. In fact, Costa Rica serves as the "other

---

*The material in the first three chapters relies heavily on the material presented in the author's book *Human Communication Systems*, 2nd ed. (Boston: American Press, 1989) and is presented here by permission of the author.

culture" in most of the analyses in this text. It is felt that using a single culture in this manner lends a consistency to the analyses that will aid the reader in grasping the concepts more clearly. The major concepts of each chapter are summarized at the end of the chapter, and their place in the cultural orientation model is explained.

Axiom: *For effective intercultural communication one's attitude is more important than one's knowledge and/or understanding.*

CHAPTER ONE
Human Communication: By Definition

When people meet they do so to communicate, but how would you define human communication? What is it? I'm sure you would know it if you saw it, but is it really as prevalent as we think it is? Is it basically a process that one can explicate and visualize, with actions that must be taken and rules that must be followed, or must it have an effect that can be measured so that when certain things have happened, we can say that human communication has occurred? Or perhaps it is an undefinable interchange of cognitive energy that functions as a vehicle for social intercourse and creates and/or maintains interpersonal relationships. Let's look at an example.

In the United States, the telephone number of the hotel and your room number are usually displayed on the telephone (or thereabouts) in your hotel room. This is not the case in Costa Rica, for example. For several years telephones were installed by a union that happened to be run by the Communist Party. When they installed a telephone in an *apartotel*, or hotel, they would put a sticker on it bearing the telephone number of the Communist Party's headquarters. A young North American female, when visiting Costa Rica for the first time, called several of her newly made friends and gave them this number, thinking it was that of the *apartotel* where she was staying. After a couple of days she found out why no one was calling her, but the Communist Party is probably still wondering why it was taking her calls!

With the telephone number on the telephone there was intent to communicate, but to whom and for what purpose? When I have finished writing this book, and you have finished reading it, has communication occurred? Or can we forget about the *process* and say that human communication occurs when one person affects another cognitively or physically? For example, is a child proof of communication between its parents? Or can we forget about the

1

effects and look at communication as the ingredient in social intercourse whose *function* is to precipitate relationships, build organizations, and create hierarchies? For example, friends, the local church, and governments.

When human communication is studied from each of these perspectives, the focus is necessarily different and leads to different conclusions about the nature of human communication. Each focus affects the definitions we give to effective communication, competence, and the term communication itself. It is the opinion of this author that human communication should be studied and understood within a context that allows all three of the above approaches to be used, depending upon the focus of the inquiry. Such a context is provided by General Systems (Borden, 1985a).

A SYSTEMS APPROACH

The basic model of the human communication process is a linear one in which the fact that communication is an ongoing process is indicated by the inclusion of a feedback loop. Basically, the process is this: The communicator sends a communiqué to a communicatee who responds by returning a communiqué to the communicator. The linear model hides the fact that both the communicator and the communicatee are sending and receiving communiqués simultaneously. The reader should be familiar with such concepts as feedback, noise, source, semantic encoder, codes, message, signal, transmitter, receptors, semantic decoder, destination, and intent.

Any message may be put into several different codes; in fact, the signal transmitted in almost every communication situation is a composite of several codes, all of which should elaborate the message coded into the signal. When they do not, e.g., when you are telling someone that you love them but your nonverbals are saying "I couldn't care less," there is noise in the system, and your communication effectiveness is diminished. Communication is, at best, approximate. The result of unintelligible, unintended, or misinterpreted signals may be a serious problem for either the communicator, the communicatee, or both, as it was in the opening example!

The fact that messages and meanings are in the mind and must be encoded into and decoded from a signal for communication to occur is an important distinction, for we have long been calling that which we speak or write "the message." But that which we speak or write is a *signal* into which a communicator has coded one or more messages and from which a communicatee may also decode a number of messages. Our libraries are full of signals (books) which, when read, deliver slightly different messages to each of their readers. Human communication is a cognitive process.

The process definition of human communication is perhaps more obvious in intercultural communication when one is learning a second language. In the beginning this is a process in which we create and transmit signals that are decoded by our host, teacher, or friend and corrected by this person, who gives us feedback by telling us what is a more precise or acceptable signal for the message we wanted to convey. Problems usually occur when one is using literal translations from one language to the other. For example, in Costa Rica if you do not hear or understand what someone has just said, you do not say *"¿qué?"* (what), as I had the habit of doing, but *"¿cómo?"* (how). After being corrected by everyone, I finally realized that you must use the cultural norms if you want to be understood.

If one focuses primarily on the effects of human communication, one is looking at the responses produced by this process and gives little attention to the process itself. The effects model was made popular in the late 1940s by Harold Lasswell in his famous *Who* says *What*, in what *Channel*, to *Whom*, with what *Effect*. With the advent of various mass media, one had to take into account the channel through which the signal was being sent. Focusing on the effects aspect of human communication often leads to misperceptions and thus, misunderstanding of the intended message.

Illustrations of this focus are abundant in U.S. foreign policy statements. For example, the United States is more results oriented and Latin Americans are more process oriented. When the presidents of the five Central American countries signed the Arias Peace Plan in 1987, the U.S. State Department commented that they had signed the agreement but there was no peace. The Central Americans were looking forward to a process that would bring about peace, while the United States was looking at the agreement as a statement of an accomplishment. Product vs. process is a serious difference in cultural orientation.

Rather than asking how communication occurs (process) or what response it evoked from the audience (effects), one might ask what function it has in the ongoing activities of life. What is the importance of communication to one's livelihood? What role does it play in being human? In the broadest sense, the functional approach to human communication focuses on the role it plays in defining humanity. This approach transcends both the process model and the effects model to look at the whole picture, with communication being only one of the variables. It relies on both of the other models to help explain how it functions, but the focus is on communication itself. It asks, What is the role, or function, of communication in the process of developing social systems? An appeal to General Systems Theory can help us ascertain this function.

General Systems Theory

Basic systems theory is concerned with: 1) wholeness—a system is composed of two or more interrelated subsystems; 2) sharing—the subsystems are bonded together through the subparts which they share; 3) synergy—the output of a system is greater than or different from the sum of its subsystems' outputs; 4) entropy—without an input of energy, an open system will "run down," i.e., become disorganized and unable to function efficiently; 5) self-regulation—a system must have a cybernetic to evaluate feedback and make corrective adjustments in the functioning of the system; 6) differentiation—the subsystem's position in a system is secured through its ability to function effectively in that position; 7) integration—the effective organization of individual subsystems gives the system its degree of synergism; and 8) equifinality—different systems may start at different points and use different means to arrive at the same end product. A system functions within an environment and its actions are constrained by the appropriate boundaries between it and its environment.

There are two basic types of systems: open and closed. Since human systems are never closed (Miller, 1978), we will only concern ourselves with the open system. The most basic definition of an open system is two or more components interrelating to achieve an objective. These components are interrelated through the attributes they share, and the sharing process *bonds* the components into a unit—a system. The attributes may be physical and/or psychological. In an open system the interrelating requires an input of energy. The interrelatedness of the components is predicated on the purpose, function, or objective of the system. Thus, the role each component takes within the system is determined by the interaction of the system's objectives and the component's characteristics. The *bonding* process has two variables: a vehicle for sharing, and attributes, or subparts, to be shared. Each variable is necessary but not sufficient. Both must exist for the bonding process to occur.

The bonding together of a system's components gives structure to the system and thus reduces entropy—the measure of a system's disorganization. It has been shown (Shannon and Weaver, 1949) that entropy is applicable to all systems. The basic principle is that unless a system has energy input, it will "run down"—entropy will *increase*. The fact that all things have a natural propensity to randomness says that energy must be expended just to keep them in a steady state. This principle is evident in all aspects of human existence. Our muscles atrophy, as do our relationships, if they are not fed and exercised. To maintain the structure of every living system there must be an input of energy-producing material, a throughput (metabolism) of this material, and an output of at least the waste (Schrodinger, 1968). For the system to do more than just survive (i.e., grow, mature, produce), it must have more than its basic requirement of energy. This principle holds for all levels of living systems, though the input may consist of more than physical energy.

The hierarchical nature of systems is basic to General Systems Theory. It is difficult to imagine a system that is not an element in a larger system (supra-system) and is not made up of smaller systems (subsystems). Thus, when we analyze a system, we do so either in terms of its relationships with other systems in its supra-system or in terms of the interrelationships of its subsystems. We can only describe a system in a superficial way without resorting to its function in the supra-system or the functionings of its subsystems. Thus, in systems analysis one must accept the notion of the hierarchical nature of systems.

Levels of Systems Complexity

Yet another aspect of systems theory is important to the understanding of a Human Communication System (HCS). Systems may be categorized according to their complexity into eight successive levels. Each level contains all of the attributes of those that precede it. Beginning with the Static system, we proceed to the Mechanical, the Cybernetic, the Organic, the Differentiating, the Mobile, the Cognitive, and the Associative (see Borden, 1985a, for a detailed discussion).

Static level systems show relative positions and relationships among parts, but essentially they are closed systems, with no way to generate or receive energy. A map is a static system, as it shows the spacial relationships of its subparts—cities, roads, geographical artifacts. *Mechanical* level systems add the variable "dynamic." At this level we can see the ways in which the parts, working together, result in the desired action of the whole system. *Cybernetic* (self-regulating) level systems have the ability to interpret information so they can regulate some aspect(s) of their own behavior. They are mechanical systems with a cybernetic unit installed, set, and maintained by an external human system.

Organic level systems mark the boundary between nonliving and living systems. At this level the control and maintenance of the system are innate functions of it. This level is also the first to have teleological behavior, an innate purpose, namely, survival. *Differentiating* level systems have many subsystems, all of which have been differentiated into systems with specialized functions. At this level we see the integration of subsystems to create complex processes for the survival of the species (trees are a good example). *Mobility* level systems can move to a new environment at their own discretion. They have a centralized cybernetic (brain) that is fully integrated into all aspects of their development (animals are the best example).

Cognitive level systems differ from the mobility level in that as humans (the only example of this level), we are self-conscious—we have a value system against which we can measure our behavior. What's more, we are self-reflexive, i.e., we know, but we also know that we know. Humans can talk about talk and discuss discussing. This tremendous sense of self can be both a help and a hindrance to our development. We have self-actuated teleological behaviors, i.e., we can set our own goals and strive to achieve them. We are also aware of some of the ramifications of our innate teleological behaviors. For example, we know we are born to die. We have a heightened sense of time, of history, and of our place in it. We are knowingly time bound.

At this level there is also a much more elaborate sense of relationship, both with other humans, with society in general, and with the environment. We play many roles in the different units of society to which we belong, e.g., parent, child, boss, politician, etc. What's more, we are generally able to see the hierarchical nature of these units and can put priorities on the roles we take. Most of this activity is carried on through the use of symbols, a behavior unique to this level of system complexity. Whereas animals *react* primarily to **signs**, humans *transact* primarily with **symbols**. The cognitive level is the highest level of living system known at the present time.

Associative level systems are the highest level of human systems of which we are aware. When human beings organize, they do so for a purpose. Thus, organizations may have the same types of teleological behaviors as cognitive level systems. One important difference is that their subsystems have life in themselves; subparts may be autonomous and make decisions that do not fit into the goals of the system. A second difference is that the role an individual plays in the associative system (organization) is usually more important than the person taking that role; i.e., practically no one is indispensable. As with the last four levels, the most basic objective of the associative level system is survival—a consideration that often interferes with its other objectives.

The first three levels of complexity are nonliving systems. However, they have served as the key models for the behaviorist philosophy of social science for most of this century. They have become ingrained in our thinking to such an extent that we often view other people (particularly those who are different from us) as controllable if we can just find the key to their cybernetic. It is stimulus-response thinking without even the mobility level of choice behavior. For example, many of the problems of the policies in the Middle East revolve around survival, but many of the participants are treated as though they had no choice in the matter. Even animals will fight for survival.

Human communication always takes place within an associative level system between two or more cognitive level systems—persons. In intercultural communication we must be aware that both persons have the same systems characteristics even though they may differ in the way these characteristics have been assimilated into their cognitive structures. The essential point is that we should never revert to treating or thinking about another *person* as though she or he were a system from a lower level of complexity. This is an extremely difficult behavior to maintain. Our ethnocentricism tells us that we are superior to other cultures and, therefore, we do not have to treat them as one of us. Our cultural heritage may confound many of our intercultural communication experiences.

Human Communication Systems

An HCS is a system in which *human communication* is the basic objective of the system. The sharing that takes place among the components (subsystems) of an HCS is accomplished primarily through the use of symbols. Thus, at least two of the components of the system must be able to use symbols in the encoding and decoding of signals. The definition of a human communication system becomes *any dynamic set of interrelating components, at least two of which are humans, functioning to achieve an objective through communication among its components* (Borden, 1985a). The key to the definition of human communication lies in the *bonding process* among the components of a system. Thus, we may use the characteristics of bonding in systems theory to explore the functions of human communication.

Communication is the sharing of information through meaningful symbols. The sharing of attributes bonds components into a functioning system; it creates a relationship. When does human behavior fill a communication function? From a systems perspective, *when it bonds two or more of the participants (components) into an HCS through the sharing of their information*. Sharing involves more than just sending or receiving a signal. Since human communication uses symbols, additional energy must be expended to encode and decode the message contained in the signal. When this cognitive energy is expended by both parties (involving the same signal), bonding occurs; a relationship is established. From a systems perspective, bonding and communication are synonymous and, therefore, the encoding and decoding of a message into/ from a common signal constitutes human communication. Since encoding and decoding are intention driven, it is only when there is intent on the part of both participants that communication occurs.

A brief example may illustrate this point. You are sitting in a park in a foreign country, whose language you do not speak, observing the people passing by. You look at another person's face and find that she or he is looking at you. As your eyes meet you can feel the bonding process occur—the expenditure of cognitive energy. Even though you do not know any of the verbal or nonverbal codes of this culture, eye contact is a universal form of nonverbal human recognition and forms an immediate, though temporary, HCS (relationship). If you are trying to "catch the other person's eye," the intent is obvious. If you catch it by chance, the intent is spontaneous. In these examples both the intent to transmit and to receive signals is apparent. Attributes of this microscopic event can be expanded into all other communication situations, both intracultural and intercultural.

DEFINING HUMAN COMMUNICATION

When defining human communication from this perspective, we must consider the meaning of the term *intent*. As used above, intent is defined as the expenditure of cognitive energy by the communicator to encode a message into a signal or by the communicatee to decode a message from a signal. Human communication necessitates the production of symbols, and these can neither be produced nor interpreted without the intent to do so (Motley, 1986). Human communication occurs when the production and interpretation involve a *shared* signal. Whether or not it has been effective cannot be known without feedback from the sender and the recipient concerning the *purpose* of the message coded into the signal, but that occurs at another level of analysis.

Intent must not be confused with purpose, meaning, motive, or the effect of the communiqué. Intent only energizes the system so it can *produce a signal or interpret a signal*, i.e., *communicate*. Most of the time it is conscious, but sometimes it is not. The crucial point is that we cannot equate *intent* with the *purpose* of the communiqué. The purpose may be to persuade, inform, or entertain, or, on a more personal level, get a date, tell someone what time to meet you, or make him or her laugh. All of these *presuppose* the intent to communicate.

Using intent to communicate as the basis for the bonding process allows us to explore the many behaviors that have been called communication; i.e., to see which ones are communication (see Figure 1) and what roles the other types of behavior play in our everyday interactions. We will see how crucial this is when we look at an intercultural situation.

The first possibility, that of no intent on the part of either the communicator or the communicatee, can be thought of as observable behavior, which may be described but to which no meaning is attributed. This usually occurs in impersonal situations in which you know you may be observed and you are able to observe others, e.g., sleeping or reading on your flight to Bangkok or London, being mindful of the other passengers but not paying attention to them, etc. The source is just being itself, and the recipient is just an uninvolved entity. There is no bonding between the two and, therefore, no communication has occurred and no HCS is created. It is merely the *general behavior* of two or more people without the intent to communicate.

The second possibility involves a source with no intent to communicate and a recipient who interprets the behavior of the source as meaningful. Perhaps the most obvious case of this type of behavior is when a person arrives in a new culture and interprets the general behavior of the people there as though they intended to communicate to him or her. It is compounded by the fact that we interpret their behavior from the perspective of our own culture rather than the culture we are now in. It is hard to believe that we can be the victims of our own perceptions. However, a great many of our misunderstandings of others stem from just this type of behavior. We observe a behavior and infer from it a meaning. But this meaning comes only from our cognitive structure and psychological set. If the other person is confronted with our interpretation, she or he may be shocked, not having had any intention of communicating with us. The observed behavior may be either verbal or nonverbal or both. There is an attempt at bonding by the would-be communicatee, but it is unsuccessful because the bonds are only attached to the recipient, as there is no communicator. Therefore, no communication occurs and no HCS is formed. It is merely *perception* on the part of the recipient.

The third possibility involves a source with the intent to communicate but no intent to interpret the signal on the part of the would-be communicatee. In this case, the source has expended cognitive energy to develop a message, encode it into a transmittible signal, and transmit that signal through some form of human behavior. She or he is trying to communicate. However, the potential communicatee has either failed to observe the behavior or, having observed it, fails to attribute any meaning to it. This is often the case when you are in a culture where you do not know the language. You know that there

Communicatee
Recipient
(Observer)

		No Intent	*Intent*
Communicator Source (Observed)	*No Intent*	1 General Behavior	2 Information Gathering (Perception)
	Intent	3 Information Dissemination (Expression)	4 Communication

Figure 1: A Human Behavior Schema

are opportunities to communicate, but you are unable to take advantage of them because of the language barrier, so you tune them out. This may be a problem if the behavior you just ignored is that of a person asking for help or a news bulletin concerning your safety. In this case there is an attempt by the would-be communicator to instigate the bonding process, but there is no reciprocation on the part of the potential communicatee and thus, the bonding process cannot be realized. Therefore, no communication occurs and no HCS develops. It is merely *expressive behavior* on the part of the source.

The fourth possibility involves the expenditure of cognitive energy on the part of both participants. With this expenditure of energy, the situation is one of transaction. Each participant intends to communicate and, in so doing, generates cognitive energy that bonds them together into an HCS. This is true whether or not the communication is effective and whether or not the purpose was negative or positive. The HCS is realized through the encoding and decoding of shared signals; it does not depend on the purpose for which the signals were sent nor the effect they had on the recipient. The most important variable at this point is the *intent* to communicate. You stop someone on the street and ask, in your broken Spanish, how to get to the closest post office. Your informant doesn't understand your question but tries to tell you anyway, and you both listen and speak intently. In this case both parties expend energy on the shared signals. The source organizes thoughts and transmits them in coded signals. The recipient takes these coded signals and expends energy trying to fit the decoded message into his or her cognitive structure. Regardless of the effectiveness of the communication, bonding occurs, and a temporary HCS is created.

In this type of human transaction there is an implicitly agreed-upon objective—to communicate, relate, share, bond. Both participants expend energy to achieve this objective. For two entities to strive for a common objective, they must be interrelated. Thus, communication brings with it all the prerequisites of a system—two or more components working together to achieve an objective. In this case the primary objective is to communicate, but this is not to say that there are no other objectives (purposes), nor that these are the same for each participant. The initial purpose may be merely to recognize the other person as a human being, but at some point in time the objective may change to friendship or some other more involved goal.

Human communication exists and continues as long as there is sufficient coherence to allow the participants to continue to interact (Pearce and Cronen, 1980) and sufficient relevance (Haslett, 1987) to make it worthwhile. The fact that we are cohering with another person, a cognitive act, says that we are bonding ourselves together into some type of human relationship. This is not to say that human communication is always harmonious or effective. It is to say that if communication takes place, it is intended. It is this very fact that creates the bonds between the participants of an HCS. The need to communicate is nearly as strong as the need to breathe, drink, or eat. However, while we may breathe, drink, and eat by ourselves, we cannot communicate without another active participant. So, it is possible *not* to communicate.

Because human communication requires intent, we *cannot* model human communication on any of the levels of systems complexity below the cognitive. We must use an anthropomorphic model and be aware of its innate, self-regulating subsystem, the cybernetic. The cybernetic (Wiener, 1961) is the label given to the control mechanisms of a system, and it is the seat of intent. It is usually thought to regulate the system's activity on the basis of feedback from the environment of the system. However, we may broaden this idea to include internal feedback and stimulation from the system itself because humans are living systems. Thus, the cybernetic is the controlling subsystem of the parent system and is composed of the components necessary to regulate all the activities of the system. These components themselves must be in balance in order to maintain a steady state in the system (von Bertalanffy, 1968). The cybernetic is the seat of decision making and, as such, controls how we behave in any context. If we are to appear to be consistent in our interpersonal behavior, our cybernetic must maintain a steady state within the cognitive system. To do this it must also maintain a balance among its components. When it fails to do this, we become erratic, unpredictable, and undesirable. It is impossible to talk about the cybernetic of a system without describing the components implicit in its functioning.

THE HUMAN CYBERNETIC

Physically, the human cybernetic has been said to be the brain. The psychological counterpart to the brain is the Self-Concept—the individual as known to the individual. This psychological construct acts as a controlling agent or subsystem in all the behaviors exhibited by the person. It is acquired through interaction with "significant" or "salient" others, is continuously being developed through social interaction, and is subject to change throughout our lifetime. However, by the time we become adolescents, our cybernetic has become so determined that it is difficult to change it thereafter. This conceptualization of self is of Anglo origin, and though the self exists in all cultures, its conceptualization may differ dramatically among them (more in Chapter 9).

There are five components of the self-concept: Bodily Self, Self-Identity, Self-Extension, Self-Esteem, and Self-Image (Kash and Borich, 1978). If one can maintain a balance among these components, then the self-concept can maintain a steady state in the person. It is easy to imagine (or remember) how one might act when one's cybernetic is out of balance. Do we still act as though we are that "fat little kid?" Can we accept praise or blame? Are we happy with our life? All of these are reflections of our cybernetic. Of crucial importance is the fact that all five of these subsystems are culture dependent and must be redefined when we move to another culture.

The Bodily Self

This is the sense of self as a physical entity. It differentiates us from all other people around us as well as the environment in which we live. We obtain this sense sometime in our first three years of life. Our sense of uniqueness as a person starts with our sense of bodily self. It is usually what we are thinking of when we use the subjective I. It is also a strong part of our sense of continuity; we see our body change, and we identify with it because it is the most immediate part of our self-concept. More and more, the advertising industry tells us what we should look like and what the consequences will be if we look that way. By the time children enter first grade, they know what a "good looking" person is for both sexes in their culture.

In a recent study Costa Rican and U.S. students were asked to describe their ideal male and female on 12 physical characteristics. For most of the characteristics there were no significant differences (women are shorter, men are taller), but Costa Ricans prefer women to be heavier, with larger hips/buttocks, and to wear more makeup than do U.S. students. When you look at the differences between the two subcultures (male/female), you find that: 1) women prefer women to have smaller busts than do men; 2) green eyes are preferred over brown by women, but the opposite by men; 3) women prefer to wear more makeup than men would like them to wear; 4) women prefer men's hair to be shorter than men like; 5) women prefer less body and facial hair on men than men do; and 6) women prefer men to wear more cologne than men do. These were all significant differences in the preferences of men and women from both cultures. What effect might they have on communication between members of these two subcultures?

Self-Identity

This is the sense of self that is determined by the roles we take in our HCSs. It is developed through communication with all those different types of people that make up the many HCSs to which we belong. Our social memberships and the degree of integration we have with these systems shape our identity. Since we are known to others by our role behavior, their treatment of us is an indication of how well we have developed that role. How do you like the way you are treated by others? When you are in the presence of others, at least three of your senses are telling you how well you are being accepted. You can see, feel, and hear how others respond to you. Much of self-identity is formed by the way we interpret the actions of others toward us. It is formed through the communication we have with significant or salient others. Thus, our self-identity is the self in relation to others.

If you are in a foreign culture and are asked who you are, what is your answer? Most often we identify first with our name and then with our culture and our occupation. The self is very closely identified with the culture, although we seldom think of this when in our home culture. This gives us an indication of just how important our culture is to the self-identity we carry with us. Another example of this is the feeling of loss we have when we find ourselves in a foreign culture. There may be little to identify with, including the language, which is our second most important identity group.

Self-Extension

How do you present yourself to the public? Self-extension, the third component of the self-concept, may be looked at as a performing self. It is the part of self that exists in the manifestation of how we feel about our behavior in public. We may be reticent, shy, extroverted, false, or real, but as we play out our role, others will become aware of how we feel about ourself. Significant or salient others can give us feedback that will help us give a more realistic performance of our self. We may extend our self by exhibiting repeated behaviors that are characteristic of a valued behavior on our part until we develop that characteristic as part of our self-concept. We may find ourselves doing things that we never thought we would do, like going for an extended vacation in a foreign culture. Once we do it and find that nothing drastic happens, we can use this experience as part of our self-extension. Risk taking is the way we find out who we really are, sometimes in spite of the values and norms of our culture. Nothing ventured, nothing gained.

Intercultural communication is almost always an extension of ourselves until we become bi- or multi-cultural. Those who never venture outside of their culture have not opened themselves to the insights about themselves that only another culture can give. It is only through extending ourselves that we come to know who we are. When we put ourselves into another culture, we realize that we must create an identity within that culture. That means we must find out what the salient aspects of the culture are so we can know how to fit into it. By extending ourselves we find out the limits of our behavior in that culture, which can easily open us up to greater endeavors in our home culture.

Self-Esteem

This is the part of self that develops through the affirmation and recognition of others for the things we have done. It is our sense of self-value or self-worth and is based on the acceptance of our behavior by significant or salient others. It comes from our perception of how well we can develop our potential in our immediate society. If we are continually put down for trying new things, or our work is unduly criticized, we may feel that we have lost the ability to develop our potential. The value judgments of others can be self-building or self-defeating. These value judgments may be on any of the other four components of the self. Depending on the level of significance or salience of the critic, we may reject the person rather than accepting the value judgment. At the same time, we may criticize ourselves even when others do not.

We usually criticize ourselves negatively when we do something we think is stupid. When learning a second language, most of us have found that we have ample opportunities for this type of criticism. The older you are, the more you seem to be set in the mechanics of your first language and the thinner your skin is to the arrows of embarrassment. Perhaps our self-esteem is affected most by our ventures into new cultures where we have few, if any, guideposts by which to find our way. The possibilities for making mistakes are abundant, and the probability that you will make one is nearly 100 percent. However, the sense of accomplishment and enlightenment from learning a second language or becoming knowledgeable about another culture is well worth the pain. It may also do great things for your self-esteem.

Self-Image

The self-image grows out of the history of our value-based images of the past. These stem from either the similarity or the discrepancy between the way we view our self and the ideal self we carry around with us. We have to realize, of course, that our ideal self is usually a product of our culture and, perhaps, a product of the media and advertising. It is usually based on culturally defined roles and norms of behavior. Thus, we may be building our image on what the culture stresses as important rather than our own value judgments. This is especially true today with the state of change in male and female roles in our society. In any case, we must ask ourselves at some time how we feel about ourselves in relation to what we could be ideally.

Of course our self-image is fostered by the feedback we receive on our activities on the other four components of our self-concept. Does our body live up to our ideal? How about our self-identity? Are we known as what we want to be known as? And our self-extension? Do we take enough risks, are we trying new things? How about spending a few months in Thailand? And in all of this, do we feel that we are living up to our potential, doing our best, or at least doing what we want to do? If the answers to all of these questions fit in with the ideal self we have developed over the years, then we will have a good self-image. If that self-image includes being able to communicate across cultures, then you must develop the other four subsystems of the cybernetic in the environment of the other culture.

APPLICATIONS

These five subparts, though they are not mutually exclusive, are integrated into the self-concept of the person. We hypothesize that maintaining balance among these subparts in the cybernetic maintains the steady state of the system we call a person. When one of these subparts is subjected to undue criticism, the whole person reacts to counter this input and bring the system back into steady state. Thus, to understand the behavior of the person, one must know something about that person's self-concept. However, since the self-concept is culture dependent, we must know its implications in both our culture and the culture of the person with whom we are communicating.

Many of our communication strategies are built around maintaining our self-concept or facilitating the self-concept of someone else. In many cultures, saving face is extremely important because it safeguards the self-concept. Are we aware of this, and do we facilitate this behavior when called upon to do so? The United States culture's tendency to be objective and blunt often causes untold damage to foreign relations. Other cultures are much more subjective and sympathetic to the other person. Their communication is heavy in relational attributes, while ours is heavy in information.

Since communication cannot take place without at least two people, it is obvious that synergy is an important construct. What and how much more can they do as a system than they can do as individuals? Does it make any difference whether two sides of a dispute (an HCS) sit down at a bargaining table and talk, or can they solve their problems as individuals? Some cultures are much more aware of the necessity of communication than others, and it appears that just the act of talking to each other (forming an HCS) aids in the resolution of problems—a synergistic function of HCSs.

The ability to communicate and form HCSs is an entropy-reducing activity (negentropic). Of course, this takes energy, and there is probably a level of communicative activity which is necessary to maintain a steady state, i.e., keep the entropy level constant in the HCS. The cybernetic should be aware of this threshold and know that increased communication or efficiency of communication or a change in the focus of communication must occur before the system can reduce its entropy. Just the act of forming an acquaintance with someone from another culture helps reduce the entropy of the world!

Many different types of relationships are represented in the different types of HCSs. We have acquaintances with whom we have very limited communication, co-workers with whom we must communicate, friends and/or lovers with whom we want to communicate, and various combinations of these with whom there is more or less communication. As we move up the scale of intimacy from acquaintance to friend to lover to spouse, we find that the system's bonds change in meaning and function. If we add to this today's lifestyles, in which neither partner wants to be dependent on the other (or interdependent, for that matter), we find that the systems' bonds are being strained to their limits. Now, if we add an intercultural dimension to this relationship, we find that the ability to maintain the system may be extremely difficult.

Of course, if all of the above relationships are with the opposite sex, we must realize that we already have one level of intercultural communication in the relationship. There are probably no cultures in which males and females are acculturated in the same way. Thus, they represent distinct, universal subcultures, and everything that is said in this book can be applied to male-female communication. If one adds the fact that these two people are from different national cultures, the problems and solutions can be much more complex.

TRANSITION

We have begun our study of communication by looking at a number of constructs that we must keep in mind as we progress through this book. All three approaches to the study and understanding of human communication will be used in the understanding of intercultural communication. The process and effects approaches were seen to be important to the function approach in that they give us information about communication that is essential to understanding when and how it occurs, the concept of noise, and the differences between process and product. The function approach was shown to fit in well with a systems theoretic analysis, which helped us define communication as that process which develops relationships.

The necessity for intent to communicate was shown and differentiated from the purpose of the communiqué. Four types of human behavior were defined—general, perception, expression, and communication. We need to keep the four main concepts of systems theory—entropy, synergy, bonding, and cybernetics—in mind as we delve deeper into intercultural communication. Of major importance are the concepts of levels of systems complexity and the components of the self-concept. The former is important because it affects the way we model and think about human communication (relationships), and the latter because it gives us a way of looking at human stability, which often suffers when we are placed in a foreign culture. We also indicated how synergy and entropy enter into the systems model of human communication. As we continue to develop this model, we will see how other concepts facilitate our understanding of intercultural communication. In particular, in Chapter 2 we will give some insights into the role of communication codes in intercultural communication.

INDEPENDENT STUDY

In this chapter we are interested in the systems characteristics of intercultural communication.

1. Give an intercultural example for each of the four types of human behavior and discuss the implications of each.

2. Choose an international organization (the United Nations, Organization of American States, the World Court, etc.) and analyze it briefly using the five components of the cybernetic. What are the problems of stability revealed by this type of analysis?

3. Discuss with several students from the same culture (not your own) how their self-concept may differ from your own based on the five components of the cybernetic.

CHAPTER TWO
Human Communication Codes

It was shown in Chapter 1 that communication functions to create relationships and that these can be studied as Human Communication Systems (HCSs). To create such a system, something must be shared among the components (subsystems) of the system. In an HCS three subparts *must* be shared by the participants for the bonding process to occur. These are *codes*, *channels*, and *messages*. Messages come in coded signals through channels. Shared codes, of course, are an integral part of communicative literacy. These codes may be verbal (all natural and artificial languages) or nonverbal (body language, art, dance, music, etc.). Obviously, if you only speak French and I do not speak it at all, it will be impossible for us to communicate on the verbal level, thus hindering our chances of developing an HCS. On the other hand, we may share some nonverbal codes and thus develop a limited HCS on that level of exchange. Shared codes are essential to an HCS, as are the channels through which the coded signals pass.

As it is given that I can receive and decode your signals, there must be a message in these signals for us to share. The primary focus of the messages we share can be either informational (sometimes called "instrumental"—goal directed) or relational (sometimes called "consummatory"—an end in itself) or both. Regardless of which one is of major importance, the other one is always present. Sharing may involve all of the attributes of each component or subsystem of the system, as well as those of the system itself, but it cannot be done without shared channels through which coded signals can be sent, and the codes must be shared so the components interpret the correct message from them. In doing this they will receive both informational and relational messages that enable them to develop an HCS.

RITUALISM

Much of our use of language is ritualistic. This is probably best seen in our greetings. As we pass someone we know, we usually say, Hi! How are you? But we are really not asking that question. (Sometimes a foreigner, unaccustomed to our ritual, will attempt to tell us and, of course, we are made to see how ritualistic our greetings have become.) It is merely a way of signaling recognition, of renewing the bond between the two of you. Thus, it has different meanings depending on the depth of the relationship. Think of all the many ways we have of greeting someone either verbally or nonverbally in both vocal and nonvocal modes. Now think of how you handle the second, third, or more meetings of the same person over a short period of time. We usually just nod or say Hi if anything at all.

Latin Americans have a more intense greeting on the first and subsequent meetings over a short period of time. They have a number of phrases to ask how you are or how things are going that tend to bother Anglo-Americans because they expect a reply—even though this also becomes ritualistic. This was the primary irritation felt by a group of U.S. college students in Costa Rica for a semester abroad program. What they were experiencing was the cultural need for affiliation. It is expressed in many ways, but the most obvious (to an Anglo) is this constant need to make what we often feel is a first-greeting-of-the-day greeting *every* time individuals meet. On a college campus, students meet quite often, and the U.S. students began to complain about not knowing how to handle the situation. They soon began to "go through the motions," but without the internal need for such. This, of course, reinforced the Costa Ricans' image of Anglos as being a cold, distant people.

Let's continue with the greetings behavior. The author was once introduced to a young woman from Argentina. Knowing the Latin American custom of kissing on the cheek, he kissed her, but as he withdrew she said, "Wait a minute. In Argentina we kiss on both cheeks," and so he did. The kissing custom is very strong in Latin America but only between females or male-female greetings—never between heterosexual males, as is common in other cultures. Depending on the strength of the relationship, one might also embrace and/or shake hands. Males always shake hands, even if they meet several times a day!

I had an opportunity to observe this custom over a three-day period in San Salvador when the USIS wouldn't let me leave my hotel because of the danger for gringos there. I spent considerable time in the lobby and dining room just observing the people. You must realize that this was primarily information gathering (they weren't intending to communicate with me) and thus, the conclusions I drew were from my own cognitive structure, not theirs. I noticed that as families met, the little kids would kiss, the men would kiss the girls and the women, and the women would kiss the women, the girls, the boys, and the men. But as I observed this happen over and over again, I began to notice that when the older people kissed, male-female and female-female, the lips never touched the cheek. They were just touching cheeks and sucking air! A *very* ritualistic behavior. However, young Latin American women tell me that the young men are different in opposite-sex greetings; they continually try to at least brush the corner of the woman's mouth in an accidental sort of way! For interpersonal relationships the nonverbal codes are probably more important than the verbal ones.

THE BASICS

We have suggested that the message resides in the mind of the person and that the signal is the external, coded, transmitted form of it. Signals are often subdivided by using two dimensions: the type of code and the mode of transmission. The types of codes are divided into *verbal* and *nonverbal*. The modes of transmission are divided into *vocal* and *nonvocal*. Though the codes and modes are often confused and used interchangeably, it will be clear that vocal is not necessarily verbal, nor is nonvocal necessarily nonverbal, and vice versa. Vocal transmissions refer to all sounds created by the vocal mechanisms, not just words, while nonvocal refers to all other types of transmissions (behaviors). Verbal codes refer only to that part of the signal composed of words and their syntactic structures, while nonverbal refers to all other aspects of a signal. In Figure 2 we make a clear distinction between these dimensions and their interactions. It is up to the communicator to choose the appropriate code and mode by which to attempt to create the desired message in the mind of the communicatee.

Both codes and modes may affect the human communication process. Is it easier to write or to speak (read or listen to) your second language? Do you understand the "meanings" of the nonverbal/vocal nuances used by native

	Codes	
	Verbal	Nonverbal
Modes — Vocal	Speaking	Stress, Pitch, Etc.
Modes — Nonvocal	Writing Signing	Body Language, Painting, Dance, Time, Space, Etc.

Figure 2:   A Four-Way Categorization of Communication Signals

speakers of your second language? How about the music, dance, art, and body language? One can distill many of the important concepts of the codes/modes construction in the following way:

Verbal and nonverbal codes exist only in the form of a signal. A signal is a physical entity that is sent by someone to be received by someone else. It can be recorded and preserved over time, but it has meaning only in the minds of the communicators. The message coded into any given signal may create different meanings for each recipient. Why is this so? The answer lies in the differences between signs and symbols. *Every symbol is a sign, but every sign is not a symbol.* If we can keep that clearly in mind, we should not have difficulty understanding these two categories.

The phrase *I love you* may be analyzed from six different perspectives.

1. *Signs*

Each letter in this phrase is a sign of the Latin alphabet. As such, they have no meaning in and of themselves. They are merely parts of the alphabet. The three groupings of these letters (what we call words) are also signs, but they are signs of the English language. As such, they have no meaning and can only be described as units with distinct sequences of letters. A sign is an integral part of what it signifies. Clothing may be a sign of civilization; a particular type of clothing may be a sign of a particular culture or subculture. There is a one-to-one correspondence between the sign and what it signifies.

2. *Symbols*

In the above phrase we see that single letters may become symbols ("I" has been given the source of the communiqué as its referent), as well as multiple-letter words. The word "love" has many more referents than the word "you," and its referents are much more subjective. The original referent for a symbol was arbitrary, but in learning a language we must learn what the normal referents are for the culture that speaks this language. As a symbol obtains more and more referents, it becomes more and more abstract.

3. *Codes*

The English language is only one of the codes formed with the Latin alphabet. It happens to be the one through which we are communicating to you right now on the verbal/nonvocal level. It has a vocabulary (a number of symbols), rules of grammar, and syntactic rules. This code is usable for communication only by those who share a level of literacy in it, and there are many facets to literacy. When learning a new language you were probably able to say what you wanted to say long before you could understand the replies you got. On a Berlitz tape I have for learning Spanish, the speaker teaches you phrases that are ritualistic expressions so you will sound like you know the culture. Being literate in a code includes being literate in the culture, and you are begging for misunderstanding if you sound literate but are not.

4. *Signals*

When the above phrase is written or spoken, it becomes a signal and can be transported from one person to another. A signal is much like a sign in that it can only be described. The message and meaning that it carries (in a coded form) will change with the context in which it exists (persons, situations, cultures). When a person smiles at you, it is a nonverbal signal. You can describe it and perhaps you know both its message and meaning, but does this signal carry the same message to someone else? Nearly everyone calls those things we write or say messages, but by doing this they have jumped over a crucial step in the communication process. We must first be able to describe the signal objectively before trying to decode its message and meaning.

5. *Messages*

The first level of decoding a signal gives us the message contained in that signal.The above phrase is a culturally acceptable way of expressing a feeling somewhere between "like" and "worship." At the message level we may analyze a signal in terms of the referents of each of its symbols and their syntactic alignment. This is analogous to the symbol perspective (2) above. There are culturally accepted norms for all messages, and these are known when we know the culture and the language. They often do not make sense when taken as literal referents to the symbols used. Language is synergistic; i.e., its messages and meanings are not always the sum of the referents of its symbols. Any metaphor illustrates this point. Have you been living high off the hog?

6. *Meanings*

This final perspective is analogous to the code perspective (3) above. Meaning occurs only in context and is completely subjective (personal). Literacy in meaning is shared by only a few—perhaps only two. The phrase "I love you," if transmitted only after the sender has been pleased in some way by the receiver, may mean "thanks" to which "you're welcome" may be the appropriate response. The phrase *te quiero* in Spanish is translated as "I love you" in English. Literally it can be translated as "I want you," which has definite sexual overtones in English. In discussing this with male and female college students in Costa Rica, the females said they never took it to have sexual overtones, while the males felt that it did. *¿Qué es amor?*

VERBAL CODES

There are thousands of verbal codes with which cultures communicate intraculturally; perhaps half a dozen can be considered international languages. All of these verbal codes share the constructs of vocabulary, grammar, and syntax. As mentioned earlier, most feedback uses the verbal code. However, there is a great deal of feedforward in speaking and writing, listening and reading. If you are trying to speak a foreign language and are not very literate, you can tell when you are speaking to a person who 1) listens, and 2) knows his/her own language. They will be able to finish your thoughts for you, help you find the right word, and give you a feeling of bonding. Sometimes we see this phenomenon of feedforward at work in our own speech. Those of us who lecture often find ourselves in the middle of a sentence with no way out. The content and the syntactic rules we started with led us into a grammatical trap. To escape, we usually just pause and start over!

Another difference between spoken and written language is that while writing allows us to choose our words and phraseology more carefully (we can think about them before we transmit them—try that while you are speaking!), it does not allow us to display the emotion connected with the communiqué nor to modify the signal if we see the recipient is upset by it. Immediate feedback and modification may be sacrificed for the permanency and precision of writing. This is why written communiqués are best for objective information, while spoken communiqués are best for subjective relational messages. Thus, most phatic communication—communicating just to relate—is in the spoken mode. We often talk just to relate with no concern at all for what we are talking about. We seldom do this with writing.

Information Management

The idea that language structures much of our reality has become the basis for considerable research. There is abundant evidence to show that reconstruing reality is a necessary part of getting through life. It is difficult to accept many of the facts of life without making up some reason for their happening. You flunk an exam or are caught doing something illegal. In cases like these we tend to talk about them from our point of view, and this talk often leads us to believe what we want to believe. We use language to relieve our internal tensions (even a good scream now and then may help) and to structure our view of reality. The legal problems of Oliver North are a case in point.

We also use language to structure another's view of reality. Information management is becoming a big business. We should be aware that this type of behavior is going on. Perhaps the most blatant use of information management was in the Falkland Islands war between the British and the Argentines. The headline in one newspaper (Sunday, July 18, 1982) read "British used lies to breed Argentine fear, turn tide." It seems that they "leaked" false numbers of troops and equipment, stories about the Nepalese Gurkhas, and plans for the invasion. This was later referred to as "official disinformation." But should we fault the British, since psychological warfare—trying to create a false reality through verbal behavior—has always been a major part of any war? And what of the reasons given for the Iran-Contra affair, the Noriega fiasco, and the language used in advertising and public relations? Any political campaign is a good example of using words to create a reality favorable to the candidate. Where is truth?

General Semantics

We live in a world of words, and we often react to them instead of what they say. This can affect our behavior and the HCSs of which we are a part. General Semantics, the study of the interaction between language and behavior, has developed several concepts that can help us be more realistic in our verbal behavior and our reactions to other's verbal behavior. The most important concept is that of *awareness*. We must become aware of our own verbal behavior, the effect it has on others, others' verbal behavior, and the effect it has on us. A heightened awareness will help us see some of the problems as they occur and allow us to make some changes in our HCSs.

A second concept is that of *abstracting*. When we say anything about anything, we must realize that we are not saying everything about it. Generally, we pick out those things that fit into our psychological set (usually subconsciously) and include only these in what we say about the topic. Since we cannot say everything, what we do say is necessarily biased by our perspective. Thus, information management occurs every time we speak. The dilemma of the trial lawyer is that no two people ever see or report the same happening identically. The process of encoding is a process of choosing what we want to say, and this requires us to abstract from our perceptions those things we feel are the most important to communicate. When we abstract, we say less and less about more and more.

A third concept looks at *words as maps*. When one makes a map, one includes only those things in it that are important to the purpose of the map. This is similar to the concept of abstracting. But a second characteristic of a map is important; the map is just a map and not the territory that it represents. The better the map, the closer it resembles the territory, but it will never be able to take its place (who would want to live on a map of the Bahamas?). The same principle exists in communication. Words are only maps of semantic space. Some are more accurate than others, but none are the semantic space itself. Thus, the recipient must interpret them to arrive at the meaning intended, just as the motorist must interpret the map to arrive at the destination.

A fourth concept, one that has plagued us for thousands of years, is that of *labeling*. Down through the ages one of our primary means of knowing has been to label the unknown, to describe it and to record its behavior. This has led us to feel that if we can place a label on something, we know what that thing is. This form of stereotyping has led to all kinds of problems. The McCarthy era is probably our best publicized debacle of this sort, and the 1988 presidential campaign had its moments, but the use of labels as forms of prejudice has been with us since the beginning of speech. If someone says, "She or he is a drug addict," then that person suffers from all the connotations of that label. We often hear someone say "Well, if they think I am a loser, I might as well be one." Even when the label is not derogatory, it will have an effect on the person so labeled.

The fifth construct that is important to our use of language will help us overcome some of the problems of the previous four. It is called *indexing* and is used to remind us that all of our perceptions take place in time and thus in some context. If we can index our perceptions, we will be able to make comparisons with more recent events and detect changes that may take place. It helps us avoid stereotyping, keep an open mind, and be less judgmental.

The language we use says more about us and our relationship with the object of our discourse than we are usually aware. If we label, we are responsible for the accuracy of that label and must take the consequences of its effect on the other person. When we let words stand in the way of our understanding of another person or a communication event, then we are probably reacting to the word and not accepting its map-like qualities. If we think we have said all there is to say about a subject, then we are probably not aware of the nature of our encoding process. An et cetera can be placed at the end of almost every statement we make! Our ability to abstract the most valuable information from a given event is a measure of our communicative competence. Our ability to verbalize it is a measure of our communicative proficiency.

SEMANTICS

How do languages communicate? Although they differ in levels of complexity and ease of writing, given the full advantage of the language you can say anything you want to say in any language. Some readers will object to this statement, but if you take into consideration the cultures involved and the use of loan words for more modern concepts, it should be true. It is also true that there are no direct translations of many thoughts from one language to another. But with sufficient knowledge of the languages and the cultures, one can evoke the equivalent idea. For example, what is the English translation of the general Spanish *ojalá* or the Costa Rican Spanish *achará*?

The creation of symbols allows humans to talk about things that are not in their immediate presence. We can talk about the past in the same way we can talk about the present and the future. One can understand something about the importance of time to a culture by the existence of verb tenses in the language. In the same way we may be able to understand the importance of various objects, concepts, actions, or relationships by the number and types of symbols a culture has for referring to them. We are known by the language we use, particularly when we are angry or surprised.

Semantic Space

The meaning generated by a single symbol may vary considerably. When two or more symbols are used together, the number of meanings may decrease or increase depending on the nature of the symbols. "House" has more meanings than "tree house" and fewer than "dog house." However, there are other ways of conceptualizing meaning. Of particular importance to communication is the notion of semantic space. It is usually thought of as a sphere; the meaning of each symbol is its normative position in it. When you encode a message you pick the symbols that map the proper portion of this sphere. Decoding is the reverse, and the effectiveness of communication is measured by the congruence of the portions of the sphere mapped by the encoder and the decoder.

Osgood, Suci, and Tannenbaum (1957) developed a method called the semantic differential by which one can measure the meaning of particular symbols. Still used today, it allows us to get some insights into our use of symbols that are otherwise rather elusive. The semantic differential allows us to locate particular symbols in our sphere of meaning, our semantic space. Semantic space is psychological, having three major dimensions: evaluative, activity, and potency. Each dimension is represented by bipolar adjectives with which we can describe the referent of the symbol being considered. The closer we feel the referent is to either of the poles, the more it has of that attribute than it does of the other.

The evaluative dimension is represented by adjectives such as good-bad, positive-negative, and pleasant-unpleasant. The activity dimension is represented by such adjectives as active-passive, fast-slow, and hot-cold. The potency dimension is represented by the adjectives hard-soft, strong-weak, and heavy-light. The semantic differential is designed to measure a person's feelings about referents. When used with a sufficiently large number of people, it measures the normative position of the referent in semantic space for a culture.

Osgood, May, and Miron (1975) created a semantic differential that could be used across cultures and studied the subjective meaning of 620 concepts across 23 cultures. They say that "Human beings, no matter where they live or what language they speak, apparently abstract about the same properties of things for making comparisons, and they order these different modes of qualifying in roughly the same way in importance" (p. 189). The three dimensions of meaning appear to be universal across cultures and languages. Thus, it is possible to locate various concepts within a universal semantic space. This can be illustrated by looking at the attributes given to the concept *girl* by U.S., Mexican, and Thai respondents. The first three adjectives were, respectively: pretty, beautiful, small; lovely, beautiful, pretty; and pretty, lovely, small. All quite similar, though the Mexicans never used the adjective small.

The semantic differential allows us to plot the normative "meaning" of various concepts, compare the opinions of various groups, measure opinion change over time, and show that the meanings of words are not additive. To illustrate the latter, if we used a semantic differential to measure the meaning of "foreign" and "policy" separately, we would find that the sum of their scores would not be the same as the score of the concept "foreign policy." One might very well say—having their country's foreign policy in mind— that "foreign" and "policy" are each good, active, and strong but that "foreign policy" is bad, passive, and weak. This is an example of synergy; meanings are neither additive nor static.

Coding Meaning

As mentioned above, labeling has always given us problems, even when the labels are nonderogatory and are used for convenience in dividing large groups into workable subgroups. For example, can you divide the people who live in the Americas into North and South/Central Americans? Not if you want the second category to represent all of the Latin Americans. Mexico is in North America and so is Quebec, not to mention the rapid increase of Hispanic Americans living in the United States. Since all of us are Americans, we cannot use either Americans or Mexicans or Canadians to designate all North Americans. The broadest categories would be Anglos and Latinos.

Other aspects of language have a strong effect on our HCSs. Albert Mehrabian (1971) indicates that we have a language within our language that is saying things of which we may not be aware. We tend to minimize both the responsibility for our behavior and the immediacy of our involvement with a person or event by using particular types of verbal behavior. We have defined 12 of these and present them in Table 1.

Table 1:   A Language Within a Language (Borden, 1985a)

1. Overinclusion:
   a. Putting the referent in a larger group.
   b. Putting yourself in a larger group.
2. Overspecification:
   Relating to part of the whole.
3. Extending:
   Attributing the action to someone else.
4. Objectifying:
   Removing yourself from the action.
5. Distancing:
   Putting the referent at a distance from you.
   a. By formality—forms of address.
   b. By demonstrative pronouns—this, that.
6. Negation:
   Using a negative statement of purpose.
7. Euphemisms:
   Calling something by a less sensitive name.
8. Conditional:
   Being less than assertive.
9. Qualifiers:
   Being tentative
10. Obligatory:
    You are obliged to do something else.
11. Oughts:
    Making the communicatee feel guilty for imposing.
12. Passive:
    Putting the blame on something else.

If you and a friend went to Mexico and later were asked if you liked your host family, you might reply (using several categories from Table 1): 1a) "I like Mexicans" or 1b) "We liked them" or 2) "I liked the children" or 3) "My friend liked them" or 4) "They were a typical Mexican family" or 6) "They weren't bad" or 8) "They could have been worse" or 9) "Seemed all right to me" or 11) "You ought to ask my friend."

To show closeness or distance you might introduce someone as 5a) "My friend, Jim" or "My boss, Mr. Blake" or just as "the cook." You can also show your involvement by saying 5b) "That is a good idea" or "This is a good idea." Euphemisms 7) soften the harshness of reality, e.g., "passed away" for died, "little boys' (or girls') room" for the toilet. We often make excuses by saying 10) "I can't, I have to study," whether we do or not. We may also put ourselves in the passive role 12) by saying "The clock tells me it's time to go" when we can think of no other way to get away from someone.

These nuances of meaning are available in all languages. Those of you who know Spanish know that blame is never taken for an accident. For example, *Se me fue la idea* (The idea left me). Do we not do the same thing? How about, "The car left the road and hit a tree." The driver had nothing to do with it! It seems that any time we use the passive voice, we are in danger of placing responsibility where it does not belong.

All of these methods use language to say more than what is usually expected. We may also use humor to say things that we are not comfortable saying up front, e.g., kidding someone about his or her weight or other characteristics that we would like to see changed. However, most people see through this type of verbal behavior. What one person thinks is funny another may think is downright repulsive. This is true in many areas of conversation, but it is probably most pronounced in dialogues where one person reads something sexual into everything the other person says. Playing with language is a good exercise for the mind, but it can also be degrading. You are what you say!

THE NATURE OF NONVERBAL COMMUNICATION

When we talk about nonverbal communication we are really talking about the codes used to encode a message and the signal that contains them. If you refer back to the definition of communication in Chapter 1, you will see that much of the encoding and decoding of nonverbal signals falls under the first three types of noncommunication. That is, either one or the other or both are unintended. Thus, we must conclude that although nonverbal signals are a great source of information, they are quite often not in the true sense of communication; they are often used instead as meta-communication, saying something about the communication that is taking place. They often set the scene, or create the atmosphere for the communication event. They are so closely associated with verbal communication that the two signals are often inseparable.

The inability to send and receive precise information through nonverbal signals, mainly because the message is most often inferred without feedback, makes us realize that we must either operate on the broadest of norms or know the person in our HCS very well. For this reason the *individual* is the most important variable in nonverbal communication. In fact, learning each other's nonverbal messages is a primary activity in getting to know someone. How do we know what they mean, if anything, by the nonverbal cues they send? We pick up a nonverbal signal (cue), *infer* the meaning encoded into this cue (usually on the basis of what it would mean if we were sending it), and then develop *expectations* from our inferred meaning. The sequence of events is cue, inference, expectations.

When analyzing nonverbal communication, either ours or someone else's, we must keep two factors in mind: first, the environment—both its physical and psychological dimension—of the communication event, and second, the participants in the communication event, i.e., the components of the HCS. Variables that are always important are sex, age, status, relationship, and cultural heritage. If you are witnessing an argument between two people, imagine the different conclusions you might draw if they are the same sex, opposite sex, the same age, quite different ages, the same status, obviously of different status, any of a number of different relationships, and from the same or different cultures. Now look at the various combinations of these variables. The individual is the most important variable in the communication process!

THE NONVERBAL CODES

Since we can only receive signals with our senses, it might appear that it would be best to categorize nonverbal codes according to the sense receptor that receives them. However, while some of the codes would fit well into this type of schema (olfactics, gustics) others do not (proxemics, chronemics). The best we can do is say that since many of the codes are codes of convenience, i.e., they have been developed because we needed some way to talk about these behaviors, they have no real interrelated structure. In this section we will present the various codes in what we feel is a coherent manner and from a U.S. cultural perspective.

Artifacts

An artifact is any object in our environment that tells us something about that environment. Artifacts may be personal or public and may be divided into fixed-feature elements, semifixed-feature elements, and nonfixed-feature elements (Rapoport, 1982). Personal fixed-feature artifacts are things like our bone structure, eye color, and skin texture. Public fixed-feature artifacts may be trees, mountains, buildings, and even whole cities. These are all objects that are not readily moved or changed, though nothing is absolutely permanent.

The semifixed-feature artifacts are those objects that may be changed at will but have enough permanence to make them habitual. Public examples are furniture arrangements, billboards, and window displays, while personal examples are hair styles, clothing, and jewelry. Any of these can be changed quite easily, and their change will be seen to an observer as a nonverbal signal.

The nonfixed-feature artifacts are those objects that are able to move under their own power. Thus, pets, robots (in the future), and people (who are not in our HCS) are examples of public artifacts, and facial expressions and eye and muscle movements are examples of personal artifacts. Each of the personal artifacts have been studied sufficiently to be given their own code.

Now think of this code in conjunction with your visit in another culture. Both public and personal artifacts will probably be different from back home. Different trees and architecture, vehicles, and people. The people may have different skin color, bone structure, hair styles, and facial expressions. How do (will) you feel about that? It is this code that gives us the feeling of being at home or away. When the artifacts do not match our expectations, we have nothing to identify with, and so we feel isolated and alone. We usually make acquaintances quickly so we have a familiar face with which to identify. If we stay there long enough, then the artifacts become familiar and we can feel at home there too.

Personal Appearance

Though this may be a strange name for a code, the signals sent by our personal appearance are so important that we must consider this as a unique nonverbal code. It has several dimensions of which we must be aware. The first is body type. Three different body types have been identified and appear to have consistent characteristics across sex and culture. These are: ectomorphs—those people who are thin, frail, and tall and are stereotypically anxious, serious, shy, sensitive, and introspective; mesomorphs—those people who are ideally proportioned, are of average height, muscular, and trim, and are stereotypically assertive, confident, energetic, and nonconforming; and endomorphs—those people who are short, plump, and soft and are stereotypically affectionate, jovial, kind, relaxed, and dependent.

A second aspect of this code is the semifixed-feature artifacts that allow a person to identify with various groups within a culture. Clothing is the most important of these features. By changing our clothing we can move from one HCS to another quite easily and in the process become a different person. Other features are our hair style and color, though these are more apt to be used by females than males. The same can be said for cosmetics and jewelry, both billion-dollar industries. Thus, we see that much of our nonverbal behavior may be dictated by the advertising we see and the desires of corporate executives. To some extent we may also think of skin color as part of these features, though present research tends to link tanning with skin cancer and this may change our image of what a healthy colored skin is.

Chromatics

The use of color as a coded message has a long history. Color has always been important to both individuals and cultures for both fixed and semifixed artifacts. In the United States, red, white, and blue (in that order) symbolize patriotism; they stand for the country. For the individual, color can be found in hair (do blondes have more fun?), eyes (dark brown eyes are more domestic), clothing (bright colors are for extroverts), food (it must be the right color or it won't sell), and our environment (different colors set different moods). We know that soft pastel colors are more conducive to relaxation than are bright colors, which tend to stimulate.

Facial Expression

This may also sound like a strange name for a code, but it is one of the most important. It is sometimes included under kinesics (as it has to do with muscle movement), but we prefer to consider it as a unique code. The face is the primary transmitter of emotional cues. Six types of emotions are generally held to be recognizable (Ekman and Friesen, 1975). These are surprise, fear, disgust, anger, happiness, and sadness. We should hasten to add, however, that there are no pure signals of emotions. All of our facial expressions are *blends*, as the face is constantly in motion.

How does a culture display its emotions? Research in facial expression has been done primarily with still photos of faces showing the emotion called for. However, since these do not appear in reality (everything is a blend) this research has tended to show significance where there is none. The more recent research is using video and finding that only happiness can be identified consistently (Motley and Camden, 1988). The context of the emotion is extremely important. Can you tell the difference between tears of joy and tears of sorrow or anger without the context? Since some cultures show their emotions much more openly than others, it is important to investigate what emotions the indicators display.

Oculemics

Our eye behavior sends many messages to our communicatees. This includes not only where we are looking but also how long we look and with what intensity. Superiors tend to hold a gaze, while subordinates tend to look away. Making eye contact can be both embarrassing and exciting. The eyes are our primary means of showing likes and dislikes. Relationships depend on eye contact, as it is the primary way a person knows how the communicatee is reacting to the communiqué. In this way it is a regulator of conversation. Our pupils dilate when we show interest and attention (Hess, 1975), and this activity may have an effect on those watching us. It will certainly affect our intimate conversations. This may be a reason why dark-eyed people are considered more domestic. It is hard to distinguish their pupils from their irises.

Oculemics has strong cultural ramifications. Many cultures (Latin Americans, for example) teach their children that looking an authority in the eye is being insubordinate. Others (United States) want the child to look at the authority when they are speaking to them. This opposite view of insubordination has been a problem for U.S. teachers of Hispanic Americans. In some cultures, to stare or gaze is a form of admiration; in others, it's a sign of disrespect. In Costa Rica the use of the eyes by the females is a well-developed art form. Perhaps the more relationally oriented a culture is, the more the eyes become important to interpersonal contact; they are the *only* contact in cultures where women wear a veil.

Kinesics

Kinesics is concerned primarily with our body movements and posture. The way we walk, sit, and stand tells others something about us. Ekman and Friesen divide body movement into five categories of signals. *Emblems* are gestures that have a direct verbal translation. They are those cues which we usually classify as gestures: the thumbs-up sign, the finger, and the familiar hitchhiker's thumb are good examples. But some emblems are used by different groups to send entirely different signals than they were originally meant to send. An example is the "hookem horns" gesture of the Texas University Longhorns. Its basic message all over the world is that the receiver of the gesture is being cuckolded (Morris, et al., 1979).

Illustrators are those gestures that complement our verbal signals. When giving directions we often point (an illustrator). We illustrate the size of the fish that got away and the look on the face of the loser. Illustrators usually accompany verbal signals. *Regulators* are body movements that help control the flow of communication. The primary one seems to be the head nod. A positive nod keeps the communication going; a negative one may stop it. Shifts of the body may also have this effect.

Affect Displays are those behaviors that indicate the intensity and the emotions we are feeling. Facial expressions reveal emotion, and body posture, tension, and hand and foot movements are the primary means of showing intensity. These cues also indicate lying. *Adaptors* are habits of self-expression that we revert to unconsciously when we are under pressure—twisting one's hair or scratching. They are idiosyncratic and, when learned by your friends, can help them and you understand your nonverbal behavior better.

Haptics

Physical contact is essential to the health of every warmblooded living thing. A child will die without it. As we develop we learn that different types of touching indicate different types of relationships. Malandro and Parker (1983) have divided touch into five categories ranging from impersonal to sexual: Functional-Professional, Social-Polite, Friendship-Warmth, Love-Intimacy, and Sexual Arousal. These may be exemplified by the doctor's touch, a handshake, a brief hug for greeting, a kiss on the lips, and stroking the G spot, respectively. However, the amount and location of touch is quite idiosyncratic as well as cultural. So is the touching of self. Both can be used for intimacy and control.

Studies comparing touching behavior in Latin American cultures and the United States (Borden, 1989) indicate that although the Anglos are much less tactile with friends (*amigos*), both same sex and opposite sex, than are their Latin counterparts, when the relationship progresses to a romantic involvement (*novios*), Anglos are significantly more tactile. This is confusing to both cultures. Anglos relating to Latinos think the relationship has progressed much further than it has because of the touching Latinos do in friendships. Unfortunately, both parties usually interpret this behavior from their own cultural perspective without the benefit of talking about it.

Proxemics

Our use of space may be a reflection of our age, sex, status, relationship with those around us, and our culture. Edward Hall (1969) has defined four categories of distances depending on the relationship of the communicators. Intimate (0"-18"), Casual-Personal (18"-4'), Social-Consultive (4'-12'), and Public (12'-). When we violate these norms we may find that our communication is misunderstood. One's personal space (a bubble of space that we carry around with us) may shrink or expand depending upon the relationships we have with the people around us. In a crowded elevator, obviously, it is hard to insist on a given amount of personal space.

Though our personal space may vary, our personal territory does not. Territory has fixed boundaries with physical locations (Burgoon and Saine, 1978). There are also four types of territories: Public, that territory that is open to all—a city park; Interactional, territory that is open for social interaction but which has restricted access—offices; Home, those who live there or own it can share it—house, apartment; and Body, your physical body bounded by your skin. Violations of the boundaries of these territories will also cause problems in communication.

Proxemics, with its territorial aspects, differs considerably from one culture to another. The hospitality of some cultures puts the United States to shame. Again, it seems to depend on the role of relationships in the culture. We have developed a highly individualistic culture; our space and territoriality are very real. This is also shown in the distances we keep from others. In some cultures they feel it's an insult if they cannot smell your breath; we feel it is an insult if we can. Proxemics is one of the most important but difficult codes to use when moving from one culture to another.

	Intimate	Personal	Social	Public
Time*	30 in.-?	15 in.-30 in.	5 in.-15 in.	0 in.-5 in.
Space	0 in.-18 in.	18 in.-4 ft.	4 ft.-12 ft.	12 ft.-?

*Minutes

Figure 3: The Time-Space Analogue

Chronemics

People growing up in the United States are said to be obsessed by time. Most of us are probably "time-line" type persons. Things have to be done in a structured way at the right time. Past- and future-oriented people structure their lives around memories or desires, while present-oriented people are ready to do whatever happens to come along. If you strive to develop an HCS with people having different perceptions of time, you are asking for trouble. Still, all of us have friends that are always late or always too punctual. The way we use time may be analogous to the way we use space, though the distances are inversely proportional (Henley, 1977). Figure 3 gives this information.

The United States time-line is future-oriented; most industrial cultures are. It seems to go with "progress." Other cultures are more present oriented, doing things as they get to them. The promptness with which people keep appointments (informal time) may be a good measure of their time orientation. The amount of time you will spend communicating with someone at the distances given in Figure 3 may also say something about you and your culture. This analogue needs to be tested to see if there are definite cultural differences.

Olfactics

Much is made of how we smell; the perfume, cologne, and deodorant industries are all getting rich from us. We have been told that human odors are offensive and should be controlled, but we keep right on sweating, belching, and farting (all Anglo-Saxon words!). In the '50s, halitosis was translated into housitosis by our ad industry, and products began to vie for our dollars to keep our house smelling clean and sterile.

The key word is sterile. Those cultures that are less, shall we say "pretentious," delight in body odors; we delight in the synthetic, chemical concoctions that deny our humanity. Although we know we are affected by various odors, both positively and negatively, very little is known about why. Like anything else, too much of a good thing is overpowering. So, we must be careful how we handle our odors and not violate the norms of our culture. If we do, our HCSs will suffer, particularly those on the intimate level (Hopson, 1979). Probably the complaint we hear most often from students is the difficulty they have working with students from cultures who do not share our fear of smelling human.

Gustics

What kinds of foods do you really like to eat? Probably not those that are the best for you. Much research is now being done on what foods are best and which ones we should eat to ensure long life. Diets are published each year, and if you aren't on one, you are probably in the minority. Yet, little research is done on taste. We know that the foods for space travel had to be made tasty even though they were squeezed out of a tube. Artificial foods and dried foods always seem to have a strange taste. So how does taste affect our HCSs? The old adage, The way to a man's heart is through his stomach, may be one answer. Taste in food or drink can be a source of bonding between two or more people, to say nothing about the social influence of food fests.

The personalness of taste and its importance to us is attested to by the numerous metaphors built around it. Many of our good and bad relationships are referred to by using sweet and sour metaphors. There may be a linguistic variable in this phenomenon, however. In English one says, "She is my sweetheart." There is no comparable expression in any of the Romance languages—French, Spanish, etc.

We know that taste must be acquired; as we go from one culture to another, we may find it impossible to eat what they eat. The hot spices of some cultural foods are beyond the acceptability of some of our stomachs!

Vocalics

Facial expression and vocalics are closely related in the show of emotion. The voice carries emotion through its intensity, intonation patterns, pitch, stress, etc. Other aspects of the voice are also a message to the communicatee (Burgoon and Saine, pp. 80-83). *Voice quality* may be characterized as breathy, tense, husky, nasal, and orotund, to name only a few. Each of these allow you to make an inference about the character of the person speaking. Other aspects of vocalics include *vocal characterizers* such as giggling, whining, moaning, and whimpering, which may characterize the speaker's way of speaking. *Vocal qualifiers* such as intensity (loud, soft), pitch (high, low), and extent (clipped, drawl) also evoke inferences about the speaker. The voice is also used to make sounds that flow along with the verbal signal but are not words. These are called *vocal segregates* and are exemplified by vocalized pauses, coughs, snorts, clicks, and sniffs.

Cultural differences in vocalics become evident when one tries to learn a culture's language. In Latin America it is easy to get a discussion going over which country speaks the best or worst Spanish. Costa Rica, Columbia, and Chile are usually mentioned in the best category, while Puerto Rico, Mexico, and Panama are mentioned in the worst category. Perhaps the close contact these last three countries have with the United States has something to do with the way they speak. Although purity of vocabulary is a variable in this differentiation, much of it has to do with pronunciation, enunciation, rate of speech, and intonation.

Acoustics

The study of sound and its effects on communication is an important part of nonverbal research. We have talked about physical noise hindering effective communication. Other types of sound may enhance it. Whenever we are involved in a communication event, we should be aware of the acoustics of the situation. This is true both in the sense of allowing the desired sounds to be propagated and eliminating undesired sounds.

Music is one of the most popular forms of entertainment and may also affect our emotional stability. Cultures are identified by the types of music to which they dance. Salsa, merengue, waltz, twist, etc., all say, or have said, something about the culture that embraced them. Are you into music from other cultures, or are you a cultural purist? For many of us it is difficult to get into some cultures' music, though with the globe getting smaller now, we are apt to hear many more "foreign" sounds.

Silence

As facial expression is to kinesics, silence is to acoustics, and we must be aware of its potential for meaning. Silence functions in a relationship as a "linkage" variable (Jensen, 1973). Its use indicates that a relationship exists. Each of its four functions can be either positive or negative.

1. *Affecting*—it can be used to heal or to wound.
2. *Revelational*—it can conceal information or it can reveal information.
3. *Judgmental*—it can give assent or dissent.
4. *Activating*—it is used to stimulate thoughts and actions.

The use of silence in different cultures is striking. Ishii and Bruneau (1988) tell us that in North America and Northern European countries, "silence is viewed as dark, negative, and full of 'no things'—all of which are considered socially undesirable," while in other cultures "silence is *often* achieved. Here breaking silence is a necessary evil, at best; speaking is a negative act" (p. 310). The strong differences between cultures in the use of this code must be considered seriously for effective intercultural communication.

NONVERBAL BEHAVIOR

As mentioned above, the inferences one draws from nonverbal cues set up expectations of behaviors to follow. Both of these cognitive behaviors are usually based on the belief structures of the observer rather than the intent of the communicator. One of the dangers inherent in this activity is the fact that we often assume intention on the part of the sender when there really is none. Until one gets to know another person quite well, it is nearly impossible to infer, with any accuracy, what their nonverbal cues are meant to communicate—if anything (Buck, 1983). Even in close relationships one would be well-advised to check their inferences, for it may be just expressive behavior and not meant to be interpreted.

There are, however, some basic nonverbal behaviors of which most of us partake in certain situations and of which we should be aware. Much of our ritualistic behavior is nonverbal, e.g., greeting and leave taking. If we know the correct nonverbal behaviors for the culture we are in, we can use them in our communication strategies or observe them in others and develop a deeper understanding of the culture. Nevertheless, we must be careful of the inferences we make, for our nonverbal behavior is not as Freudian as some would have us believe (Fast, 1971).

TRANSITION

In this chapter we have taken you through many aspects of verbal and nonverbal codes that will be used later in the book to explain some of the problems in intercultural communication. The primary concepts are: ritual, information management, the five aspects of General Semantics, semantic space, and coding meanings. Language is a good example of the systems concepts of synergy (meaning is not additive), entropy (language organizes), and bonding (our codes must be understood by someone else). It should be obvious that both verbal and nonverbal behavior may also add to the noise in communication—jargon and deceit are the chief offenders. Since language is symbolic it is only produced at the cognitive level of systems complexity and is used to form the associative level of systems complexity. The five aspects of General Semantics play a major role in the development of the human cybernetic. They are also of great use in intercultural communication. If we maintain an awareness of our language, both verbal and nonverbal, and that of the culture we are in, many of our communication problems can be short circuited and kept from building into international incidents.

You can observe the 14 different nonverbal codes given to you in this chapter in your daily interactions. They may help you find why you are a competent communicator, for the nonverbal signals we send have a significant effect on our acceptance in any communication event. They should also help you see similarities and differences between your cultural habits and those of another culture, thus helping you be a more competent intercultural communicator. Their role in rituals, as well as the way in which nonverbal cues can be used to manage information, should become obvious. The most difficult aspect of nonverbal communication is a knowledge of the intent of the communicator. Most of the cues we pick up are not communication at all but only a means of gathering information, from *our* perspective.

This completes our presentation of codes and modes. In the next chapter we will discuss the environment of communication acts. However, before we move on, there is one question that has been nagging me for years: Why are we so reluctant to talk about our nonverbal behavior? It would seem that this is the best way to find out what we meant or didn't mean by what we just did. But alas, it's hard to talk about things you cannot put into words.

INDEPENDENT STUDY

In this chapter we were concerned with languages, both verbal and nonverbal, and meaning. The only way to really understand a language is to experience it, so the following questions will try to put you into situations in which you can experience some of the differences between cultures using verbal and nonverbal codes.

1. Ritualistic language, both verbal and nonverbal, is a fundamental part of every culture. For a short paper, discuss the ritualistic codes used in greetings with two or three members of a culture other than your own. Do a comparative analysis. For a longer paper, do this for several different cultures.

2. Pick one or two nonverbal codes and discuss their usage with members of a culture other than your own. Do a comparative analysis and write a report. You may want to compare several cultures.

3. Take an activity, such as a first date or an interview for a job, and compare two or more cultures on their use of a number of nonverbal codes. Similarities? Differences?

4. The differences between formal and informal (street) language are important to understanding the semantics of a language. Choose your favorite second language, find a professor who teaches it, and discuss with him or her some of the differences in the two. Now take what you have learned and discuss it with some members of the culture who speak this language as their first language. Write up your findings.

CHAPTER THREE
Human Communication: Dimensions and Constraints

When I was 16 years old we moved from New York state to New Mexico. I graduated high school there knowing several Mexican-Americans but not having any as close friends. Most of them were first generation immigrants, but I knew almost nothing about their cultural heritage. A couple of years after graduation, I took a job on the highway and drove the pickup to the construction site each morning, picking up some of the crew on the way. There were two other Anglos and one Mexican-American whom I had known in high school as an acquaintance. All three of the riders had to walk from their homes out to the main highway where I picked them up at a specified time each morning.

We always had to wait for the Mexican-American, sometimes 10 or 15 minutes. Each night he would promise to be on time the next morning. Finally, we told him that we would not wait for him any more. The next morning he was not at the pick-up spot when we arrived, and we could not see him coming down the street. I stopped, and the other two guys pitched a fit, reminding me of the warning of last night and saying that he would never learn to be on time unless we kept our word and left without him. As I pulled back out onto the highway I caught a glimpse of him coming around a corner three blocks away, but I gave in to the arguments of the other two riders and left. He thumbed his way out to the site, beat us there, and was waiting for me when I came into the office. Most of what he said was in Spanish but enough was in English for me to know that he didn't hold my family in very high regard!

How many times do we offend people because we do not understand their cultural background? We view a situation and put constraints on it based on our cultural norms or personal preferences without taking the demands of the situation into account. Since all communication takes place within an HCS, the context or environment for this communication is an essential ingredient in the communication process. In this chapter we will show that variables on the three dimensions of the communication environment place constraints on the communication that can take place.

DIMENSIONS OF HUMAN COMMUNICATION

Every system exists within an environment from which it receives energy and information and to which it returns its own specialty. The environment for a human communication system may be thought of as the context in which communication takes place. Since the basic component in an HCS is the person—having physical and psychological attributes—it seems imperative that the environment in which the HCS exists also have physical and psychological attributes. Communication decisions at any given instance are made on the basis of the constraints we feel from the variables contained in the three dimensions of the HCS environment.

The three dimensions are:

1. Situational—all the externally perceived variables which set the scene for the communication event.
2. Personal—all the internally perceived variables affecting the communication event, presenting the communicator with a choice of communicative behaviors.
3. Cultural—all the nonconscious ideologies we carry with us that may suggest what our normal communicative behavior would be.

These three dimensions define the environment in which an individual functions in an HCS. The interaction of the environments of two or more persons constitutes the environment of the HCS. The compatibility of the individuals' environments affects the development of their HCS. True to the systems definition of environment, the components of an HCS may interact with the environment on these three dimensions. In return, these dimensions place definite constraints on communicative behavior.

Situational variables are all the external aspects of the communication event (physical and psychological) that affect the choices we make in our communicative behavior. For example, the weather, our deadlines, the time, the place, the tension you perceive in the other person, and his or her sex, age, status, and culture. All of these have a profound effect on what we feel we can do and say in a given encounter. The exigencies of the rhetorical situation fit into this dimension quite well (Bitzer, 1968). They ask what the situation demands, or what is required to achieve the goals of the HCS. Situational variables are all those external forces and contingencies that stimulate, facilitate, or impede communicative behavior. They all affect our behavior, but we can always deviate from the path that external stimuli might seem to dictate.

Personal variables are defined as those factors that precede actions. They are internally perceived and may best be categorized by the extent to which they are doable and the extent to which they require investment in the communication event. Since we are looking at the person as an active agent, we can ask what choice she or he has in the behavior she or he is about to display or has been displaying in any given communication event. Unfortunately, our doables usually do not include behaviors that we do not do normally. When faced with a new communication event, we resort to our old way of doing things and begin talking about the weather!

Kelly's (1963) personal construct theory is particularly valuable here, especially the idea that "a person's processes are psychologically channelized by the ways in which he *anticipates* events" (p. 46, italics added). Our choice behavior in any communication event is forward-looking, concerned with achieving the objectives of the system; it is teleological. This is true primarily because the person is reaching out, setting up anticipations of events, and making choices based on these anticipations. The degree to which we invest ourselves in the event will make a great deal of difference in what we feel are the doables. The personal dimension contains all the internal, physical, or psychological pressures we feel in any communication event and is focused primarily on the future and our self-image.

Cultural variables are composed of the attitudes, beliefs, and values we have developed over our lifetime. These are often referred to as our attitudinal frame of reference (Rokeach, 1960). That is, they take into consideration all of the beliefs, fears, desires, and expectations we have developed as a result of our exposure to the culture in which we live. Most of our attitudinal frame of reference is nonconscious; i.e., we are not consciously aware of these feelings. Bem (1970) calls them nonconscious ideologies, and they surface when something happens that questions the status quo. We then have the tendency to say, "But how else could it be?" The attack on male supremacy is a good example of a nonconscious ideology being made conscious. When women first began to question their existence as the homebodies and caretakers they were pictured to be in the media, many males *and* females asked, "How else should it be?" Current events show how difficult it is to change these nonconscious ideologies, particularly in macho cultures.

CONSTRAINTS ON HUMAN COMMUNICATION SYSTEMS

In a general systems approach to human communication, one of the most disturbing questions is, Where does the system stop and the environment begin? The boundary of an HCS also has physical and psychological aspects,

Figure 4:   Human Communication Constraints

and as one would expect, it can be located on the above three dimensions of the environment.

On the situational dimension, the boundary that constrains the system is its use of time, space, and artifacts. Any of these can determine the limits of an HCS. On the personal dimension, the boundaries are our physical energy, our knowledge, and our degree of self-actualization, i.e., the degree to which we are aware of our self and our human potential and are able to constructively assert our individuality (Maslow, 1970). The boundaries on the cultural dimension are the cultural norms. If a component of the system or the system itself tries to step over this boundary, it is immediately in danger of being ostracized. It may communicate across the boundary, but the norms put definite constraints on the system and its development. All of these boundaries constrain any HCS.

The Situational Dimension

The situational dimension has both physical and psychological properties. We may be able to control what situations we find ourselves in, but once there we have few choices. We do have the obligation to explore all of the physical and psychological aspects of it and to develop our expectations accordingly. If we misread the situation, we may be adding more constraints than are there or not realizing some that are there, and then partaking of inappropriate communicative behavior (as in the opening example). You can probably think of instances where the situation demanded something other than what was going on.

As we have said, the situation stems from the perceptions of the communicator. We never come in direct contact with reality, for it is always filtered through our perceptions. Thus, the situation—all externally perceived variables—is affected by our senses, knowledge, and psychological set. We shall say more about each of these as we continue. Since we are dealing with perception, we must be aware of the fact that we are only dealing with the reception and decoding of a signal. This is information gathering at its best, but remember, there can always be some missed cues and/or miscues. Furthermore, it is based on inferences that come from our cognitive structure, not some objective sensing device. Therefore, the best we can hope for is the proper perspective on the situation. Our receptors and decoders stand between us and reality. Thus, we must work on improving our perceptive abilities, but enter each communication event with the awareness that we are functioning on the basis of our perceptions.

Communication events have physical settings: They take place in some time-space continuum and with some artifacts. We must also realize that some of the artifacts in the situation may be people like us. Thus, we must be aware of our perceptions of them: age, sex, status, and psychological set. We must add to this perception of the physical setting our perception of ourself; how do we fit into this situation?

As there is a physical setting for every communication event, there is also a psychological setting. We call this our psychological set, as it molds our perceptions of the situation and the activity that occurs. This is our mental set that gives us our anticipations and expectations for the communication event. If we are an astute communicator, we will continually check our anticipations with our perceptions to see if they agree. If they do, then we can feel confident that we are correct in our inferences. If they do not, then we must revise one or the other. Communicative competence is developed through knowing our anticipations for a communication event and checking to see if they were confirmed by our perceptions of the event. It might help if we check our perceptions with an outside source as well.

How does psychological set affect our communicative behavior? If we enter a communication situation anticipating acceptance of our ideas, we will act in a way that will give others this feeling. Our anticipatory behavior may help get them accepted, but the main point is to see if the communication event unfolds as we had expected. This gives us a check on how close our image of reality is to that of those with whom we communicate. Our psychological set gives us a focus that facilitates selective perception, i.e., biasing our perceptions of an event in the direction of our attitudinal frame of reference. This means that it is psychologically difficult to be objective about anything we perceive. As we mentioned earlier, we often change our perception of the communication event rather than our view of reality. This may mean that we are living in an imaginary world and need outside help to become realistic.

One other aspect of the situation must be mentioned. We would like to think that life is stable and uncomplicated. Actually, it is neither. In any communication event we must be aware of the dynamics of the event. Objectives, behaviors, and reasons continually change. A communication event is always in a state of flux. We must keep this in mind as we communicate. Each point in a discussion changes our cognitive structure and thus, should change our perceptions. An HCS does not remain constant. If we do not recognize or are not aware of the dynamics of a communication event, or an HCS, we will make effective communication impossible.

When we have defined the situation, we have defined the behaviors that are possible. Situations themselves have rules for proper conduct. Funerals call for different behaviors than picnics. What are the rules? Are they consistent across cultures? Parties, classes, luncheons, and board meetings call for different kinds of behavior than does making love. This is an extreme example, but perhaps it makes the point that we must be aware of the situation and its purpose before we can determine what the rules are for appropriate conduct. These behaviors stem from the exigencies or demands of the situation.

Knowing the relationships that exist in an HCS allows us to assume the appropriate role for us in that HCS. When a male first enters a male/female relationship, he usually assumes the dominant role. This may not be appropriate, but until the couple has communicated about it, his culture may dictate that in this type of relationship, he should be the dominant one. Since first encounters are usually based on stereotypes, this isn't a bad way to begin, but he must be aware that this is one aspect of HCSs that is changing rapidly, so he must be prepared to adjust his communication to fit the circumstances. If he is unperceptive, or set (psychologically) in his ways, he may miss the opportunity for an exciting relationship. The role we assume initially may not be the one we take permanently.

The exigence in a situation comes from the persons, events, objects, and relationships that are a part of the communication event in which we are partaking. Nonetheless, only those of which we are cognizant can play a role in our communicative behavior. Therefore, one of the constraints or boundaries of the HCS on the situational dimension is our perception. If we are not perceptive, we will limit the communication possibilities and thus the potential of our HCS. Our perceptions require the integration of past events with the possibility of future events, as they impinge on the present event. Thus, perception is much more than just seeing, hearing, or feeling what is in the physical setting of the communication event. It also means being aware of our perspectives and those of others in the HCS. Much of this depends upon our psychological set and the selective perceptions it precipitates.

The Personal Dimension

The humanists talked about a third force, that of the individual's active conscious choices that may direct his or her behavior. The personal dimension is that part of an HCS's environment that lies inside the psyche of its members. Perhaps this is a strange conceptualization, saying that part of our environment is internal, but if, when you are confronted with a decision, you ask yourself, What can I do in this situation?, you realize that some of the constraints on your behavior are self-imposed.

Our dominant evaluative characteristic is identified by the sets of values we bring to bear on various decision-making situations. At the same time these values are developing, we are experiencing different decision-making situations and seeing which values work the best. A child's first conscious valuing process may reflect only the good-bad dimension, but subconscious feelings involving such qualities as wet-dry, pleasant-unpleasant, and hot-cold may have been in use for some time. We assume that children begin to develop their personal values by internalizing purely physical feelings, such as hot-cold and wet-dry, and progress to abstract symbolic values, such as good-bad and honest-dishonest, as their conceptual abilities grow.

The clustering of specific feelings in relation to various events is interpreted as fear, desire, trust, etc. Each of these states may be expressed as a specific cognitive construct, e.g., fearful-fearless, desirable-undesirable, and trustworthy-untrustworthy. However, any given decision-making process is not definable by these specific feelings alone. Our choice in any real-life situation must be operationally defined in terms of a cluster of personal feelings; i.e., most of us are not single-dimension people. We do not "help or not help" a friend because the action is good or bad; many other dimensions are involved, such as time, depth of involvement, projected outcomes, etc.

Another aspect of the decision-making process is important for us to consider. When confronted with a decision, what are the possible actions that can be taken? What are the doables, or "sayables," that I have at my command? The three variables that must be considered are: 1) the objective, or end product, of the communication event, 2) all possible actions that might attain this objective, and 3) which of these actions will fit into the collective cognitive structure of the HCS.

We all have other values that play a major role in our development. When we communicate with others, we not only say something about how we feel about ourselves, we also reveal our other values. By doing this, others begin to get a symbolic picture of us, and we begin to see where we agree or disagree with others—that is, if we are aware of our communicative behavior! The process of revealing our values can be extremely difficult because it usually means that we will be evaluated by the person with whom we are communicating according to his or her value system. If that person is a significant other (one whom we feel we must please), and to some of us everyone is a significant other, we are apprehensive about stating our position before we find out what theirs is.

If we could take a more macroscopic view of our life and of reality as we see it, we would probably see that an overall structure functions in our life. This level of structure is often difficult to see either by us or a therapist, but we all have one. That we are able to use it to actualize our own life processes is not sure, for we often find ourselves striving for the myths of society rather than trusting our own inner structure. Frankl (1963) talks about this problem in terms of an existential vacuum.

> The existential vacuum is a widespread phenomenon of the twentieth century. This is understandable; it may be due to a twofold loss that man had to undergo since he became a truly human being. At the beginning of history, man lost some of the basic animal instincts in which an animal's behavior is embedded and by which it is secured. Such security, like Paradise, is closed to man forever; man has to make choices. In addition to this, however, man has suffered another loss in his more recent development: the traditions that had buttressed his behavior are now rapidly diminishing. No instinct tells him what he has to do, and no tradition tells him what he ought to do; soon he will not know what he wants to do. More and more he will be governed by what others want him to do, thus increasingly falling prey to conformism (pp. 167–168).

We are there! Tradition has given way to Madison Avenue; now our advertising agencies tell us what we need, what we want, and implicitly how to act in any given situation. So we can either let them make our decisions for us, or we can make our own decisions and take the responsibility for them.

You cannot take the responsibility for your life unless you are aware of yourself and the choices you have. The influence of others cannot be denied (as in the opening example). Thus, we would like to emphasize the point made earlier; namely, when people see you as different from them, this does not make you any more deviant than they are, for they cannot act out of your cognitive structure anymore than you can act out of theirs. At the same time, we must realize that they are a critically important source of information to us. By utilizing this information we can better establish our own sense of self, our direction and meaning in life. This sense of direction or meaning is called "intentionality" and implies both a focus on an objective and an active striving to attain it.

To develop realistic intentions requires an in-depth awareness of ourselves. Among other things, this means bringing our locus of evaluation back inside us, i.e., centering the evaluative process for any decision in our feelings and values and not in the feelings and values of others. It takes the "I shoulds" and "I oughts" out of decision making and puts in the "I wills." It also brings the acceptance of the responsibility for behavior back to the person. Along with moving the locus of evaluation back inside us, we must also move the locus of control back inside us, viz., the feeling that we are not pawns in a huge chess game, but rather, we have some control over our actions (Lefcourt, 1976).

Since all HCSs have objectives, we must know what we can do to facilitate attaining these objectives. As we have seen, much of this depends on our knowledge of ourselves, others, the communication process, and our ability to make decisions. All of these become constraints or boundaries on the personal dimension of the environment of our HCSs because they facilitate or limit our ability to find the doables for attaining the objectives. Our knowledge of what is possible and our ability to create new approaches, determine how efficient and effective a communicator we are. Of all the things that may affect our decision-making process (and thus, the attainment of the objectives), the most significant one is our values. Thus, we must know our values and those of the other components in our HCSs if we expect to achieve our objectives.

The Cultural Dimension

Growing up in any culture forces us to assimilate at least some of the norms of that culture. This we call enculturation. Rogers (1972) calls this process "introjection," by which he means taking on the values and behaviors of those around us to obtain or maintain love. As these values and behaviors slip into our subconscious cognitive structures, we are unaware that they are becoming a part of us. We then are filled with a number of values and ways of behaving for which we have no reasons, but which we cannot imagine changing. These values have a definite effect on the communication strategies we develop, for they give us a way of seeing each communication event, such as the opening experience in this chapter.

Some of the introjected values we view as positive—good looks, having money, and being clean—while others are negative—being fat, growing old, and having skin problems. Sounds like our television commercials, doesn't it? As long as these values are clear-cut, with few dissenting voices, they cause us little concern. But what happens when we have two major segments of a culture competing for our values? Take cigarette smoking, for example. We are constantly bombarded by advertisements for and against the behavior. How do we decide which to follow? Regardless of which choice we make, we will be taking on the values of our culture; either from the national norms or the norms of the group (HCS) with which we run. Having inculcated these norms, we behave accordingly without even thinking about it.

Cultures develop through years of interactions among their members. They are usually associated with a specific geographic area, but this is not a necessary condition. A culture is made up of unique ways of behaving in given situations, along with unique ways of looking at both ourselves and others. We carry around with us an image of who we are culturally, and how we differ from some other cultures or subcultures. Since our behavior is predicated on the mental image we create, rather than objective facts, we must become aware of where these images come from. It is our culture that influences us to create the mental images we use in our interactions with others. It has an effect on us through introjection, assimilation, and learning, and we have an effect on it through our acceptance or rejection of cultural norms.

Our culture tells us what type of behavior is good, valued, expected, proper, etc. It does this through its norms as we become enculturated by acquiring the rules of our cultural norms. As we begin to use these rules to develop our own lifestyle, they take on further nuances of our culture. Regulative rules may be stated generically as: within context Z, if relation Y is desired, then behavior X is preferred, obligatory, prohibited, permissible, or irrelevant (Shimanoff, 1980; Reardon, 1981). Thus, if in the context of our family (Z), we want to be accepted (Y), the following rules may apply:

Being conservative is preferred.

Obeying our parents is obligatory.

Taking drugs is prohibited.

Being a little avant-garde is permissible.

Knowing a second language is irrelevant.

You may be able to come up with contexts (cultures) in which most of these rules would change places.

Depending on how isolated a culture is, the differences between it and other cultures may be extreme or barely noticeable. This is of importance when we look at subcultures as well. For example the male/female subcultures coexist but maintain noticeable differences in spite of this. Cultural differences appear in at least four areas of communicative behavior:

1. Verbal behavior is an obvious difference between most cultures. It ranges from completely different languages, e.g., Russian and Spanish, to subtleties within the same language, e.g., coke, pop, and soda may all refer to the same drink depending on where you are from.

2. Nonverbal behavior is similar to verbal in that it may have extreme differences, e.g., personal space of the English and Arabs, or the subtle differences in dress that indicate status in some cultures.

3. The values of the culture, which will be discussed in detail later.

4. The mental images that are typical of the cultural members. If the members of two different cultures hold similar views of reality, it will be much easier for them to communicate than if they are vastly different.

It is not enough to try to change one norm of a culture without changing the norms that are affected by it. In Costa Rica, after the Peace Corps had trained local women for specific jobs, they found that these women would not apply for the jobs because they felt it would be infringing on male territory. Sex-role stereotypes must be broken on both sides of the equation. If a male sees himself as the dominant member of an HCS, he will act that way. If the female also sees him in that role, the HCS will function smoothly. But, if the female sees herself as equal (or superior), there will be problems in the HCS. If the male doesn't take the dominant role, but the female expects him to, there will be problems in this HCS as well. The expectations you have of the behavior of other people will make a great deal of difference in the way your HCSs function. These expectations are based on your mental programming. You will continue to have these expectations as long as they are confirmed by the behavior of others. Unfortunately, sex-role stereotypes are far more universal than they are unique to any one culture (Williams and Best, 1982).

As we indicated above, some of our mental programs are conscious and some are nonconscious. If we put all of these together, we find that we have a way of behaving that requires little or no thought. Perhaps we can define this as a predisposition toward certain communicative behaviors. We designated this aspect of communication as our attitudinal frame of reference. It is a broader concept than nonconscious ideologies; it shows up in almost all of our communicative behavior because it guides our thinking. In our HCSs we may come down on the side of democracy, freedom, equal rights, abortion, etc. Our friends know this about us and expect it of us. In this sense, our attitudinal frame of reference is our *personal culture*; it has a large component of the culture in which we were raised, but is also uniquely us.

The best way to find out what some of your cultural attitudes are is to spend some time in another culture. You may have felt this culture shock when you first came to the university. It sometimes represents a culture quite foreign to the one you grew up in. However, if you are sent to a foreign country by your company with the expectation of managing local people as you did back home, you may find it almost impossible to overcome some of your biases. This is especially true if you have a tendency to be ethnocentric, i.e., you think the characteristics of your culture are superior to those of other cultures. It is hard to have effective communication when two members of an HCS have been enculturated differently; it is impossible if one or both are ethnocentric (Harris and Moran, 1979). The phrase "the Ugly American" came from the tendency of so many people from the United States to think and behave as though they were superior to the host culture. This is really brought home when you are in another country and think all the people there are foreigners! Who is the foreigner? Our enculturation, especially if we have been sheltered from other cultures, can give us an ethnocentric view of reality (Bochner, 1982).

The norms of behavior in any culture will form boundaries for any HCS that has a component from that culture. What do we mean by boundary? We usually think of boundaries as physical things that we can see, touch, or hear. The boundaries of the playing field for any sport are good examples. You cannot violate these boundaries without paying a penalty. The rules of the game are written with the boundaries in mind. They become part of the structure of the game. The same can be said for HCSs. The rules by which they are established take into account the norms of the culture in which they reside. Attempts to violate these norms, whether they are norms of consent or force, will result in penalties. The creation of Solidarity in Poland is a good example. That is not to say that we should never challenge the norms of a culture; if they were never challenged, they might never change, and progress would be impeded.

Though boundaries are usually thought of as constraining the activity which they bound, they may also facilitate it. A pitcher uses the boundaries of home plate to make himself effective. If he threw every pitch down the middle of the plate, it would be a disaster. The same is true of cultural norms. We can use them to explore differences in expectations of the members of our HCSs, or we can let them force us into seclusion for fear of breaking one of them. They make it easy to communicate because if we do not violate them, we can feel sure that we will be accepted by others in our HCSs. They may also force us into certain communication patterns. Clinging to them allows us to maintain our present course without having to exert any effort in that area of our endeavor. It's the path of least effort. Unfortunately, it may also be the path of least creativity, involvement, and commitment to the objective. If we never challenge our culture's views of reality, we have a good likelihood of never becoming anything more than we are right now. Richness in personal maturity comes from the ability to see beyond our cultural programming and transcend our cultural norms.

TRANSITION

This chapter has introduced the three dimensions of human communication systems. The rest of the book will say much more about each one. The main point is that we should be aware of these three dimensions and take advantage of the analytical possibilities they offer. We must realize that when we are communicating across cultures, the situation is much more difficult to perceive. Perhaps this knowledge can help us become better intercultural communicators, particularly when we realize that most of our perceptions come from nonverbal cues, which are interpreted from our cultural norms. The communicators' purpose is also important, since the behavior may be ritualistic, with a purpose different than what we perceive.

Much of what we perceive in a foreign culture may be noise rather than what it would be in our culture. The same is true of the behaviors we intend to be communicative but are ignored by those around us because in this culture they are not communicative signals. Both of these situations give us a feeling of increased entropy, as we realize that our attempts to communicate are not controlling the situation as we thought they would. We may be able to discover the source of our problems if we can look at the communication event from the three dimensions discussed in this chapter. In the following chapter we will delve deeper into the situational dimension of human communication.

INDEPENDENT STUDY

The assignments for this chapter are more general and therefore less likely to have well-defined answers. However, by delving into the three constraints that are placed on our communicative behavior, we can begin to get a picture of how cultures differ.

1. Situational constraints: Get two or three students from different cultures and go to a public gathering place, like a shopping mall, where different types of people can be observed. Over a period of time choose several different-looking types of people and ask each of your cohorts to write down as many of their perceptions about each of these people as they can (sex, age, occupation, etc.). When this exercise is finished, discuss the similarities and differences in your perceptions. Is there a common source for your differences? Write a report.

2. Personal constraints: Choose a specific communication event (such as being questioned by the police) and determine how personal values and cultural norms overlap by discussing this situation with a group of foreign students (representing at least four different cultures) and write a report.

3. Cultural constraints: Choose a specific communication event (such as asking for a date) and, using the five rules of cultural norms, discuss this situation with a male and a female from a culture other than your own to see how the norms differ from yours and how they differ between the two sexes. Write up your findings.

CHAPTER FOUR
Situational Orientations

I once helped a young Costa Rican mother get a passport for her daughter. When we arrived at the passport office, she insisted that we go to another location in the same ministry to find a friend of hers because he could help us. We finally found this young man, who had obviously never met the mother, and she explained to him that she was the cousin of one of his uncles. That made the link, because they then began talking about people they both knew. He left his desk and escorted her back to the passport office where he introduced himself to the agent (whom he hadn't met before) and identified himself as an employee of the ministry. At this point the agent reviewed the mother's application (although there were 20 or 30 ahead of her) and said that something was wrong with her daughter's birth certificate.

I then drove her to the lawyer's office where the original work had been done on the passport papers. Three lawyers with nothing to do were there, but she would not let them work on her documents because the lawyer who had done the original work (a friend of her uncle) had stepped out for something. We waited! He finally returned and corrected the problem. The documents had to be recertified by a government office—this was done by a clerk who asked no questions—and then a new application had to be made for the passport. I waited for another hour (in the car) while she went through another friend to get the new application. With this we returned to the ministry, found our original "friend," who took her back to the first agent (who now placed the necessary stamps on her application), and then to the passport dispatching office. He introduced himself and the mother to the manager (it was nearly closing time and there were many people waiting), who discovered that he knew this woman and her family and would have done all of this for her if she had asked him in the first place!

In this chapter we will look into the way in which we perceive communication situations. Perception is a two-step process: sensation—the reception of stimuli from the external environment, and interpretation—the creation of a cognitive image of the external environment. It is a subjective process in which we perceive particular things and associate them with other things that are going on at the same time and place. We may also associate them with other things in our mind, as our perceptions are influenced by cognitive structures and processes.

DEFINING THE SITUATION

Friendship, a basic attachment between two people, is the cornerstone of most human relationships. The behavior of friends may very well be a significant cultural indicator. Perhaps the primary schema that is formed for friendships is that of expectations: what kind of behavior do you expect from a friend? Experience tells us that friends and acquaintances in some cultures are the chief means of accomplishing one's objectives (as in Costa Rica), and that what one culture may call an acquaintance another calls a friend. The expectations of friendships in some cultures are close to what we in the United States have labeled Machiavellianism—using other people to achieve one's own objectives (Christie and Geis, 1970). In a study of Costa Rican and U.S. students, Borden (1982) found that Costa Rican and U.S. males had identical scores for Machiavellianism, while the Costa Rican females had significantly higher scores than the U.S. females.

In the opening illustration, the physical aspects of the situation included a foreigner (me) trying to assist a national in the process of obtaining a passport for her daughter. It included all of my perceptions of the actual physical offices, people, and environment of San José, Costa Rica. Some of it was familiar to me, but most of it was not, so I was learning about the city and the bureaucratic red tape as we went along. Whenever I asked a question, I always got the answer, "This is how we do it in Costa Rica." The physical aspects of the situation also include the languages spoken (we are talking about "situation" in an intercultural communication event), both verbal and nonverbal. The major nonverbal code in which differences were noted between our two cultures was time (chronemics). The woman seemed to be in a desperate hurry but willing to wait for hours to talk to just the right person.

Time bridges the gap between the physical and psychological dimensions of the situation. My evaluation of her "need to hurry" was created from my own cognitive patterns of what constitutes this concept. In her own culture she may have appeared relaxed and unhurried. Another psychological perception was what I deemed persistence, or perseverance. At each juncture she persevered until she got what she came for. A third psychological construct that amazed me was the notion of "friend." The young man who first became her friend through a linkage to her cousin later introduced her as his friend. In the United States, many of our cousins are probably not our friends! It was also notable that she would not do business with anyone who was not her friend. Networking behavior is pursued in the United States, but not to this extent. Our perception of using a friend for our own gain still smacks of being unethical.

There is another side to this story of Machiavellianism. While I watched, amazed at how deftly this young woman worked her friends (who never seemed to be perturbed by the inconvenience—but perhaps it was only an inconvenience in U.S. terms), I grew more and more frustrated by her expectations of me. She never asked if I had the time to do this running around. I bought her lunch and paid the parking fees when necessary. She never asked me to do anything (just told me how to get to the next office) until we were through, when she asked me if I would drive back into the city to pick up her brother from his work because his car was in the shop. But she didn't know exactly where he worked, so I saw much of San José that I never knew existed! I felt that she was treating me as both a Costa Rican friend and a rich gringo. The psychological dimensions of any situation consist of both the perceptions of the foreigner and those of the nationals; but can a foreigner ever be treated completely like a national?

Stereotyping

In keeping with the nature of human communication, we must always bear in mind that perceptions of the situation are being made continuously by both of the communicators. These perceptions can take many forms, but of primary interest are the cues that tell us who the other person is. Who do we think we are and who do they think we are? Singer (1987) suggests that we have a number of *perceptual identities* and defines them as "a number of individuals who perceive some aspect of the external world more or less similarly, but who *do not communicate* this similarity of perception among themselves" (p. 38). He distinguishes perceptual identity from that of group identity by saying that, "A number of people who perceive some aspect of the external world more or less similarly and *recognize and communicate* this similarity of perception form an identity group" (p. 40) (italics added).

In intercultural communication our strongest perceptual identity is that of our home culture; we perceive an identity between ourselves and other members of our culture though we seldom, if ever, communicate this similarity. These perceptual identities are also the strongest barriers to effective communication, as most of us are unaware of our cultural perceptions. Most of the group identities we have within our culture become only perceptual identities when we communicate across cultures. We may see the person we are communicating with as a member of our identity group, say a university student, and treat him or her as we would a student from our culture when, in reality, the aspects of the external world that you perceive alike are minuscule in comparison to the cultural differences you do not perceive at all. What happens in such a situation? We are usually confused if our communicatee does not behave the way a student should behave. The pattern of behavior or schema or stereotype we have developed for the concept "student" does not fit the perceived behavior of our communicatee. The same is probably true for the opposite side of this dyad; they do not see us fitting into their concept of a student.

Negative stereotyping results from shallow perceptual identities and has been "regarded as the product of an erroneous and atypical thought process in which the person adopts conclusions he would not normally make" (Hamilton, 1978, p. 82). Hamilton continues this argument by stating the three assumptions on which this definition of stereotyping is based. They are 1) it fulfills the motivational need of the stereotyper (perhaps the need for power), 2) it is based on illogical thinking, and 3) there is always some truth in the stereotype. The evidence he presents indicates that most stereotypes stem from a legitimate differentiation among social groups. He says that:

> As human beings, we exist in a world of many individuals performing many acts. As perceivers, however, we find it difficult to live in such a world and hence we seek out similarities and differences, reducing the degree of complexity confronting us by sorting people into groups and by sorting acts into behavior patterns. When, as a consequence of this categorization process, the perceiver comes to associate certain patterns of behaviors or traits with certain categories of persons, then stereotyping has occurred (p. 83).

Our most common categorizations are 1) people who are like us and 2) people who are different from us, and the characteristics we use to make these categorizations can be anything. Human beings seem to find it impossible not to separate others into these two groups. But we find a wide range of differences in the ability of people to distinguish similarities and differences between themselves and others. The process of categorization based on limited perceptions is absolutely necessary for us to remain sane, for who can go through the entire list of female or male characteristics every time they meet a person to determine which sex they are? Our cognitive processes automatically chunk data, probably through some kind of pattern recognition, in order to speed up our information processing time.

So, if our cognitive processes operate on the basis of categorizations, what is wrong with stereotypes? First, we should recognize that there are both good and bad stereotypes. Good stereotypes are those that are based on sufficient characteristics and categories to give us a first approximation of how to communicate with the other person. They provide sufficient commonalities for us to identify with some aspect of another's culture. Bad stereotypes are too limited, based on too few characteristics or categories. Second, we should realize that stereotypes are only good for the initial encounter and must be checked and modified as is necessary. Third, we must realize that when we place value labels on our stereotypes, we cease to use them in the most optimal way; we are letting our ego involvement dominate our communication processes.

Making Sense

We have seen that it is both necessary and impossible not to have stereotypes about the environment, including the people, making up our communication situation. If we assume that both sides in an intercultural communication event have these stereotypes of the other, how do they go about making sense out of the communicative behavior of the other? A more cognitive aspect of the communication situation is the ability of the communicators to recognize the scripts, schemas, and motives of the other, or at least to recognize that the other person has them. Of course, these probably vary more by individual than by culture. However, the cultural orientation model given in Chapter 6 will give some cultural characteristics that will help us to make an initial approximation.

If we are the foreigner in the communication event, we must realize that we have the obligation to accept the legitimacy of the other's culture. *This is no small task.* With the prevalence of ethnocentricism, one of the leading causes of ineffective intercultural communication is the unconscious (or conscious!) refusal to accept the other's culture as sovereign and equal. It points out clearly the we/they dichotomy and the inability of either or both to accept culture as a legitimate variable in the communication process. When this occurs there is a battle over who will serve as superior and who will be subordinate. Schmidt (1975) talks about this as the difference between the expert and the novice. Certainly, the expert has a better grasp of the situation, in this case the host culture, but usually from the perspective of his or her cultural attributes (of which he or she may be unaware). To be sure, it may not be the persons from the more complex culture who are the experts, though they tend to think they are.

Another important point that must be taken into consideration when defining the situation is that not everyone will perceive it to be the same. Certainly, the cultural orientation will have an effect on the person's perception. The foreigner may be at a great disadvantage in that artifacts and behaviors of the host culture will stand out to him or her in contrast with his or her expectations. How does he or she interpret these differences from the remembered culture? We know that two people can see the same object and interpret it differently as well as seeing two different objects and interpreting them as the same. Add to this the confounding nature of the different cultural orientations and it is a wonder we can communicate at all!

Glenn (1981) says that "1. perception depends on the subject and not only on the object; 2. the contribution of the subject to the total transaction depends, at least in part, on the previous experience of the subject, i.e., on memory; 3. different subjects, and the same subject at different times, may bring different contributions to cognitive transactions" (p. 51). When defining the situation we must keep these ideas in mind, else we set up a situation that does not resemble reality. And what is reality? When we have done our best to describe the situation with all of its variables, we still must remember that we cannot rid ourselves of our own culture, for it is us; we must work within the knowledge that we are different from every other culture and that our culture affects the way we perceive all others.

It appears that the possibility of making sense out of the communication situation rests on the basic assumption that our behavior is motivated by a stable cognition. The foundation for this cognition is our belief systems. Ajzen and Fishbein (1980) have developed a means by which we can predict behavior if we have sufficient knowledge about a person's beliefs, attitudes, and intentions. Whether or not this process is reversible is not known (knowing one's behavior, can you predict their intention, attitude, and beliefs?). Nonetheless, this is the intuitive process we use when we attribute reasons for behaviors. They say,

> At the most global level, a person's behavior is assumed to be determined by his intention. At the next level, we showed that these intentions are themselves determined by attitudes toward the behavior and subjective norms. The third level explained attitudes and subjective norms in terms of beliefs about the consequences of performing the behavior and about the normative expectations of relevant referents. In the final analysis, then, a person's behavior is explained by reference to his beliefs (p. 79).

None of these links should be considered autonomous; rather, the one level has an influence over the other. Being able to predict behavior based on this chain of constructs assures us that knowing the belief and disbelief systems of a culture is an important part of making sense of the communication situation. Besides belief systems, one must also include in the situation a knowledge of past behaviors and what obstacles, both physical and psychological, might interfere with the performance of the expected behavior (Chaiken and Stangor, 1987). Past performance is still the best predictor of present behavior. Thus, an experiential knowledge of the culture is essential.

Some Examples

What happens when we find ourself in another culture? We are all so familiar with some basic experiences in our own culture that we will follow these cultural standards without even thinking. Since the language being spoken is probably not our first language, the verbal differences are much easier to pick up than are the nonverbal. For this reason we must observe the nonverbal cues given by our host culture. They may be subtle but meaningful.

Self-Presentation   But what difference does it make how you present yourself? Can't you just be yourself? Perhaps, but unfortunately, the first impression we make on others may be the last impression we make on them if they do not accept us. Therefore, we must meet their standards to some extent—thus, the ritual. Although first impressions do not last a long time if we go on to get better acquainted with the person, they do have a great deal to do with the possibility of continuing to get acquainted.

First impressions are usually based on personal appearance and all of the nonverbal codes associated with it. Besides our physical attributes (body type, hair style, age, sex, culture, etc.), we must be concerned with our clothing (artifacts), body language (kinesics), touching behavior (haptics), promptness (chronemics), how close we stand (proxemics), the feelings we project (facial expression), where and how long we look (oculemics), how we sound (vocalics), how we smell (olfactics), and in some cases the color of our clothing (chromatics). Can you think of an occasion where acoustics, gustics, and silence might also be applicable?

The presentation of self has attributes from the five dimensions of Self-Concept presented earlier. The bodily self is the primary object of our first impressions. Self-identity is seen in the role we play in the communication event. (Do we continue a role we have in one HCS over into another HCS?) Self-extension is seen in the behaviors we exhibit to gain acceptance from those in the HCS. (Are we ingratiating, unassuming, extroverted, etc.? How do we show this—Kinesics? Vocalics? Haptics? Chromatics?) Self-esteem is closely akin to self-identity, but the way we show it is usually seen in the way we treat others—chronemics, haptics, kinesics, vocalics). Finally, self-image, the way we feel about ourselves, can be heard in our voice (vocalics) and seen in our face (facial expression), our posture (kinesics), and sometimes in our eye behavior (oculemics). Can you think of other codes that might project these dimensions of self? Are you the ugly American or just another person?

Relating to Others   Most relationships are started with eye contact (oculemics). The contact is made and held a bit longer than is correct for polite, uninterested interaction in that culture. This action was probably brought about because you saw something in the other person's appearance that you liked. If the look is reciprocated, the next signal is to move into the other's personal space (kinesics, proxemics). Now you may use a personal or environmental artifact as the subject to open up a conversation (the weather, the room, their appearance).

You may find that it was the color of their eyes, hair, or skin that interested you, and that may become the subject of conversation (chromatics). If you are observant of the facial expression and tension in the other person's body, you can infer a like or dislike for you or the subject you are discussing. You may also infer this from the tone of voice used in your conversation (vocalics). Both of you will probably be aware of the odors that both you and the environment are giving off (olfactics).

You will also be acutely conscious of the use you make of time, though you may not be aware of the quantity that has passed (chronemics). In this situation, the presence or absence of touch may indicate the progress that is being made in the development of this relationship (haptics). Depending on this progress, one of you may suggest that it is too noisy (acoustics), and that it would be better at his or her place where he or she has a bottle of vintage Gallo (gustics). Does silence give consent?

Fantasy is great, isn't it? The principles are there, but the time sequencing is shortened. The point is that all the nonverbal codes play a role in the development of a relationship. Personal appearance is almost always the first code used. We are drawn to those we like and avoid those we dislike. Our initial contact may be through haptics rather than oculemics, or it may be through vocalics. However, it is nearly impossible to develop a relationship if we do not approach a person (kinesics) and get inside their personal space (proxemics). Of the other codes, facial expression, artifacts, and chronemics are of great importance, and in our culture maybe even olfactics. But what difference does it make whether you are in your culture or another? Think of all the variables (codes) with which you can err!

Controlling the Situation   Manipulation is a form of control, as is persuasion. But everything we do in an HCS controls it. Three rituals have been established to control the flow of communication between two or more people: initiating, structuring, and terminating interaction. They all have set rules of conduct in every culture, but may vary drastically from culture to culture. They are probably the first rituals children learn for communicative interactions, but their use may cause us to become tense throughout our lifetime.

Initiating signals are those that allow us to become involved with someone and create an HCS (Krivonos and Knapp, 1975). They usually involve the codes of oculemics, vocalics, haptics, kinesics, proxemics, chronemics, and facial expression. We greet someone with a handshake and later say "It was like shaking hands with a wet sponge (or a dead fish)!" Most of our greetings are ritualistic, but we pick up a great deal of information about someone from the way they greet us because we know what to expect—at least in our culture. What are the rules for meeting people?

Structuring is done because we feel that it is the most efficient way to communicate. We "take turns" being the speaker and the listener (Wiemann and Knapp, 1975). How do we know when to switch? We never seem to time our utterances, but we speak on the average of six seconds before giving the other person the floor. To keep the speaker role longer, we may use sustained intonation patterns, verbalized pauses, and audible inhalation (vocalics), the continuation of a gesture (kinesics), or breaking eye contact with the receiver (oculemics). To give up the floor and let the listener become the speaker, we merely have to complete our verbalizing. Silence, the rising intonation pattern of a question or the falling of a statement (vocalics), the making of eye contact (oculemics), turning toward the listener, and a positive head nod (kinesics) will all yield the floor.

The listener may signal a desire to take the floor by leaning forward, raising a finger (kinesics), or catching the eye of the speaker (oculemics). She or he may also try to interrupt by speaking over the speaker. Males are more likely to do this than are females. Usually, the sounds the listener makes are those that reinforce the speaker in that role. These vocalic signals, along with head nods and body positioning (kinesics), are called backchanneling and reassure the speaker that the listener is involved. Of course, if the listener gets up and moves away, sets his or her attention on other things, or begins to ignore the speaker, it is evident that the speaker's turn is over—as well as the whole conversation.

All of these cues are from the U.S. culture; they are what we start with when we visit another. But we should be keenly observant and quick to pick up on cultural differences.

Terminating cues are those signals that indicate we are no longer accessible (Knapp, Hart, Friedrich and Schulman, 1973). As noted above this may be one-sided termination, but usually it is agreed upon through subtle nonverbal cues, which indicate the conversation is over. Kinesic movements indicate readiness to leave: leaning forward, nodding, moving toward the exit, physically getting up, shaking hands, breaking eye contact, and leaving (actually terminating the interaction). Some of these nonverbal signals add to the summarizing and supporting behavior of the verbal signals. It seems that it is our custom to leave most interactions on a supportive note even if we haven't agreed much with the other person.

You may find that terminating a conversation and leave-taking behaviors are ambiguous in many cultures. They seem to be drawn out, left up to the guest, but never discussed—you just have to know when to leave. With the U.S. culture being so uptight about time, this sometimes becomes a problem.

PERSPECTIVE TAKING

In defining the intercultural communication situation, we have indicated that a number of perspectives must be kept in mind. However, the major perspectives are those of the communicators from the two different cultures. What do we know about them, and how can we take their perspectives? Oden (1987) tells us that "For some time now, researchers have realized that much of what people know is structured in terms of explicit internal models of aspects of the world they experience" (p. 217). Our world view as well as our perspective on the particular situation in which we are involved resides as a model, or memories, in our cognitive structure. These models are formed in the process of our making sense out of the environment. Oden continues by saying,

> In each case, the appeal to the use of a mental model is based on people's abilities to "run internal simulations" of what would be expected to happen under various hypothetical situations as a means of evaluating alternative problem solutions and making reliable predictions of outcomes in the world. Being able to perform this obviously powerful thinking procedure requires having a systematic body of knowledge about properties of relevant objects and operations. However,

people's models by no means need to be complete or even consistent in order to be effective (p. 218).

To be an effective intercultural communicator one must be able to role play the situation and to take the other person's role in it. In fact, Burleson (1982) tells us that, "the possibility of coordinated social action depends on the individual's capacity to 'take' (i.e., imaginatively construct) the perspective of others. One must be able to represent and anticipate the other's view of a situation in order to mesh one's line of action with that of the other" (p. 473). As you can see, the ability to mesh the two lines of action depends on your knowledge of the other person's cultural, personal, and situational orientation. Our knowledge of any situation and our ability to take the other person's role in it are all part of our situational orientation. If we do not know the other person's cultural and personal identity, then we will find it difficult to take his or her role. On the other hand, some of us, even though we have all of the information, find it difficult to take on different roles.

Wiseman and Abe (1986) go further than just talking about taking the other person's role; they specify the nature of the perspective one must take. "For the intercultural communicator, the ability to take the other's perspective through person-centered attributions, rather than through cultural stereotypes or other position-centered attributions, should enable him or her to be more interculturally effective" (p. 613). The difference they are pointing out is between knowing why a person takes such a perspective and knowing what perspective a person will take. For example, I may know that Costa Ricans will hire a friend or relative rather than the person most qualified for the job, but if I don't know why they do this, then I cannot generalize this principle to other situations.

Nor can we generalize this principle to other cultures, for as Saral (1979) says, "Each world view has different underlying assumptions. Our normal state of consciousness is not something natural or given, nor is it universal across cultures. It is simply a specialized tool, a complex structure for coping with our environment" (p. 81). Though the magnitude of cultural differences may not be great, the fact that they exist means that we must be aware of them when we attempt to take the other person's perspective. Perspective taking is an integral part of any communication situation, but it takes on added importance when the communicators are from different cultures. The probability of misconstruing the other person's perspective decreases with the increase in our knowledge of the other's cultural orientation.

The degree to which our communication is effective has long been equated with the congruence of message(1), in the mind of the source, with message(2), in the mind of the recipient. Since 1966 (Laing, Phillipson, and Lee) we have been aware that this congruence is intimately connected with our perspective-taking abilities. The idea of perspective taking stems from the realization that the way we see an issue may not be the way the issue is seen by others, and thus we may end up with misunderstandings, poor relationships, and failed negotiations.

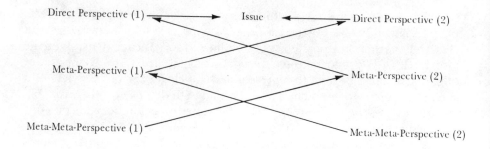

Figure 5:   Levels of Perspective Taking

Laing, et al., suggested that in every communication act there are at least three levels of perspective taking:

1. *Direct Perspective*—your personal attitude toward the issue,
2. *Meta-Perspective*—what you think the other person's attitude is toward the issue, and
3. *Meta-Meta-Perspective*—what you think the other person thinks your attitude is toward the issue. These three perspectives may be visualized as in Figure 5.

At each level your perspective and the other person's may be congruent or incongruent. Incongruency leads to misunderstanding and communication problems. "Comparison between one person's view and another's on the same issue tells us whether they are in *agreement* or *disagreement*. If one person is aware of the other's point of view, we say he *understands* him or her, but if he or she fails to recognize the other's point of view, we say they *misunderstand*. In agreement and disagreement we are comparing *direct perspectives on the same issues*" (p. 60). "*Understanding* can be defined as the agreement between the meta-perspective of one person and the direct perspective of the other.... *Being understood* is the agreement between the meta-meta-perspective of the one person and the meta-perspective of the other.... *The feeling of being understood* is the agreement of one's own direct perspective and one's *own* meta-meta-perspective" (p. 29).

The ability to understand each other is central to effective communication. The problems encountered in cross-cultural communication are exacerbated by the cultural variables that confound perspective taking. The more ethnocentric the communicators, the less they are able to realize that incongruent perspectives, and thus misunderstanding, may be playing a role in their communication. On the other hand, it may be that disagreement over the correct perspective, or not respecting the other person's right to their perspective, is at the root of the communication problems.

LaFeber (1983) shows in considerable detail how the perspectives of the politicians in the United States and in the Central American countries have differed since the very beginning. The United States had severe problems with Figueres in Costa Rica, Sandino in Nicaragua, Martinez in El Salvador, Morales in Honduras, and Arbenz in Guatemala, to name only a few. In each case the United States sent messages that conflicted with its stated policy and confounded the perspectives of both countries. A most confusing behavior has been the United States' backing military dictatorships while espousing democracy. The U.S. perspective behind this behavior seems to be that voiced by Theodore Roosevelt. He believed that Central Americans were unable to govern themselves and therefore unable to maintain order, and for him maintaining order seems to have had the higher priority.

We can use the above information to explain the perspective-taking model. If the issue is trust in the Central American countries to govern themselves, then we see that the rhetoric and the stated policy of the United States showed strong belief in this. However, when the Central American countries believed this and made moves toward strengthening self-government, they were undercut by a different policy, that of stability and pro-U.S. sentiment at all costs, e.g., Arbenz in Guatemala and Sandino in Nicaragua (we might also add Allende in Chile). By the time one gets to the meta-perspective, many different possibilities prohibit diplomats from taking the perspective of the other country. Thus, at the diplomatic level—where the real agenda is so often hidden from the other side—it is impossible to negotiate in good faith; the perspective that each side should take is that of uncertainty and continued close negotiations.

Kim (1986) says that "understanding and accuracy (are) the most important concepts" (p. 35) for communication to be effective. In the above example neither of these exist; neither side could understand the other because they could not predict with any accuracy the real direct perspective of the other. Diplomats should have ways of finding out what the direct perspectives of the other country are. If they cannot, what are the chances for a common citizen to know these? In a study (Borden, 1985b) of U.S. and Costa Rican perspectives on the problems in Central America, the direct perspectives of the U.S. and Costa Rican students were found to be significantly different, but a group of U.S. students who had spent from three to five months in Costa Rica had perspectives that were halfway between the others' perspectives. Lee and Larwood (1983) found the same phenomenon with expatriate managers in multinational firms and called it "cultural resocialization." It indicates that one possible way to change one's perspectives in the direction of another culture is to live in that culture for a time.

Another way of looking at the need to know and to take the other culture's perspective is presented by Newmark and Asante (1974). They say,

Culture provides the individual with a frame of reference in which to function, and has a strong role in the formation of values, attitudes, and communication styles. . . . A person must be able to modify his own frame of reference to become more aware of the roles and values of other cultures. In the intercultural environment one is confronted with people having different personal as well as cultural realities. Therefore one is faced with a whole set of new perceptions to interpret. This means that one must become more acutely aware of his own cultural cues; our cultural cues take on different meanings in different cultures (p. 55).

Being late for an appointment in Costa Rica does not mean that you are being disrespectful to the person you are seeing, nor does having to wait hours past your appointed time mean that you are being put down. However, it may be a constant struggle to see time as Costa Ricans do.

PERCEPTION

Perspective taking rests on our perception of the situation. Higgins and Bargh (1987) tell us that "people apparently encode environmental information fairly accurately without supplementing the original information with previous knowledge. But it also appears that some kind of abstract summary representation of the data may be encoded along with the data themselves, and the summary may influence subsequent processing and decisions" (p. 373). These "abstract summary representations" may differentiate one culture from another. Korten (1976) says that "different cultural groups use very different systems of categories in perceiving other people. . . . cultural needs affect the importance of particular perceptual categories and in this way shape the interpersonal perceptions of the culture's members" (p. 133). Since even basic associative cultures use a linguistic code, we know that some abstracting goes on. These abstract summary representations are the encoding of the experience we have just had into the language of our cognitive structure. The summary representations are the schemas we attach to the coding of these experiences.

When we experience our environment, it is not necessary to encode this experience into a linguistic code (at least at a conscious level), but as it is stored in our cognitive structure, it is given verbal and/or nonverbal terms by which it can be retrieved from our memory. We can use these codes to retrieve it, or if the experience is recalled by itself, the codes attached to it are also recalled. For example, the basic abstract summary representation used for associative memories are those of time, location, and emotion. If you have done much traveling, all you have to hear is the name of a country or city you have visited to recall the good or bad experiences you had there along with the dates when you were there. Or, if you are thinking of good or bad experiences, this country or city will be recalled along with the time when you were there.

Another aspect of perception is that when we encode environmental information, we also generate and store inferences based on this information. These inferences (based on old expectations) aid in establishing new expectations. The importance of these inferences is that "perceivers are continually directed in their interpretation of information by features of the current or recent situational context that activates particular constructs. In addition these influences on interpretation are automatic and uncontrollable" (Higgins et al., p. 376). Thus, our associative memory is continually linked with past experiences, and we build up a tremendously complex cognitive structure from which memories of disparate experiences may be recalled by any number of different cues.

As we construct this complex cognitive structure, Higgins, et al., say that our "expectancies or hypotheses about what is likely to happen in a social situation play a critical role in the selection of information from the environment to be encoded, as well as in how that information will be encoded into memory" (p. 378). This is akin to the concept of selective perception. We see what we expect to see through the selection of the information that fits into our expectations. The more dangerous aspect of this type of perception is that in the process we are reinforcing the schemas that produced the selective perception in the first place. This chain of events can lead to stereotyping, closed mindedness, and ethnocentricism. Again, Higgins, et al., say that "Once a social judgment is made it has pervasive effects on the processing of relevant information, which mainly serves to perpetuate the belief" (p. 382).

One can see, then, how our cognitive processes function in a situation to help us make sense out of it. The schemas we form function in our perspective taking and also direct our search for the truth (as we see it). When we take our perspectives in a communication situation, our expectations are for schema-consistent behavior (Boski, 1988). But look at the problems. Unless we have sufficient experience in the other person's culture to know his or her schemas, we will be using the schemas from our own culture, and our expectations will not be in line with the reality of an intercultural communication situation. What is our hope for effective communication?

Wedge (1972) reviews a number of mechanisms of perception that are used to develop stereotypes or images of cultures by citizens of other cultures. A few of them are 1) mythic stereotypes for which there is no hard data but it sounds true (it's what we want to hear); 2) thinking by analogy, which takes a host cultural schema and applies it to another culture (since we would do it so will they); 3) overgeneralizations and connotations of words, which make the image subjective and may result from the fact that local preoccupation focuses the perceptions of the people on the popular stereotype of the other culture; and 4) the need of a scapegoat to take the heat off the local government. Another problem in developing our image of a culture is "attributors have a strong and reliable tendency to overemphasize negative information about the individuals being judged" (Ehrenhaus, 1982, p. 725).

TRANSITION

Our situational orientation rests primarily in our cognitive structure. How we perceive the environment is not like how anyone else perceives it. We get used to the artifacts in our environment and do not have to go through the differentiation process to know what we need to know about it. The environment is much like our language; redundancies in it make it easy for us to collect the information we need and fill in much of what we do not perceive. Eco (1979) says that

> There are a lot of phrases and indeed entire discourses that one no longer has to interpret or decode because one has already experienced them in analogous circumstances or contexts. There are a lot of circumstances in which the hearer already knows what the speaker is going to say. Interactional behavior is based on redundancy rules of this type, and if people had to listen to (or read or look at) every expression they received, analyzing them item by item, communication would be a pretty tiring activity. As a matter of fact one is continuously anticipating expressions, filling up the empty spaces in a text with the missing units, forecasting a lot of words that the interlocutor may have said, could have said, will certainly say, or has never said (p. 136).

Thus, our main concern in the situational orientation is the expectations we bring to it. The schemas and the stereotypes we have will help us know what to expect, but unless we operate from an open mind, these can also spell disaster.

The constraints placed on the human communication system by the situation (the participants' perceptions of the situation) are seen in what each of the communicators feel is demanded of them by the situation. The United States perceived the situation of Arafat coming to speak before the United Nations in 1988 as demanding that they not let him into the country. The cultural norm has been to let the leaders of any culture into the country for U.N. purposes. There were many possible doables by which the United States could have circumvented the policy they had established in relation to the PLO. But in this case the government chose to let their personal orientation to Arafat confound their perception of the situation and refused him an entry visa. One could look at this from the perspective of cultural and personal constraints as well, constraints that will be explicated in the next two chapters.

INDEPENDENT STUDY

It is difficult to objectify the perception of situations. One can discuss situations with friends and see that there are always different perspectives.

1. Gather some acquaintances from three or four different cultures, choose a world crisis situation, and see how many different perspectives are represented in this group. Can you step into any of the other's positions?

2. Using a semantic differential, elicit the direct perspectives and meta-perspectives on a world situation of students from at least two different cultures. Are they in agreement? Do they understand each other? Where are the problems, if any?

3. In a group discussion, see if you can get people to open up on their stereotypes and how they developed.

CHAPTER FIVE
Personal Orientations

Our personal orientation, i.e., the way we perceive reality based on our cognitive structures and processes, can be detrimental to our ability to "get along" in another culture. A female graduate student from the United States was doing research for her thesis in Costa Rica. She was an intelligent young woman who spoke Spanish fluently, and in general she had a good disposition. Her upbringing in the United States, however, had conditioned her to expect equal treatment with males (though she was not a "women's libber"). The machismo of the Costa Rican males had already turned her off, particularly their use of *piropos* (a thinly veiled sexual comment meant to compliment a woman). Costa Rican women have been known to return to their homes to change clothing if they do not receive these comments from the males! Although it is part of the culture, it is also sexist. (A strong movement to eradicate this behavior is now underway, as it is inappropriate in today's world of equality.)

When the graduate student began to collect data for her thesis, the university officials with whom she had to work were all males. In presenting her request for permission to do the study, she was ignored as they carried on the negotiations with her male supervisor. This would never be tolerated in the United States, and she barely tolerated it in Costa Rica, proclaiming that their macho system had to change. That is probably true, but when in another culture you cannot be closed-minded to the way they do things. After all, it is their culture and you are the foreigner. Your ability to differentiate between cultural norms and personal indignities (at least considered such back home) is essential to effective intercultural communication.

We know that knowledge consists of facts, concepts, and processes. In the last chapter we saw that perception consists of sensory reception and information processing, if we accept that information processing consists of both the association and abstraction of information. In this chapter we will look at one's personal orientation in terms of one's cognitive processes and structures and their effect on understanding intercultural communication. Now we need to see how we form our cognitive orientation through these processes.

COGNITION

Cognition refers to one's cognitive processes. We use the term information processing to cover the same idea. It has two basic aspects: Content—the actual memories one has (units of knowledge), and Processes—the means by which psychological constructs are created, linked, and stored. One's particular memories are necessarily associative in that they are linked together by the places, times, and activities that generated them. They form a basis for conversation whenever we meet family, friends, or acquaintances. They also form the basis for tests of intelligence, as we are usually asked to regurgitate pieces of associated knowledge. The presence of cultural bias is obvious. Better intelligence tests take into consideration one's cognitive processes as well, but we will see that these are also culturally biased. Scott, Osgood, and Peterson (1979) point out that

> The task of studying cognitive content is essentially different from that of studying cognitive processes. To describe the contents of cognition is to describe a representation of reality, and thus to describe the facts from some person's point of view. Though a subject's cognitive contents are not directly known to an observing psychologist, they are known to the subject. Cognitive processes on the other hand involve not beliefs, but mechanisms, structures, and states. Neither the observing psychologist nor the subject can know these processes directly; they must be inferred from behavior and reports (p. 8).

The constructivist's approach to communication says that it is through communication that we construct our individual view of reality (Delia, O'Keefe, and O'Keefe, 1982). This construction of reality makes us "who we are," both to ourselves and those who know us. Both aspects of cognition (content and process) are involved in the definition of ourself, for it is not only what we know as fact but also how we arrive at new facts and how we reason from those we have accepted. All of this is involved in the personal dimension discussed in Chapter 3 and is the personal orientation of the individual within his or her culture.

PERSONAL CONSTRUCTS

In his work on Personal Construct Theory, Kelly (1963) presents the basic assumptions about personal orientations that are fundamental to the present work. For him, the Personal Construct is the basic unit of cognitive structure. Personal constructs are "transparent patterns or templets which he (man) creates and then attempts to fit over the realities of which the world is composed. . . . They are ways of construing the world" (pp. 8-9). The development of one's personal constructs is the processing aspect of cognition. Kelly says that ". . . man creates his own ways of seeing the world in which he lives; the world does not create them for him" (p. 12). He goes on to say that

> We assume that all of our present interpretations of the universe are subject to revision or replacement. . . . We take the stand that there are always some alternative constructions available to choose among in dealing with the world. No one needs to paint himself into a corner; no one needs to be completely hemmed in by circumstances; no one needs to be the victim of his biography. We call this philosophical position *constructive alternativism* (p. 15).

Thus, we have two basic assumptions: the freedom of the human being to create his or her psychological constructs, and the freedom to change these constructs with the admission of more information. A person is neither environmentally nor biologically determined; rather, he or she must bear the responsibility for his or her view of the world, i.e., personal orientation. Constructive Alternativism means that one can and does alter one's personal constructs. Kelly says, "In general man seeks to improve his constructs by increasing his repertory, by altering them to provide better fits, and by subsuming them with superordinate constructs or systems" (p. 9). Thus, we build up psychological constructs that are abstractions from the experiences we have had and the memories we have stored.

Constructive alternativism is one of the most important concepts in intercultural communication. It says that we do not have to remain ethnocentric but can reconstrue our reality to include other world views, other cultures. Those of you who have tried it probably found it difficult to reconstrue your experiences to fit into another's frame of reference.

The situation with which most of us have had the most experience is in the area of opposite sex love. With males and females being two diverse subcultures within all cultures of the world, this is an example of universal relevance. Do you really understand your lover? Can you get inside his or her head to see how he or she views the events that you experience together? What is your personal orientation toward your sex and the opposite sex? If both of you have grown up in the U.S. culture, then you have a modicum of similarity in your cultural background. How would it be to fall in love with someone from another national culture? Even so, the fact that you are in love may help you overcome (understand, accept, acknowledge) many of the differences you encounter. Think of the differences between this type of situation and that of two diplomats who have no respect for each other's government or culture.

One of Kelly's (1970) basic corollaries is that "To the extent that one person employs a construction of experience which is similar to that employed by another, his processes are psychologically similar to those of the other person" (p. 20). This position seems reasonable since, if we have like belief systems and attitudinal frames of reference, we would probably get along just fine (it might also be a bit boring). However, since no two people can ever be exactly alike, we must always be prepared to deal with diversity. The problem arises in that our personal constructs (attitudinal frame of reference) set up our expectations for each communication event we enter; they give us a means for *anticipating* events. Being teleological, we enter each event with a purpose and have anticipations as to how it will turn out. We can then modify our personal constructs to agree with how closely our perceptions of the event match our anticipations of it. Our sensitivity to the discrepancies between perceptions and anticipations is a measure of our self-awareness. Cognitive stability comes from our ability to anticipate correctly the events we experience.

One's cognitive stability is also affected by the total make-up of his or her cognition. Hofstede (1980) says,

> each person carries a certain amount of mental programming which is stable over time and leads to the same person showing more or less the same behavior in similar situations. . . . we cannot directly observe mental programs. What we can observe is only behavior, words, or deeds. When we observe behavior, we infer from it the presence of stable mental programs. . . . "mental programs" are intangibles, and the terms we use to describe them are *constructs* (p. 14).

We call them psychological constructs. One aspect of these mental programs has been referred to as Cognitive Style, which "refers to the characteristic ways in which individuals conceptually organize the environment" (Goldstein and Blackman, 1978, p. 2), and this involves both the content and the processes in our cognition.

DEFINING COGNITIVE STYLES

There are several different approaches to cognitive style, each representing a slightly different view of this general construct. Nonetheless, common to all approaches is an "emphasis on the structure rather than the content of thought" (Goldstein, et al., p. 3). Structure in the sense used above refers to *how* knowledge is organized, while content refers to *what* knowledge is stored. The primary problem for researchers is that the development of cognitive structures "is seen to occur in specific domains of activity and involvement" (Burleson and Waltman, 1988, p. 3). This means that cognitive structure may be influenced by content areas (domains), and you may organize your thoughts about interpersonal relationships differently from your thoughts about politics. Thus, one's cognitive style may be content bound and not a general construct as originally thought. Some types of cognitive style are more content bound than others, however.

We will look at five different approaches to cognitive style to see how each focus might affect the development of our communication strategies when contacting a person from another culture. The five approaches move from more content oriented to less content oriented, and each plays a significant role in the development of our personal orientation and in the type of communication strategy we might use in striving for effective communication.

Authoritarianism

Research on this approach to cognitive style began in the 1930s and '40s with the rise to power of Adolph Hitler. "The studies began with a focus on anti-Semitism, were conducted within a psychoanalytic framework, and led the researchers to the conclusion that prejudice is not an isolated aspect of an individual's functioning, but rather an integrated component of personality" (Goldstein and Blackman, p. 15). Although this research seemed to be isolating a personality type, two important correlates of Authoritarianism marked the beginning of research on cognitive style: rigidity and intolerance of ambiguity.

Goldstein and Blackman define rigidity as a "continuation of former behavior patterns when a change in the situation requires a change in behavior for more efficient functioning" (pp. 39–40). (Does this describe the situation in 1988 when, after the PLO had met the demands of Israel and the United States, they were still not allowed to speak to the United Nations in New York on the Middle East problems?) They also say that

> The concept of rigidity refers to thought and behavior that is exceptionally resistant to modification. Rigidity was evident when the authoritarian individual refused to relinquish ethnic stereotypes when faced with information contradicting the stereotype. Another characteristic of rigidity is that the individual's cognitions are compartmentalized and walled-off from each other, resulting in an apparent lack of consistency (p. 19).

The last characteristic is similar to Bem's concept of the opinion molecule. He gives evidence indicating that one can hold several contradicting beliefs with no feelings of inconsistency because they are isolated from each other and the person holding them will not let them be juxtaposed. This would facilitate the rigidity of a person holding such beliefs.

The other characteristic of authoritarianism is intolerance of ambiguity and is defined by Goldstein and Blackman as "the unwarranted imposition of structure when the situation is unstructured" (p. 40). A person with this type of cognitive structure prefers symmetry, familiarity, regularity, oversimplified dichotomies, premature closure, and stereotyping. She or he wants things to be simple, with easy or no decisions to be made. For example, is it really true that all of the strife in the world can be blamed on East-West political differences, or is there room for unaligned strife, other types of power struggles, and neutrality?

Other cognitive characteristics that correlate with rigidity and intolerance of ambiguity are concreteness (as opposed to abstractness), political and economic conservatism, concern for status and success, and ethnocentrism—"the tendency to rigidly accept the culturally alike and reject the culturally different" (Goldstein and Blackman, p. 17). In plain terms, someone with an authoritarian cognitive style says, If you are like me, you are OK, but if you are different, forget it!

Dogmatism

Dogmatism is the name given to the cognitive style that is similar to, but more content free than, authoritarianism. "A person who is dogmatic in one area is likely to be dogmatic in another" (Goldstein and Blackman, p. 63). Rokeach (1960) was the primary researcher of this construct and produced the open-minded/closed-minded continuum to depict the cognitive range of a dogmatic person. This type of cognitive style can be applied to either right or left wing groups with equal sensitivity (Tetlock, 1983, 1984). The dogmatic person has a "relatively closed cognitive organization of beliefs and disbeliefs about reality" (Goldstein and Blackman, p. 63). Compared with an authoritarian person, a dogmatic person has an authoritarian outlook on life in general and intolerance toward those with opposing beliefs.

In an intercultural situation this type of person is best described as the Ugly American—an ethnocentric individual who feels that nothing in the present culture can match that of the home culture. They stay in Holiday Inns around the world because they want to feel at "home," and they tend to think that the people in the country they are visiting, rather than themselves, are the foreigners. They seldom become comfortable in another culture, and often become problems for both their home culture and the one in which they are visiting or working.

This type of cognitive style is concerned with the structure of one's beliefs. The resulting cognitive system is "organized into belief and disbelief systems. The belief system is made up of the ideas an individual accepts as true. The disbelief system is comprised of a number of subsystems of ideas the individual rejects as false" (Goldstein and Blackman, p. 64). This means that disbelief systems are not just the negative of belief systems, they are composed of definite conceptual units. For example, democracy and socialism may be in your belief system while communism and dictatorships may be in your disbelief system. With these belief and disbelief systems, we build our personal constructs by which we create our view of reality.

Dogmatic persons are closed-minded; they are not open to information unless it is consistent with their beliefs. This makes it extremely difficult to negotiate with them. They are intolerant, rigid, and less able to perceive dogmatism in others than are open-minded persons. Dogmatism seems to decrease with education, although there is some concern that one's cognitive structures are not well formed until adulthood, and many of the research results are from studies with children. In sum, this type of cognitive style indicates that some people are more or less rigid, intolerant, dogmatic, and closed-minded than others. A number of examples could be raised here, but consider the situation in the Middle East. The religious and nationalistic fervor that motivates these countries to war is a good example of dogmatism. One doesn't negotiate when one has the "truth."

Cognitive Complexity

A basic premise of cognitive style is that we do not know anything directly but only through the symbolic representations we make of our environment, e.g., each aspect of that thing we call a tree is mediated through the symbols we use to talk about it—trunk, leaves, bark, roots, etc. If this is the case, then whenever we study the workings of the mind, our findings will be affected by the domain of knowledge within which we work. Since we are interested primarily in cognitive style as it pertains to human communication, the domain of knowledge within which we work is that of interpersonal constructs. Goldstein and Blackman take from Personal Construct Theory the idea that

> man is actively involved in cognitively organizing the world around him; the essence of man's activity is his forecasting of events. The individual makes predictions about what will occur and modifies his ideas based on the outcome of these predictions. Kelly termed these ideas *constructs*. A basic notion of Kelly's formulation is that man is capable of *representing* the environment, not merely *responding* to it, and that differing representations lead to different behaviors (p. 104).

Cognitive complexity is concerned primarily with a person's ability to differentiate, i.e., find the characteristics that make one person, object, or concept different from another. It is closely related to one's analytic ability, the ability to subdivide a problem into its relevant parts to see what courses of action might solve the problem. One's ability to differentiate is correlated with one's cognitive complexity. At present, there is no conclusive answer as to whether one's cognitive complexity is generalizable over different domains; apparently it is not generalizable. We become expert in domains, and part of this expertise is the ability to differentiate the subject matter into essential units. A carpenter is not a plumber is not an electrician, etc.

Research has found that persons with high cognitive complexity can accurately predict the differences between themselves and others but not the similarities. They focus on the differences. Persons with low cognitive complexity see others as similar to themselves. They have a limited category system by which they can compare themselves with others. Cognitive complexity appears to be independent from intelligence, verbal ability, and personality. It increases with age and has a positive correlation with one's ability to "infer and represent the cognitions and feelings of another. . . a major social-cognitive ability underlying competent and effective communication" (Burleson, et al., p. 14). In intercultural communication, the more personal constructs we have, the more differentiated we are, and the more categories there are with which we can characterize a person and his or her culture. We can then get deeper into the other person and thus, we are more likely to understand that person and engage in effective communication.

Integrative Complexity

While cognitive complexity is concerned primarily with differentiation, Integrative Complexity is concerned with both differentiation and integration, i.e., the division of an object into its relevant subparts and the grouping of these subparts into meaningful units, or concepts. This is essentially the process of abstracting, and Goldstein and Blackman describe it as follows:

> people engage in two activities in processing sensory input: differentiation and integration. Differentiation refers to the individual's ability to locate stimuli along dimensions. Integration refers to the individual's ability to utilize complex rules, or programs, to combine these dimensions. The individual who is low in differentiating and integrating ability is said to be *concrete*; the individual who is high in differentiating and integrating ability is said to be *abstract*. All people may be ordered along a continuum from concrete to abstract, depending on their ability to differentiate and integrate information (p. 136).

The domain of the sensory stimuli has a definite effect on the differentiations that one makes. The more familiar you are with a subject, the more differentiations you can make. However, this is not true of integration. Integration is achieved by applying rules or schemas to the differentiated subparts. One's ability to integrate (abstract) depends on one's knowledge of the subparts and the rules by which they may be related. Sometimes it is necessary to create your own rule for the integration of the units, and this ability makes one a truly innovative thinker. The rule by which subparts are related is contained in the concept that describes the relationship. For example, family is a concept with the underlying rule of blood-kinship, but we know that it can be extended to contain other types of relationships. The more types of relationships contained under a single concept, the more abstract is that concept.

An example may help clarify the abstraction construct. Most U.S. students, if shown pictures of two light-skinned males, a dark-skinned male, and a light-skinned female, would differentiate and integrate (abstract) on the basis of skin color, thus grouping them as three whites and one black. Most Panamanian students would abstract on the basis of sex, thus grouping them as three males and a female.

Goldstein and Blackman say that some of the differences between persons who think in concrete terms and those who think in abstract terms are that concrete individuals show:

1. Poor differentiation and incomplete integration
2. A bifurcated view of the environment
3. Reliance on authority
4. Intolerance of ambiguity

5. Rigidity under low levels of stress
6. Collapse under high stress
7. The inability to see alternative solutions to problems
8. A poorer ability to role play and to think in hypothetical terms
9. A poorly defined self-concept (p. 139).

As a person becomes more conceptually complex she or he moves away from the above characteristics and toward their opposites. As you can see, some of the characteristics fit into the earlier types of cognitive style, authoritarianism and dogmatism, and some are found in the type called cognitive complexity. Characteristics number seven and eight are the two that set the integrative complexity type of cognitive style apart from the others. It still may be affected by the subject matter, but it goes beyond the other types in that it adds the integration process. Thus, it is more applicable than the first three approaches to the understanding of human communication in general and decision making in particular.

Field Dependence

The final type of cognitive style is that of field dependence/independence in which a person's perceptions are measured in relation to how much they are affected by external and internal stimuli. A field dependent person has trouble differentiating the salient aspects of a stimulus from the background noise, while a field independent person is adept at differentiating. This problem of differentiation is not found in the stimulus but in the mind of the individual. Do you see what is actually happening or what you want to happen? Can you pick out the meaningful symbols from the noise? It was found that "an individual's characteristic way of perceiving was consistent from one situation to another, that it was not easily altered, and that it was stable over periods of years" (Goldstein and Blackman, p. 174). We speak of tunnel vision, a critical eye, and selective perception to indicate some of the ways people "see" things. All of our senses "see" in the sense that we collect information through them and must do something with it. Field dependence/independence can be applied to all five senses.

Field dependence/independence is concerned with both differentiation and the two aspects of integration, complexity and effectiveness. As the occurrence of differentiation does not ensure the occurrence of integration, so the occurrence of integration, with its various levels of complexity, does not ensure effective use of the information. "Complexity refers to the elaborateness of the subsystem relationships; effectiveness refers to how smoothly the subsystem components function together. Differentiation must precede integration, but its presence does not necessarily imply that integration will follow" (Goldstein and Blackman, p. 176). One may be able to develop a highly elaborated system, but are the subsystems meaningful? We may be able to differentiate among people on the basis of many different physical features and integrate these differentiated features into a highly complex system of human features, but what does this system tell us about their ability to communicate, or their need for love, etc. The effectiveness of the integration is evaluated by the usefulness of its constructs.

Studies of this type of cognitive style revealed that females are more field dependent than males, and that Mexicans are more field dependent than Mexican Americans, who are more field dependent than Anglo-Americans (Buriel, 1975). Field independence seems to increase with age for the young, but it decreases with advanced age and infirmity. Persons who are field dependent are more socially sensitive and more likely to conform. They are also more open in expressing thoughts and feelings and favor social over solitary situations. Persons who are field independent have higher levels of differentiation and integration, are more intelligent, and are better at solving individual, analytic problems.

COGNITIVE STRUCTURE

While cognitive styles are concerned with the development and structure of one's personal constructs through differentiation, integration, and the structuring of one's belief/disbelief systems, cognitive structure refers to the various ways in which cognitive entities, including content and processes, may be psychologically structured and what constructs are hypothesized to control this structure. For example, we have based much of our thinking in this book on Kelly's Personal Construct Theory, which says that we build personal constructs (belief systems) for each object in our cognition. Then, each time we interact with an object, such as a friend, we have expectations as to how the interaction will go. This type of structure differs from the semantic space of Osgood, et al. (1957), in that their research shows that objects can be represented in a three-dimensional space. The dimensions of Osgood, et al., are: the evaluative (good-bad), activity (active-passive), and potency (strong-weak) upon which all concepts can be mapped. Osgood, May, and Miron (1975) showed that these three dimensions are universal dimensions of cognitive structure and can be used to map affective meaning from one culture to another. Since each object (concept) is uniquely positioned in this three-dimensional space, both of these structural methods can be used to differentiate between or among objects.

Another aspect of cognitive structure is that of movement or cognitive change. Few of us are so authoritarian or dogmatic that we never change an opinion, attitude, or belief about some object. Thus, part of the theorizing about cognitive structures has been about how these representations of objects (meanings, opinions, attitudes, beliefs, values) change over time and experience. Most of these theories are based on Heider's (1958) balance theory in which he hypothesized that maintaining a balance among one's cognitive structures was essential to a healthy personality. Festinger (1957) extended balance theory by considering how people altered their cognitive structures when two or more concepts were seen to conflict (were dissonant). We usually interpret the experience that led to the dissonance or change the structure of one of the concepts so that the dissonance is reduced to a tolerable level.

For example, you go to a Latin American country and become very close friends with a person there. After you leave, you write this person several times but receive no letters in return. What do you think? Here, the concepts of friendship and communication have become dissonant (you think that one attribute of good friends is to keep in contact, to communicate). You will probably be uncomfortable about the situation and make all kinds of excuses at first, then begin to find other attributes that you can apply to your so-called friend. When you find out, or realize, that not communicating with someone who is not in the immediate vicinity is characteristic of Latin Americans in general, you may feel better about it, and this may reduce your dissonance to a tolerable level. Nevertheless, you will probably still feel some resentment.

Scott, et al., take an "object-attribute" approach to cognitive structure; i.e., for each object in our content system we can associate various attributes and we can differentiate objects on the basis of these attributes. Again, this is similar to the semantic space of Osgood, et al., with the exception that the attributes are not limited to bipolar adjectives. The attributes that are ascribed to each object are said to bear an associative relationship in that they are associated with the same object. Attributes may also have the relationship of implication; if we find that an object has the attributes X and Y, we imply that it also has the attribute Z.

A common stereotype is that if a person is very social and is not on time for appointments, he or she is probably lazy (social + tardy = lazy). We use implications to form judgments. Of course, these judgments are really just extrapolations of our attributional structure and, therefore, in reality have no connection with the object being evaluated. This aspect of cognitive structure has serious negative implications for effective communication. It is probably more serious in intercultural communication because of the lack of similarity in the cognitive structures of persons from two different cultures.

TRANSITION

We have seen that several factors are involved in the various approaches to cognitive style: rigidity, intolerance of ambiguity, consistency, openness, differentiation, integration, concrete, abstract, intelligence, and conformity. For some of the types of cognitive style—authoritarianism, dogmatism, and field dependence—the characteristics seemed to be stable over time, while for cognitive complexity and integrative complexity the measures varied with the domain. All types of cognitive style should be subject to change with education, but dogmatism and authoritarianism were the least likely to do so. All of the characteristics of cognitive style have real consequences for human communication.

One's personal orientation is based on his or her cognitive style and cognitive structure. From their style we can find their way of dealing with others based on their ability to receive and process information. From their structure we can obtain their value systems as they are revealed through the attributions they use to define various concepts. With these two insights into the behavior patterns of an individual, one can make some prediction about how he or she will act in a particular situation. As we will say many times in this book, the problem this raises in intercultural communication is that the personal orientation we perceive in someone from another culture is based on the meaning of the attributes we find in our own culture. Thus, we may be, and usually are, disappointed to find that our expectations are not met.

Personal orientations are also affected by the individuals' cybernetic, as detailed in Chapter 1. The bonding between individuals with similar personal orientations may be easy or impossible. Think of two authoritarian or dogmatic individuals who have opposing views. Could they ever be friends? The bonding that would be created between them would be one of anger or frustration. Though this is a bond, it is not one that would be conducive to growth and maturity; the refusal to accept new knowledge would prohibit change in the HCS. The probability of having counteractive personal orientation as we move from our culture to another increases dramatically. In the next chapter we will consider a general cultural orientation that will help us understand intercultural communication.

INDEPENDENT STUDY

1. Is the variation greater between individuals or cultures? Choose a measuring instrument from one of the cognitive styles and record the responses of ten people from each of two different cultures. Look at the results, statistically or otherwise, and see which respondents are similar and which are different. Write a report.

2. One measure of personal orientation is to see if the person can interpret the events he or she has perceived to give them different meaning. Make up a story, or find one, and ask several of your friends from different cultures to posit reasons for the outcome of the story. Analyze and report the findings.

CHAPTER SIX
Cultural Orientations

My first trip abroad was to attend a conference in Edinburgh, Scotland. Before I went, I asked my English research assistant what the people were like in her country. She characterized them as being quite private, making friendships over an extended period of time. She also told me several times that she and her husband couldn't get over the differences they had found in the people of the United States from what they had expected. Their image of a U.S. citizen was of a loud-talking, back-slapping, buffoon wearing a big hat and boots (an impression they got from the U.S. tourists they saw visiting Great Britain). Her husband had seriously considered not accepting the position he had been offered in the United States because they did not think they could live in such a culture.

With this limited knowledge of England my wife and I flew from Boston to London, changed planes and flew on to Edinburgh, Scotland. We were the only passengers from the United States on the second leg of our flight, and in trying to converse with other passengers, we found that our neighbors, at least, were not as open to conversation as the people we had met in our travels in the United States. After landing in Edinburgh we had to wait for our transportation to the conference. While sitting in the bar we heard this loud booming voice say, "Hi chappie. How you all doin'? Bring me a beer. Not one of those thick, warm English things, but a real cold U.S. of A. beer." I turned around to see who was making all the noise, and sure enough, there was this big guy, wearing cowboy boots and a ten-gallon hat, slapping the waiter on the back as he ordered his beer. Your cultural stereotype may jump out at you when you least expect it!

In this chapter we want to get a working knowledge of culture to carry with us throughout the rest of the book. We know that culture is a systemic concept; i.e., for a culture to exist there must be some bonding agent among its components (sub-systems). We will see that this agent is communication. Through it we develop norms of behavior for the culture which reflect our basic belief systems. However, because of the complexity of the bonding process for cultures, two cultures may have similar belief systems but different behavioral norms and vice versa. Thus, we must get below the surface differences in verbal and nonverbal behaviors to find the cultural orientations upon which to base our understanding of other cultures.

PERSPECTIVES ON CULTURE

When Kelly (1963) was expounding his Personal Construct Theory, he raised the question, "Might not the individual man, each in his own personal way, assume more of the stature of a scientist, ever seeking to predict and control the course of events with which he is involved?"(p. 5). The important part of this statement is "each in his own personal way." If we can understand the diversity among people rather than force them into similarities, we will be able to see why there are so many approaches to the construct we call culture.

A second statement by Kelly (1970) elaborates on the diversities with which we see events. He says, "Whatever the world may be, man can come to grips with it only by placing his own interpretations upon what he sees" (p. 2). Our basic teleological behavior is survival. How we construe the world and our survival within it is up to us. We may choose to accept someone else's interpretations and directions, but ultimately maturity demands responsibility for our own actions. This does not mean that we must investigate every event for which we must make a decision, but rather that we learn to evaluate other's interpretations of many events and choose which interpretation we will build our lives upon.

So it is with understanding culture and its role in intercultural communication. Many perspectives on culture have their consequent theories; none of them may be correct, or all of them may be correct. You must choose which one(s) best fits into your own perspectives on life, and then use it in developing your intercultural communication strategies. The following perspectives on culture may clarify the various types of analyses used to understand the differences among cultures.

Cultural Materialism

Cultural materialism "... is based on the simple premise that human social life is a response to the practical problems of earthly existence" (Harris, p. ix), and this fits in well with our assumption that survival is our basic teleological force. It is based on the behaviorist's stimulus-response model. Its problem is that of all social sciences: Is truth what I observe, or what you tell me? As Harris says, "Extreme caution is called for in making inferences about what is going on inside people's heads even when the thoughts are those of our closest friends and relatives" (p. 39).

Cultural materialism is based on a systems model. It strives to understand "the relationship among the parts of sociocultural systems and with the evolution of such relationships, parts, and systems" (p. 47). It is primarily an etic approach in which the "nature of the human groups is inferred from the density of interaction among human beings found in a particular spatial and temporal locus" (p. 47). Culture is defined as "the learned repertory of thoughts and actions exhibited by the members of social groups—repertories transmissible independently of genetic heredity from one generation to the next" (p. 47). Read these quotes carefully; they contain a lot of information.

Cultural materialists try to find universal biological and psychological constants with which they can discriminate among cultures. They operate within three levels of systems: infrastructure, structure, and superstructure. The infrastructure is concerned with the mode of production, i.e., how the culture physically and psychologically maintains its existence and the mode of reproduction—how the culture maintains its population size. The structure level is concerned with domestic economy, i.e., how the culture *organizes* itself physically and psychologically to accomplish the activities in its infrastructure within the domestic economy (e.g., family structure and sex roles), and within the political economy—how the culture is organized to accomplish the activities in its infrastructure within and among social units such as villages and states (e.g., political and military organizations). The superstructure consists of those activities and organizations that lead to "recreational, sportive, and aesthetic products and services" (p. 52), e.g., art, music, games, etc. Such activities are "the conscious and unconscious cognitive goals, categories, rules, plans, values, philosophies and beliefs about behavior" (p. 54).

For cultural materialism, language—both verbal and nonverbal—functions as the coordinator among the activities on the three levels of structure. In systems terms, language is the vehicle for the creation of the subsystems that exist on each level and facilitates the interactions among them. Different infrastructures do not cause certain languages to be spoken; nor do different languages cause certain types of infrastructures to be developed. Language is an all-pervasive component of each level and all of the systems within each level.

A culture's basic response to survival determines the structures that evolve in their society and the way its members explain their behaviors. Human decisions are made on the basis of cost-benefit analysis. If the benefits are taken as those for survival, then the researcher can make some inferences about the actions of individuals, groups, and societies. Since this perspective assumes a sociocultural system consisting of infrastructure, structure, and superstructure, a change in any one of its components will be reflected in the other components. For example, as the mode of production has changed in the United States, so have the domestic economy systems changed, e.g., family size, structure, sex roles. Change in any culture is the only thing that is certain. Knowing how it affects the various components of the culture may be crucial to our efforts to communicate with members of this culture. This is a basic concept that has gone unrecognized by the United States in much of its aid to developing countries.

This behavioral approach is important because we must first be able to describe the behavior of a culture before we can ask why they behave this way. However, just because we find that culture A and culture B have the same behaviors does not mean that they have the same reasons for behaving that way. It is difficult to link behavior and cognition.

I recall a professor telling our class about his trip to the top of Mt. Sinai. At that time it was a narrow one-lane gravel road. On the way down his Islamic driver let the jeep go as fast as it would. My professor thought that it had no brakes and was sure they were going to be killed. When they arrived at the bottom, he managed to ask the driver why he went so fast on such a narrow, twisting, dangerous road, where there was a good possibility of meeting someone coming up. His driver replied that all things were in the hands of Allah, and if they were to die at that time they could do nothing to prevent it. Some one else might have said "que será, será" without any belief in a higher being.

The Evolutionary Perspective

Several schools of anthropology go no further than a description of the cultures they investigate. They can tell us what the similarities and differences are among several cultures, but we are interested in *why* there are similarities and differences among cultures.

Farb (1968) puts his faith in a social evolutionary model of culture. As humans confronted different obstacles to their livelihood, they solved those problems by creating social structures that best fit the situation as they perceived it. The choices resulting in both simple and complex structures are culturally unconscious, though they may be conscious to the individual making them. The primary mechanism in this explanation is adaptation to the environment. "By examining the ways in which men have organized themselves socially, it is possible to explain why certain culture elements appear in one kind of society but disappear in another. It is also possible to place societies into evolutionary stages of increasing complexity" (p. 14).

The cultural evolution model of cultural development does not say that every culture must pass through all stages of evolution. It says that a society moves from simple to more complex organizational units, and that the stage in which a culture is found can help to explain its behaviors. Unfortunately, this method of analysis does not help us differentiate among several cultures that are at the same level of complexity. It does, however, give us an added dimension of analysis when seeking to understand intercultural communication—that of cultural complexity.

The Cognitive Perspective

Others try to explain the similarities and differences among cultures based on a psychological model. Unfortunately, they can go no further than a psychological description of the similarities and differences much like those in the personality of humans. They cannot say why they exist nor how they came into being. Although the Freudian perspective gave them a mental basis for some of their theories, it did not give them a basis for their theories in the behaviors manifested by different cultures. Perhaps this would not be a serious defect if they could predict or anticipate these behaviors, since their underlying premise is that thought precedes action. The cognitivists based their information gathering on an emic approach with little or no concern for the coincident etic behavior.

Most cognitivists make no claim for the predictability of their theories; they are intent on determining "how people acquire the normal and/or deviant mental and emotional complexes typical of different sociocultural systems" (Harris, p. 258). To do this they use the etic behavioral aspects of culture but not in the sense of cause-effect. Rather, these behaviors are there because of the mental and emotional complexes of the sociocultural systems. They are the justification for the validity of the mental structures that have been created by anthropologists.

"An adversary situation exists between cultural materialism and cognitivist and psychological strategies only when cognitivists and psychological anthropologists claim that the mental, emic, and personality aspects of sociocultural systems determine the etic and behavioral aspects, or when they claim that cultural materialism cannot explain the causes of mental and emic sociocultural differences and similarities" (Harris, p. 259). Again we see the importance of the direction of action. While cultural materialists hold that the infrastructural conditions give rise to mental and emic personality characteristics, the cognitivists say that it is vice versa. Regardless of which comes first, this perspective makes us realize that one must consider the cognitive aspects of culture when doing an analysis for intercultural understanding.

Cultural Interpretation

Looking at culture from an interpretation perspective takes us out of the description phase of analysis and focuses us on the *messages* that the described behaviors have encoded into them. Messages, if you recall, are normative, social, and public and are encoded into signals that have been transmitted by a behavior that is intended to communicate. The central point is that human behavior is seen as symbolic action (Geertz, 1973). However, the analysis of this behavior is at the message level, not at the meaning level (even though Geertz and others use the two terms interchangeably). Meaning (in this text) is subjective, personal, and unpredictable from an objective, public perspective.

Cultural interpretation focuses on the public messages found in the signals sent between communicators. These signals may contain both verbal and nonverbal codes and be transmitted in vocal and nonvocal modes. What cultural interpretation tries to do is decode the messages in these signals as a native of the culture would—to expose the norms of the culture, to parse out the relational from the informational parts of the messages. For them, culture is the context within which communication occurs. To understand and participate in the communication process, one must know the message norms contained in the communicative behaviors of the culture. That is one reason why, when learning a second language, students are given a limited dictionary of vocabulary terms. With these one can encode the normal messages of the culture. When you find that these words are used for different messages than you were taught, you may be startled, but this is part of understanding the normative messages contained in the language of that culture. Normative messages become obvious when you travel from one culture to another, both of which speak the same language but convey different messages with the same word or phrase. For instance, a "güila" is a little girl in Costa Rica but a whore in Mexico.

Cultural interpretation focuses on the analysis of social discourse. As such, it looks at the "public world of common life" (p. 30), the most normative behavior one can study. However, as Geertz says, "Cultural analysis is intrinsically incomplete. And, worse than that, the more deeply it goes the less complete it is" (p. 29). How true this is, and you can feel it as you do it. The deeper you get into unraveling the connections between words, messages, and meanings, the more you realize that communication is at best approximate and understanding is never complete. It should make us aware of our incomplete knowledge and temper our communicative behavior in the culture we are striving to understand. Being tentative is almost always better than being certain of what you have just said or heard (a lesson from General Semantics).

A Taxonomic Perspective

All of the above perspectives give rise to classification systems—categories into which cultures may be differentiated. When we find similarities and differences among cultures, we naturally group them according to these discriminators. As with people, this categorization process tends to lead to stereotypes, and the people or cultures that have been so stereotyped treated as though this stereotype is the sum total of their essence. A person or a culture may be classified as aggressive, untrustworthy, or vulgar, but we cannot let these impressions dominate our attempts to communicate because there is always the possibility that the classification is wrong. We should try to find out why this category was used.

There are an endless number of taxonomic systems. Cultures may be classified as to geographical location—European, African, Asian, Far East, Northern or Southern, etc., etc.; by development—first, second, third, and fourth world; or politically—democratic, dictatorship, communist, or any number of other classification systems. Because the categories are derived from similarities and differences among the cultures, they are apt to become value laden, e.g., a Third World culture isn't as good, productive, educated, progressive, etc., as a First World country. This valuing process is insidious in that it creeps into our thinking and affects our communication with other cultures. Theodore Roosevelt's evaluation of Latin Americans is an example. He felt that "they were incapable of either governing themselves or—most important in T.R.'s hierarchy of values—maintaining order" (LaFeber, p. 35). Thus, the continued intervention into their affairs.

In developing various perspectives on culture, despite anthropologists' concern with similarities, differences, and change, little research has been done on the effect one culture may have had, has had, or is having on another. Contact between cultures not only affects the cultures, it also affects the ability of the two parties to communicate effectively. Smith (1979) proposes a taxonomy based on the "total amount of foreign contact." This approach highlights two relevant features that are not found in other taxonomies. The first comes from the term "foreign." Total foreign contact would include contact with all cultures outside one's own; and this is important because it gives one an orientation to other cultures in general. However, we are particularly interested in foreign contact with our culture, as this will affect how foreigners will perceive us. The second comes from the word "total." What is the nature of foreigners' contact with other cultures, especially ours? Is it primarily through the media (film, television, newspapers, and magazines), or is it with ambassadors, missionaries, or tourists? Did they spend time in foreign cultures, and if so which ones? What types of images do they hold? Both of these points are worth remembering as we develop the constructs for understanding intercultural communication.

CULTURAL IMAGES

If you have traveled much outside of your home culture, you have undoubtedly found situations in which the people of that country liked the people of your home country but did not like its government or its foreign policy and vice versa. You have found that you like the people of a country but do not like their government's policies. When we think of cultural orientation, which of these two facets of a culture represent it? If we are aware of world news, then we probably form our images of the various national cultures on the basis of the political orientation of that country. Only if we have met the people of a culture either as foreigners in our culture, or better, we as foreigners in their culture, will we be able to differentiate between the images of the people and their government.

As we see, hear, meet, talk to, listen to, or read about people of different cultures, we begin to attribute to them various characteristics—to fit them into our cognitive structure. They become loud, pleasant, ambitious, kind, stubborn, etc. etc. and the image becomes more or less permanent. Depending on our particular cognitive style, these structures may become stereotypes from which we judge all people of that culture, or they may become working stereotypes that are modified as we collect more information about them. In either case, developing an attribution system for the people of a culture is one way of construing them and their world so we can better cope with our environment. If we are open-minded, this attribution system is in a constant state of flux and is used primarily as an initial guide to communication.

Cognitively complex persons use their personal constructs to continually refine their ability to differentiate among different types of people and cultures. This ability should increase our effectiveness when communicating with people from other cultures. Wiseman and Abe say that "For the intercultural communicator, the development of more flexible, complex, and psychologically differentiated perceptions of others should enable him or her to communicate more flexibly across different social or cultural settings" (p. 613). However, their research did not support this statement. This leads us to hypothesize the existence of other dimensions of cognition that interfere with effective intercultural communication. One of these dimensions is that of open/closed-mindedness. We may be able to develop complex personal constructs, but we hold to them rigidly.

Adler and Jelinek (1986) say that the concept of culture "emphasizes the shared cognitive approaches to reality that distinguish a given group from others. . . . that the full range of human attitudes and behaviors exists within any society, but that each society favors certain behaviors and attitudes over others. . . . There is no single, universal pattern. . . . Instead, each society develops a cultural orientation that is descriptive of the attitudes of most of its people most of the time" (p. 74). Thus, they take a common denominator approach, and in most cases this would be the norms of the middle class.

This type of cultural model is based more on observable actions and therefore, is a more descriptive model of a culture's behavior. While this is one way of differentiating among cultures and would give us a template for our behavior in that culture if all cultures could be thus described, it does not give us a reason for these differences in behavior. If we can look behind these behaviors perhaps we can find a cognitive model that will precipitate them.

DEFINING THE CULTURAL ORIENTATION MODEL

Glenn gives us a glimpse of what I have called the cultural orientation model for understanding intercultural communication. It is based on his vast knowledge of intercultural communication, only a small amount of which will be found in his book. His approach to intercultural communication was based on a simple observation:

Communication among men is made possible by their having something in common; it is made difficult by the differences which exist among them. That much is obvious. Where the difficulty arises is in discovering and describing the elements of commonality and of differences, and in doing so in a way capable of explaining misunderstandings and pointing towards understanding (p. 1).

His effort to "point towards understanding" was based on his belief that

The methods of organizing information differ depending on the amount of information to be organized and on the numbers of people to whom the information is to be *communicated*. An overall methodology of the acquisition and storage of information is used in this book as a *paradigm*. The forms of the paradigm are used to compare and to describe different cultures and sub-cultures (pp. i-ii).

This paradigm is used as the basis for the cultural orientation approach to the theory of intercultural communication explicated in this book. With this statement, Glenn has taken the study of cognition out of the purely personal perspective and given it a more global importance. He is saying that what we called cognitive style in the last chapter may have far more extensive implications than the comparison of persons on the various measures; there may be cognitive constructs that will allow us to differentiate among cultures and/or subcultures on the basis of cognitive behaviors. Glenn explains his approach as:

The cognitive approach, suggests that different cultures structure knowledge differently and that these differences will largely determine many aspects of behavior and communication, e.g., the topics which are felt to be worth talking about, the organization of information during communication, the types of information which are accepted as evidence for any given opinion (p. 2).

This cognitive approach analyzes the psychological constructs by which individuals, and thus cultures, use information to make sense out of their environment.

What does a cognitive orientation approach entail? Glenn says that there is an important distinction between the processes and the products of cognition.

With regard to the processes, it will be argued that it is possible to talk of cognitive styles, that is, patterns of thinking or ways of organizing information which become habitual and which can be used in a number of situations and on numerous types of information. . . . Turning to the product of cognition, it becomes clear that individual events are generally not evaluated or interpreted in isolation. They are more generally organized with other events, forming more or less extensive networks or cognitive structures. These structures can be concepts, or beliefs, or complex systems of interrelated beliefs. It is obvious that cognitive processes and cognitive products are logically distinct but psychologically intertwined; the product is a reflection of the process (p. 2).

What Glenn calls products we have called cognitive structure. The emphasis is necessarily on the process rather than the product because:

> An emphasis on the products is necessarily static; it will produce dimensions along which concepts, beliefs, institutions, etc., can be placed. The issue that is being raised here is the question of the nature of description versus that of explanation in the social and behavioral sciences. An emphasis on the products will be descriptive, while explanation requires that the origin of cognitive products be determined. Thus, only by understanding the process, i.e., how people organize information, can we understand the products and make predictions about how an individual or a culture will react to new situations. The ability to make predictions is central to an explanatory theory (p. 4).

In some way we organize the information available to us into our own view of reality, our own cognitive style and structure. The process is our style; the product is our structure. Hofstede (1980) says that "... each person carries a certain amount of mental programming which is stable over time and leads to the same person showing more or less the same behavior in similar situations" (p. 14). Intercultural understanding, then, may be enhanced by understanding the cognitive style and cognitive structure from which a person is communicating. A cultural orientation approach to intercultural communication is designed to facilitate this understanding.

Three dimensions of cultural orientation can be drawn from Glenn's material. One can characterize cultures much as one would characterize a person. Thus, when we think of determining the orientation of a culture we can pursue the same type of research as we would in seeking to find the orientation of a person. The accumulation of individual orientations gives us a meaningful cultural norm that can be used as a first estimate to orientate communicators in their interpersonal negotiations.

The three dimensions (continua) that will help us understand the general behaviors of a culture are: associative-abstractive, which is a measure of the cognitive processes of the members of a culture; universalism-particularism, which is a measure of the preferred behaviors of the members of a culture; and closed-mindedness/open-mindedness, which is a measure of the mental rigidity with which the members of a culture negotiate (see Figure 6). Glenn defines these as:

> (1) The associative-abstractive. Knowledge acquired through a largely spontaneous experience within an environment is associative. Such a knowledge fits closely with the feelings of individuals and the shared preoccupations of small or relatively small groups. The codification of thought into precise meanings and well organized lexicons is carried out by abstraction. The results of abstraction do not reflect the spontaneous experience of small groups, but the specifically stated systems of knowledge of large groups—potentially of all mankind. . . .
> (2) Universalism-particularism. Universalism sees the world through the conceptualizations reflected in the definitions of words. It is abstractive; it does not care for all those experiences which make one person different from another. It knows "dog" but not "Fido" or "Mandy." In opposition, particularism does not know

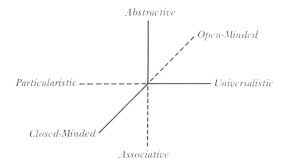

Figure 6:   Dimensions of Cultural Orientations

"man" or "woman" but "Dick" and "Jane." It is usually associative, reflecting personal lives and personal feelings. . . .

(3) Broadening vs. narrowing the frame of reference. . . . Where one broadens culture through the expansion of common learning, the other narrows it by accepting information only from those sharing a common origin or a supposedly unchangeable body of 'truth' (p. ii).

This latter dimension is what we called the open-minded/closed-minded dimension. We shall consider this dimension first because it, and the associative/abstractive dimension, have been discussed in the preceding chapter.

Closed-Minded/Open-Minded

In the preceding chapter we presented five cognitive styles, two of which were measures of rigidity, intolerance of ambiguity, and the inability to accept information that is dissonant with their beliefs. The authoritarian and dogmatic cognitive styles are examples of the closed-minded/open-minded dimension. Numerous examples of cultures display this dimension of cultural orientation. The *glasnost* movement in Russia under President Gorbachev is an excellent example of a national culture trying to move from a closed-minded to an open-minded orientation. One of the most significant aspects of this movement is the acceptance and presentation of information in opposition to the status quo.

Glenn speaks of broadening vs. narrowing the frame of reference in terms of freedom. Both ends of the continuum can produce a sense of freedom, but they have very different consequences.

A feeling of collective freedom can ... be compounded from two elements: (a) the adaptation of society to its environment, and (b) the blocking of the channels of communication through which might penetrate information contradicting the culture's world view. ... the elements under (a) call for a broadening of the flow of information, while the elements under (b) call for the narrowing of such channels. Strategies under (a) are developmental; strategies under (b) are defensive and potentially regressive. Situations in which (a) is likely to be selected are those in which the level of anxiety is moderate; strategies under (b) imply a high level of anxiety (p. 63).

The closed-mindedness end of the dimension (*b* above) reflects one's rigidity of thinking. Thinking in stereotypes, being authoritarian, inflexible, going strictly by the book, unable to put oneself in another person's position, having one solution to all problems, and egocentric/ethnocentric are all part of closed-mindedness. On the other hand, being aware of differences in perspectives, accepting other people's opinions, seeking information, being willing to discuss and/or negotiate, using rules as guidelines, and being mindful of situational variations are all part of open-mindedness. This does not mean that open-mindedness is to be equated with an inability to make decisions or to take firm stands on one's beliefs. It does mean that these positions are taken with the aid of maximum information, and they are the decisions of the individuals.

Associative-Abstractive

The last three cognitive styles presented in Chapter Five fall under the associative-abstractive dimension of cultural orientation. As discussed there, they all are involved with various levels of the ability to differentiate the perceptions of our experiences and integrate these facts into more complex systems of knowledge. Glenn says that "the terms 'associative' and 'abstractive' can be interpreted in a narrow or in a broad sense. Interpreted in their narrow sense, they define two learning mechanisms which are distinct and mutually exclusive. Interpreted in a broader sense, they define general ways of thinking. In the latter context, they are relative terms; arguments can be regarded as more or less associative or abstractive" (p. 53). It is the latter sense in which this dimension plays a role in intercultural communication and may form a basis on which cultures can be differentiated.

Since we are acculturated through our learning processes, we will look first at the associative-abstractive role in the learning process. Glenn says that "Associative learning and abstractive learning constitute two qualitatively different ways for connecting informational units in memory" and that for associative learning "the basic assumption is that the connection between elements or units of information cannot introduce any information beyond that contained in the units themselves. Thus, the connection or link in memory between two associatively connected informational units, A and B, is not labeled; A and B are simply associated with each other or listed. There is nothing in an associative theory which would allow us to define the nature of that connection" (p. 54). Of course, this type of learning cannot explain the learning of language and many other complex systems.

Learning complex systems necessitates the use of abstractions: the differentiation of the units of the systems and the integration of these units into related subsystems. Glenn says that abstractions "can include (1) any dimension which equates or contrasts two or more elements (e.g., semantic features such as big, narrow, beautiful); (2) any dimension specifying the relationship of one element to another (e.g., hierarchical relationships such as 'a robin is a bird; hands are parts of the body'); (3) rules which specify relationships between several elements (e.g., linguistic rules such as those defining a sentence or proposition; or mathematical and logical rules)" (p. 55). He explains the learning process in more detail when he says,

> In associative learning, units are connected into informational clusters primarily because they occur together in time or space. Thus, the primary boundary on what is learned is the spatiotemporal context. Informational clusters which are learned in different contexts can become associatively connected by chaining; that is, two informational clusters may be connected because of shared units. For example, if an A-B cluster and a B-C cluster have been learned, A may become associated with C. There are no conceptually defined boundaries to an associative cluster of units; that is, there are no criteria for limiting what can become associated with what. In contrast, abstractive learning is based on the abstraction of a relationship between items. The definition of that relationship provides clear boundaries for what can be included in a cluster and what cannot be, i.e., all and only those informational units which contain the relationship can be included. Thus, abstractive learning is not particular to a given situation but is situation independent. Furthermore, it is marked by the search for clear boundaries defining informational structures (p. 56).

Glenn further states that in a broad sense of the term, associative and abstractive

> refer to general modes of reasoning or thought and are relative terms rather than absolute terms. Associative reasoning is marked by "arbitrary" ties between informational units. Abstractive reasoning is marked by (1) the definition of information which is relevant to a given situation, and (2) the definition of the relationship between informational units. . . . Association and abstraction appear to be complementary mechanisms for the acquisition and the organization of knowledge. New items are incorporated primarily by association. However, association depends to a large extent on random coincidences and lacks organization. Large amounts of information cannot be retained and utilized in a largely amorphous state; organization, generally of a hierarchical nature is necessary. Abstraction provides the mechanism for such an ordering of knowledge, defining the imbrication of classes and the mutual relevance and irrelevance of items. Concepts, contrarily to associative clusters, never appear as isolates but as parts of networks of relations—in their simplest way as Piagetian groupings (p. 57).

An example may help to illustrate this concept. Every school child has had to perform the task of grouping objects according to their inherent characteristics; it is a standard test of one's ability to abstract. Such a task was given to illiterate peasants from Soviet Western Asia. The degree to which associative thinking predominates their thinking is illustrated in Glenn:

> The subjects were given the array *hammer-saw-log-hatchet*. The subjects stated that all four objects shared a similarity, and none of them could be eliminated from the array:
>
>> They all fit here! The saw has to saw the log, the hammer has to hammer it, and the hatchet has to chop it. And if you want to chop the log up really good, you need the hammer. You can't take any of these things away. There isn't any you don't need! (Luria, 1976, as quoted in Glenn)
>
> Even when the experimenter mentioned that three of the objects could be described by one word, tools, which did not fit the fourth one, the subjects insisted on keeping all objects in the array. What is the use of a hammer, a saw, and a hatchet, if there is no log to work upon? (p. 224)

From the above discussion we see that the associative-abstractive dimension of cultural orientation is operational in both the learning and the thinking processes. It should be pointed out, however, that although a person may grow up in a culture whose educational system is based on associative learning, this does not mean that this person cannot adjust to a system that is based on abstractive learning. When one works with Latin American and Asian graduate students in a U.S. university, one sees the difficulty of the transition, but it is also apparent that some of these graduate students can outperform U.S. students once they make the transition.

In comparing these two types of thought, some of the differences are: associative thought cannot integrate novel information; it is bound by tradition, whereas abstractive thought builds new systems based on systems of abstractive rules; abstractive thinking tends to increase with higher socioeconomic classes in which individuals define themselves in terms of roles rather than the association with family or groups. Thus, they relate to others on the basis of roles, whereas associative types relate on a person-to-person basis. Abstractive thinkers are able to defer gratification rather than the fulfillment of immediate impulses; thus, they are future oriented while associative thinkers are more present oriented.

Particularism-Universalism

Glenn indicates the close relationship between the associative-abstractive and particularism-universalism by stating that "the structuring of the social world in terms of kin or acquaintance suggests particularism" while "social structures based on categories or roles suggests universalism" (p. 106). The difference between these two dimensions is the difference between thought and behavior. He says that another characteristic of abstractive thought is the type of behavior it precipitates.

The core of the law of contract is the clear statement of either general or particular obligations and rights. In its general aspects it prescribes penalties or rewards to the perpetrators of specific actions, regardless of who they might be. Thus, it is abstractive and universalistic. It is abstractive because the definition of what is relevant and what is irrelevant to judgment is very specific, i.e., only the actions which occasion the legal procedure are regarded as relevant to a decision; all other characteristics are deemed irrelevant. It is universalistic because the laws are stated in general terms which can be applied in a number of different instances; moreover, they are based on principles which are equally binding for all people regardless of other characteristics, e.g., status (p. 14).

The fact that abstractive thought leads to universalism (the application of laws, rules of behavior, etc., to all people of a given culture) allows us to expand our conceptualization of cultural orientation to include a behavioral dimension. This has been designated the particularism-universalism dimension. Some aspects of universalism have been given above, but it is necessary to note that "The basic tool of universalism is reason. It may be expected that the reorganization of knowledge according to its tenets will stress logic at the expense of experience in the elaboration of programs of action" (p. 19).

In the extreme, universalistic thought "emphasizes criterial boundaries to the extent of seeing everything in blacks and whites, of ignoring the greyness not only of compromise, but also of most situations encountered in reality" (p. 235). It often leads to the belief that there is "only one solution to the problems of life, and at that of an absolutely true solution derived from doctrinal rather than observational considerations" (p. 279). A person who has moved to this level of universalism structures the world according to her or his conceptual categories and not according to observational data. We often speak of this as stereotyping in the negative sense and as closed-mindedness, since it does not allow for information, nor is it influenced by the situation.

The particularistic person is not able to reason hypothetically; it is difficult for them to put themselves in roles in which they have no previous experience or which are outside their estimates of possibility. For example, when asking Costa Ricans to answer questions about how they would behave in various male/female relationships (Borden, 1989), many answered that since they had never been in a particular relationship, they could not know how they would behave, nor could they guess.

Thus, we can characterize particularism as being more concerned with the immediate, personal, and associative nature of human relationships, and with interpersonal behaviors in which relationships (subjectivity) are more important than laws or rules, e.g., one might lie to protect a friend from the law. On the other hand, universalism is characterized by being more concerned with the mediate, social, and abstractive nature of information, and with interpersonal behaviors in which rules and laws (objectivity) are more important than relationships, e.g., one would obey the law even though it might destroy a friend.

APPLICATIONS

The closed-minded/open-minded and associative-abstractive dimensions of the cultural orientation model are well-researched constructs in the psychological literature. However, there has been a dearth of research on particularism-universalism (Borden, 1985). Loyalty to a friend and loyalty to society's norms and laws was called "particularism" and "universalism" by Parsons and Shils (1951), but it was Glenn, 30 years later, who first used them in the development of a theory of intercultural communication. He showed that some cultures are more particularistic while others are more universalistic in their actions. Zurcher (1968) concluded that Mexicans were significantly more particularistic than Anglos in both management and worker positions, but he cautioned that comparability of samples must be met. Borden (1983), using Mexican, Costa Rican, and U.S. students, found that the two Latin cultures were more particularistic on three different dimensions of inter-personal behavior—language used, equality of persons, and Machiavellianism.

Sex differences in particularism and universalism were also apparent in the subjectivity/objectivity measures used by Borden in the above study. Studies by Gilligan (1982) revealed a consistent difference in the behavior of males and females in terms of their commitment to relationships and their commitment to cultural norms and laws. Females were found to define their identity in the context of a relationship, while males defined their identity in the context of individuation and achievement (measured by cultural norms). When called upon to make value judgments, females responded from the relationship responsibility (particularistic) and males responded from a sense of responsibility to society (universalistic).

Drawing on the above data, one might hypothesize that Latins tend to be more particularistic than Anglos and females tend to be more particularistic than males. Since the above information on the presence of particularistic and universalistic behavior is based on friendships (Stouffer and Toby, 1951, Zurcher, 1968), the question arises as to the ability of different types of personal relationships to precipitate these types of behavior. Borden (1985c) found that indeed the degree of universalism increased from Latin females to Latin males to Anglo females to Anglo males. This indicates that the Latin Americans are more particularistic than the Anglo Americans and females are more particularistic than males. It was also found that the degree of particularism increased as the relationship became more intimate (from stranger to spouse).

TRANSITION

When one thinks of the infinite number of behaviors that must be accounted for, and the infinite number of cognitive structures which may evoke them (Durbin, 1973), it is possible to see the futility of trying to set up a system of predictive rules. To "account for behavior," however, is a different goal altogether (Frake, 1964). If we can develop systemic schemas that will allow a person to anticipate appropriate behavior in a cultural event, then the person will be able to build on these schemas to develop his or her own understanding of the culture and eventually assimilate the orientation of this culture. The problem rests on the fact that a person can behave in many ways in any given context, and no one has been able to factor in our most human attribute, choice. Thus, appropriate behavior in any given cultural context ranges freely over a wide variety of behaviors that are more or less acceptable in that context. An individual still has the freedom to choose how he or she will behave, and that behavior may or may not be acceptable even in their own culture. The crux is to understand the other culture well enough to know how your behavior will be received.

The cultural orientation model may help. Cultural complexity is measured in the same way as cognitive complexity. It can be placed somewhere on the associative-abstractive and the closed-minded/open-minded continua. The coincident physical behavior is an etic measure and places cultures somewhere on the particularistic-universalistic continuum. The range of acceptable behaviors must be determined on a personal level. When our behavior gets close to the edges of this range of behavior, we are creating noise in the communication process. This affects the bonding, entropy, and synergy of the HCS. The principles of General Semantics can help us alleviate the problem of noise.

Wagner (1981) says "The understanding of another culture involves the relationship between two varieties of the human phenomenon; it aims at the creation of an intellectual relation between them, and understanding that includes both of them. The idea of 'relationship' is important here because it is more appropriate to the bringing together of two equivalent entities, or viewpoints, than notions like 'analysis' or 'examination,' with their pretensions of absolute objectivity" (p. 3). In knowing another culture, we get to know our own because in the process of creating the other culture, we necessarily create our own. We must make visible those constructs of both cultures that are important to the present relationship.

With Glenn's three dimensions of cultural orientation we can approach intercultural communication with some feeling of what to expect. As we develop the concept of culture and the relevant systems for dealing with it, Glenn's cultural orientation model will help us develop communication strategies that will ensure more effective intercultural communication. Because we are now operating at the associative level of systems complexity, we can use what we know about the cognitive styles of the individuals with whom we are communicating to modify the general cultural orientation of his or her culture. For example, Costa Ricans in general are associative and particularistic, while U.S. nationals are more abstractive and universalistic. However, my Costa Rican colleague, Dr. Francisco Escobar, is more abstractive and universalistic than I am. The individual is still the most important variable in the human communication system.

The cultural orientation model cannot be reduced to the mechanistic or cybernetic models that we are so used to employing in our study of human communication. The complexity of the human communication process insists that we be observant of the congruence or incongruence between the verbal and nonverbal signals in order to make sense out of any communication event in which we find ourselves. To do this we must be able to see the situation from the other communicator's frame of reference. This means seeing it from his or her cultural orientation. In the next chapter we will begin to study the concept *culture* by looking at the belief systems that underlie a culture's orientation.

INDEPENDENT STUDY

It is time for you to begin developing your own perspectives for intercultural communication.

1. We have said several times that survival is the basic teleological purpose. What other reasons might we have for behaving the way we do? Can these reasons be attributed at the cultural level as well? (This may be a group project involving different cultures.)

2. Several different cultural perspectives were given in this chapter. Using them, the other information we have given you, and your library, develop your own cultural perspective. Remember, it must address both the physical dimension (behavior) and the psychological dimension (cognition) and show a relationship between them. What are its implications for intercultural communication?

3. This study is best done in a group. Using the three dimensions of cultural orientation shown in Figure 6, develop the characteristics of a culture that would be in each of the eight sectors of the sphere. Using these characteristics as a model, develop some hypotheses about the difficulty or ease with which each of these cultures can communicate with the others.

    a. What are the primary difficulties?
    b. What are the advantages?
    c. How can the communication problems be reduced?
    d. Where do you see yourself in this model?
    e. What existing cultures fit into your model? (You may want to consult your local cultural anthropologist for help on this.)

There are two types of reports for this project: a research report on the development of your model, answering the question above, or a script which can be role played for the class.

CHAPTER SEVEN
Cultural Belief Systems

Cultures do not have belief systems; people do. However, as a culture develops and structures are established to ensure the stability of the culture, various belief systems congeal to permit a uniform approach to the problems of the culture. These beliefs and values are then operationalized in the actions of a government in both their foreign and domestic policies. The United States fought a war to claim its independence, wrote a Constitution with a Bill of Rights, and established a political system to maintain order and govern the nation. It also fought the Civil War to assert the equality of all of its human inhabitants. We say that we live in a democracy dedicated to the freedom of its people, and in fact, to the freedom of all peoples of the world. Some would go so far as to say that freedom is only possible in a democracy.

The belief systems of Costa Rica formed in a little different manner. They declared their independence without a war (no one else wanted the country!), and had an elected government for over 100 years before the present social democracy was established in 1948 as the result of an internal revolution, a civil war. Fortunately, it happened so fast that no outside powers could intervene. Strange as it may seem, instead of the army holding the power of the government in its hand, as has been so often the case in Latin America, it was abolished and its budget transferred to education. They still resist the pressures to form an army and put nearly a third of their budget into education (Biesanz, Biesanz, and Biesanz, 1988). They, too, believe in freedom but without the use of force.

There are many differences between the belief systems of the U.S. culture and that of Costa Rica. Even though both are fiercely independent, they interpret their independence differently. For example, in the United States the government believes that all businesses should be free of government control; in Costa Rica all of the basic businesses—health, insurance, energy, communication, etc.—are autonomous agencies of the government. In the United States, the government owes no one a living, while in Costa Rica you are taken care of from the cradle to the grave. U.S. political parties campaign according to the amount of money they can raise, which leads to uneven exposure of many of the candidates; in Costa Rica all campaigning is funded by the government, so all parties have "equal" exposure. At most, 50 to 60 percent of the eligible voters in the United States vote in presidential elections; 90 to 95 percent of their Costa Rican counterparts vote in presidential elections.

From the brief comparison given above, what are some of the values of these two countries? Which are similar, which are different? In this and the next four chapters, we will be comparing the belief systems of these two cultures (and some others) to see if we can determine some of the similarities and differences that will affect communication between them.

Additionally, we will see that all cultures possess a core of basic beliefs and values, but no culture has a completely consistent set of beliefs and values. Whereas we usually consider the beliefs and values of the middle class to be the norms for the culture, there is generally a difference between the official beliefs and values of a culture and those projected by its internal and external behaviors. With close observation we can see that the beliefs and values of individuals within a culture may vary more than the beliefs and values between cultures.

BELIEF STRUCTURES

Everyone believes in something! Some are Pollyannas; some are prima donnas. Our life is built on faith, most of which we have no awareness. This obvious truth is one of the first to make itself known when we meet a crisis in our life. We have faith in our churches, schools, and neighborhoods, so we don't teach our kids about drugs, sex, and character. We have faith in our lover or spouse, so we don't have to put any effort into the relationship (and they lived happily ever after!). We usually call this type of belief "taking for granted" because we are seldom aware of doing it until we are hit with a crisis. What other beliefs are so commonplace that we do not think about them? Democracy—how many of you voted in the last election? Peace, technology, science, law, medicine; the list is endless. Do you ever wonder why these beliefs exist? Why living within certain cultures allows you to take certain things for granted?

In the last chapter we briefly mentioned Bem's work on belief systems. We will return to that work now and develop the constructs that he uses to investigate our belief systems and report some of his findings. This ground laying is important because "Collectively, a man's beliefs compose his understanding of himself and his environment" (p. 5). Thus, to understand our culture, and that of another, we should know the origin and developmental processes of our belief systems.

All of our beliefs rest upon two basic beliefs that Bem calls "primitive beliefs." The most important of these beliefs is our faith in the credibility of our senses, i.e., in their trustworthiness. They will not play tricks on us. They are reliable transformers of external stimuli into internal neuronal impulses. This is so fundamental that we almost never challenge it, but there are some who are born with faulty sense organs, so we must take this as the most basic belief. It is a "zero-order" belief. Every time we make an observation about something in our physical environment, this zero-order belief is called into play. We look out the window and see crisp contrasts between light and shadows and say, "The sun is out today." Seldom do we go through the reasoning process that would be necessary if we started with our zero-order belief to arrive at this conclusion. The conclusion and the basic premise are psychologically equal. But because it is possible to go through this reasoning process, we call the conclusion a "first-order" belief. First-order beliefs form the basis for most of our reasoning processes.

The second basic, or zero-order, belief is our faith in external authority. It is a necessary result of our human development in a family situation. Faith in the honesty of our parents is fundamental to our sanity. Of course, as we grow older we realize some authorities can be trusted and some cannot. Finding out which is which is one of the joys of life! As with sensory information, so with authoritative information; if we trust the source, then it is a given that what they say is true. What the authorities tell us is a first-order belief. The difference between zero- and first-order beliefs is the difference between the source and the information presented by the source.

When my children were quite young, we took a trip across the United States, and in one state we passed a huge flock of sheep. My son was at the age when he was just learning the names of different animals, so I played a little game with him. "Curt," I said, "look at all the pigs." He said, "Oh dad, those don't look like pigs." He paused and then turned to his sister and said, "Are they, Sherrie?" She picked up on the game and said, "Oh yes, Curt, look, they are all white, and little, and look at their snouts." It took us about five minutes to convince him that they were pigs. At that point we passed another flock of sheep and I called them sheep. He was quick enough to say that they looked like the pigs we had just seen, and we confessed that we had been playing a game with him and praised him for his powers of observation. In this case faith in the senses was undermined by the arguments of two authority figures. It was an innocent game and proved a point. However, there are times when this contradiction can interfere with effective communication, especially when such arguments are politically determined.

Primitive beliefs may lead to stereotypes as we abstract the similarities and/or differences from our experiences. We then generalize to other situations or people and clump them all into one package. We do this automatically, as it is not possible to deal with every experience as a unique experience. We have neither the time nor the mental capacity to do this. As long as we treat it as a working stereotype (i.e., one that is open to change with new experiences), then we have a useful tool for communication. It is only when we close our mind to more information that we jeopardize effective communication.

As we mature, these core beliefs are elaborated and differentiated into our values and higher order beliefs. Higher order beliefs are built up from lower order beliefs in two ways: through vertical structures, i.e., a single line of reasoning from a central belief to the present belief; or horizontal structures, i.e., building it from a number of different central beliefs. Our reasoning processes may be inductive or deductive. Since we only have to satisfy our-selves, our line of reasoning may not be the same as others'. We have mentioned psycho-logic before, and it fits in well here. Our belief systems are built up through our psycho-logic—the logic by which we structure our psycho-logical constructs. The broader the base (horizontal structure), the more difficult it will be to shake it. It is only as strong as its weakest link. Think about this in terms of some of the more noteworthy beliefs. If you believe in, or do not believe in, some of the following, ask yourself why. How broad a base do you have for this belief? God, democracy, freedom, equality, friendship, justice, capital punishment, and patriotism.

For each of the above concepts, as with all concepts, we have built a schema such that we have expectations attached to each belief we hold. If these schemas match those of our communicatees, then we have a good chance for effective communication. Each of the beliefs we hold are also placed within an affective semantic space, i.e., they can be located somewhere on the evaluative (good-bad), the activity (active-passive), and the potency (strong-weak) dimensions of semantic space (Osgood, et al., 1957). This is not only true within our own culture but in other cultures also; the differences in their locations indicate a difference in the meaning of that concept between any two cultures (Osgood, et al., 1975).

VALUE STRUCTURES

The fact that the concepts in which we believe or disbelieve can be placed on the evaluative dimension means that we can (and do) make value judgments concerning these concepts, e.g., democracy may be good, capital punishment may be bad. These value judgments help form our attitudes (likes and dislikes), but they are not synonymous with them, for we may dislike something that we know is good for us—exercise! Rokeach (1979) says,

> values differ from attitudes (as well as from such other concepts as needs, norms, interests, and traits) in providing us with standards of competence and of morality, guiding or determining attitudes, behavior, judgments, comparisons of self and others, rationalizations and justifications, exhortative attempts to influence others, impression management and self-presentations. Thus defined, values are moreover fewer in number than attitudes, are conceptions that transcend specific attitude objects and situations, are determinants of attitudes as well as behavior, are dynamically closer to needs, and are more central to that core of the person that we identify as the self (p. 10).

Rokeach (1973) determined that we possess basic values that are relatively stable, central to our beliefs, and help us predict behavior. They have "cognitive, affective, and behavioral components" (p. 7): cognitive, in that we know what we desire; affective, in that we are often emotionally committed to them; and behavioral, in that they are the basis for many of our actions. Our values are important aspects of cultural literacy. They guide us in the development of our schemas and help us determine what is normal and deviant behavior in our culture. They are abstractive and universal as opposed to associative and particular; they are also intimately involved in the development of our closed- or opened-mindedness.

Rokeach found that our values were of two basic types: instrumental—the preference for certain ways of behaving (honest, ambitious, open-minded), and terminal—the preference for certain end states of existence (security, peace, wisdom). These belief structures are thought to influence our behaviors and to result from our interactions with the environment (enculturation). Together, they give us our world view and form our *attitudinal frame of reference* against which we measure experience. Obviously, there will be some commonalities among people of the same culture but also individual differences stemming from the personal nature of enculturation.

Unfortunately, there are also inconsistencies among the values and beliefs of a single individual. Although we may have a primary central value (belief in God) that will direct our behavior in most cases, there are always exceptions. I once worked with two scientists (both had Ph.Ds. in geology) who were also bishops in their church, which believed in biblical creationism and condemned the theory of evolution. Every weekday they worked with the principles of evolution in their search for oil, and every weekend they preached the "truth." I asked them how they could live with such dissonance (hypocrisy?), and they answered that they never let the two world views come in contact. One was a job and a theory of how the earth was formed that seemed to work; the other was their life and not a theory at all but the word of God. They never tried to reconcile them. Bem says that two seemingly contradictory beliefs held by the same person are contained in opinion molecules and shows that they can be maintained indefinitely. Cultures have opinion molecules also—strongly opposed to dictatorships but supporting Samoza, Marcos, and others!

Rokeach (1968) used his value systems to measure differences between various ideological groups. Using just two values, freedom and equality, out of a 12-value list, he found that policemen ranked freedom first and equality twelfth while unemployed blacks ranked freedom tenth and equality first (p. 170). From a list of 17 terminal values, using writings of each of the following people or groups, he found that socialists ranked freedom first and equality second; Hitler ranked them sixteenth and seventeenth; Goldwater ranked them first and sixteenth; and Lenin ranked them seventeenth and first. It is obvious that our values are an integral part of our belief systems, and it is probable that our values precede our beliefs.

Table 2:   Human Belief Systems

TERMINAL VALUES	INSTRUMENTAL VALUES
A COMFORTABLE LIFE (a prosperous life)	AMBITIOUS (Hard-working, aspiring)
AN EXCITING LIFE (a stimulating, active life)	BROADMINDED (open-minded)
A SENSE OF ACCOMPLISHMENT (lasting contribution)	CAPABLE (competent, effective)
A WORLD OF BEAUTY (beauty of nature and the arts)	CLEAN (neat, tidy)
A WORLD AT PEACE (free of war and conflict)	CHEERFUL (lighthearted, joyful)
EQUALITY (BROTHERHOOD) (equal opportunity for all)	COURAGEOUS (standing up for your beliefs)
FAMILY SECURITY (taking care of loved ones)	FORGIVING (willing to pardon others)
FREEDOM (independence, free choice)	HELPFUL (working for welfare of others)
HAPPINESS (contentedness)	HONEST (sincere, truthful)
INNER HARMONY (freedom from inner conflict)	IMAGINATIVE (daring, creative)
MATURE LOVE (sexual and spiritual intimacy)	INDEPENDENT (self-reliant, self-sufficient)
NATIONAL SECURITY (protection from attack)	INTELLECTUAL (intelligent, reflective)
PLEASURE (an enjoyable, leisurely life)	LOGICAL (consistent, rational)
SALVATION (saved, eternal life)	LOVING (affectionate, tender)
SELF-RESPECT (self-esteem)	OBEDIENT (dutiful, respectful)
SOCIAL RECOGNITION (respect, admiration)	POLITE (courteous, well-mannered)
TRUE FRIENDSHIP (close companionship)	RESPONSIBLE (dependable, reliable)
WISDOM (mature understanding of life)	SELF-CONTROLLED (restrained, self-disciplined)

Rokeach (1973) finalized his value system with 18 terminal and 18 instrumental values (see Table 2). The terminal values can be grouped into self-centered and society-centered values, and the instrumental values into moral and competence values. To determine the hierarchy of values in a culture or subculture, members are asked to rank each set of values. We have seen that the rankings change with ideological stance; they also change with age. Most of the research on values has been done using terminal values. In the early 1970s, college students ranked freedom first and happiness second, with equality coming in eleventh (Rokeach, p. 76). In a series of administrations of this values test to college students, this author found that the terminal values changed to happiness first, freedom second, and equality fifteenth in 1984 and to happiness first, true friendship second, freedom fourth, and equality fifteenth in 1988. Perhaps we are beginning to take freedom for granted!

One way of interpreting the hierarchy of values is to say that those values are ranked highest of which we feel we have the least. The present climate in the United States seems to be one of less interpersonal commitment and more of personal freedom, so we may long for the commitment of a true friend. Some backing is given to this idea when we look at the instrumental values. Honesty ranks first for all groups in every time period. Responsibility was second in 1973 but had slipped to sixth in 1988. Independence was sixth in 1973 but second in 1988. Obedience was and is in the eighteenth spot.

In a study comparing Latin and Anglo-Americans, Borden (1983) found that honesty and responsibility were ranked first and second as the most desirable characteristics of same-sex friends in all three cultures (United States, Costa Rica, and Mexico). However, the Latinos believed significantly more strongly than the Anglos that "honesty is the best policy in all cases" and "there is no excuse for lying to someone else," but also that "the best way to handle people is to tell them what they want to hear" and "never tell anyone the real reason you did something unless it is useful to do so." There appear to be two different values at work here—honesty and utility—but that is from a U.S. point of view. For Latinos the value of a friendship far outweighs objective "truth;" the immediate, the subjective, and the particularistic are what is "true."

VALUES AND ETHICS

Every communication event involves the management of information, whether it is interpersonal or international. Each utterance we make requires us to make a decision as to what information that utterance will contain. In each of these decisions we must weigh the purpose of the statement against a myriad of other forces. The major force in this process is our values. Differences in values can destroy relationships whether they are across cultures or in the same family. However, when they occur across cultures, they are most likely to affect more than interpersonal relationships (Lustig, 1988). When this happens something must be compromised if the relationship is to be preserved.

Our values are "standards that guide ongoing activities"; they are guides for our decision making. When we act or say something that compromises one or more of our values, our psychological structures let us know that something isn't quite right by the feeling of dissonance that arises. If we put this in the context of communication and ethics, we can say that when we compromise our values we are unethical, and being ethical means keeping our values in balance. This definition of ethics is based on the premise that all human beings are responsible for their own behaviors, whether these behaviors are part of an intimate interpersonal relationship, a complex multinational corporate transaction, or international politics.

Compromising our values usually occurs between one or more terminal values and one or more instrumental values. To illustrate this we can look at an example using just one value from each system with an application to intercultural communication. If we use "a comfortable life" (terminal) and "honest" (instrumental), we can put ourselves squarely in the position of many international business transactions where the mode of transacting is affected by the belief systems of the cultures. The U.S. culture holds success as one of its highest values and graft, bribery, and extortion as some of its lowest values. If your company is trying to land a contract with a culture that has always used gifts to show interest in, and appreciation for, consideration, what happens if you refuse to send a gift along with your bid? To you it is dishonest, but it might mean getting the contract. To them it is the only proper thing to do, and not doing it means you are really not interested in the transaction. Would you compromise your honesty or your desire for success? Either way you will feel some dissonance and a sense of unethicality.

The major problem in ethics is that although ethical behavior can only be personal, it is only recognized when it is evaluated in a social or public situation (Borden, 1986). Inasmuch as our personal values are affected by our cultural values, we will be a creature of our culture and will react to the differing values of other cultures. If I were in a position to hire someone for a position in a Costa Rican company, I would feel unethical hiring my boss's child if he or she was not qualified rather than a qualified applicant, but that is what is done. In trying to understand, accept, and behave acceptably in another culture, or as an intermediary between two cultures, our ethical standards are often called into question. Perhaps this is most evident in situations where belief systems are the focus—missionary crusades, civil wars, and revolutions.

VALUES AND COMMUNICATION

Because we all have some form of ethics, we all feel dissonance when we must compromise our values. Unfortunately, we all also show a certain amount of ethnocentrism in that it is difficult not to judge another culture's behavior on the basis of our own culture's values, or our own, if they differ. This being the case, how is it possible to communicate across cultures? Sitaram and Haapanen (1979) tell us that

> the first rule of intercultural communication is that each participant should understand the other's values. That understanding should precede any attempts to communicate interculturally. Because communicative techniques are manifestations of one's own values, the participants communicate differently. The second rule is that each should adapt his/her communication to the other's values. Adaptation implies respect for the other value system. Without such respect one

cannot adapt his/her communicative behavior to the other system. Adaptation should be an on-going act. A person should know the art of constant adaptation to other cultures (p. 159).

Making one's values visible so others can understand and adapt to them is similar to making our schemas and our cultural constructs visible. There have been some attempts toward doing this on an objective basis, but when you are communicating with someone, you must be able to do this in the immediate time frame. This would seem to call for full authenticity and openness in the communication process, but supposing that is not one of the values of the person with whom you are communicating—and it almost never is. The emphasis in the above quote should be on "*each participant*," but it is immediately clear how difficult this is to obtain. At the same time, if we are both trying to understand and adapt to the other's values, will we not pass each other in the attempt, and, perhaps, end up communicating from the other's value orientation? This happens, and both parties are confused in the process. Better that we define the process of adaptation as that of negotiating a mutually acceptable value orientation for our transaction. This means that we must know each other's value orientations and be open in our communication to the point of recognizing them and being able to negotiate a compromise position. Is this ethical? It may depend on whether the values compromised are less important (culturally) than the success of the transaction.

Stewart (1972) develops a number of U.S. cultural value orientations that make intercultural communication difficult. Among these are:

1. our focus on the individual's responsibility in decision making;
2. the conceptualization of the world in a rather mechanistic model, in which problems can be defined and solved in an objective mode;
3. a rather linear, cause-effect model of reality;
4. an emphasis on doing—goal oriented behavior, competition, precise demarcations between work and play; and
5. a nearly fanatical commitment to time.

We seem to measure success by how much we have done in a given period of time, often with little regard for the quality of the product. The process of living has been changed from an interpersonal involvement to involvement with things—consumer items, roles, status. We are often characterized as a fast-food culture. Most of our values have helped us achieve a high living standard, but when they are coupled with vigorous ethnocentrism our ability to negotiate across cultures is diminished (Harris and Moran; Smith and Luce, 1979).

A SYSTEM OF VALUES

You have been given one system of values (Rokeach) that has a U. S. cultural bias (it was developed using only U.S. enculturated subjects). Hofstede (1984) reviews a number of other value systems in the process of developing his own. These value systems are all applicable to intercultural understanding as long as one realizes the cultural values underlying the system. Hofstede's system consists of four dimensions (or subsystems) and was developed through research into the value systems of 53 different cultures. The subjects were all employees of the same multinational corporation and its subsidiaries. The investigation concerned the values involved in work-related decisions. One might argue from this that the resulting four dimensions cannot be generalized to non-work-related situations. Nonetheless, in his attempt to discover the universality of these dimensions they were compared with most, if not all, other research results and found to be as, or more, general.

Since Rokeach's value systems are the most widely known and used in the United States we might wonder how well Hofstede's value dimensions compare. Hofstede and Bond (1984) compared the two systems and found that many, but not all, of Rokeach's values loaded on one of the four value dimensions of Hofstede and were intuitively important to it. Further, when the question was asked, are there other value dimensions identified by Rokeach's 36 values, the answer was no. It would appear that the resulting four dimensions of belief systems of Hofstede are universal and applicable to all levels of intercultural negotiations.

Hofstede (1984) found that all cultures make decisions based on the importance placed in the values which load on four subsystems he called Power Distance, Uncertainty Avoidance, Individualism, and Masculinity. It would appear, then, that these are the dimensions around which we should search for the basic values of a culture.

With these four value dimensions Hofstede has been able to differentiate among many different cultures (see Table 3). By comparing the position of two cultures on these four dimensions, one can get an idea of the relative importance of these values to these cultures and, perhaps, enhance the effectiveness of the communication between them.

Writing about power distance, Hofstede (1984) says that "The basic issue involved, to which different societies have found different solutions, is human inequality. Inequality can occur in areas such as prestige, wealth, and power; different societies put different weights on status consistency among these areas. Inside organizations, inequality in power is inevitable and functional. This inequality is usually formalized in hierarchical boss-subordinate relationships" (p. 65). Power distance is present at all levels of society. We see it in families, bureaucracies, and even in friendships. The fact that every society has to handle inequality in some way makes the knowledge of the cultural values subsumed in this dimension critically important to intercultural communication.

Hofstede says of the uncertainty avoidance dimension that "Uncertainty about the future is a basic fact of human life with which we try to cope through the domains of technology, law and religion. In organizations these take the form of technology, rules, and rituals. . . . Sex differences in uncertainty avoidance are negligible . . . (and) the most important correlations are with national anxiety level. . . ." (p. 110). As we look back at cultural evolution, we see that uncertainty has been a major facet in the organization of families,

Table 3:   Country Ratings on Hofstede's Value Dimensions

COUNTRY	POWER DISTANCE R* #		UNCERTAINTY AVOIDANCE R* #		INDIVIDUALISM R* #		MASCULINITY R* #	
Argentina	25	49	10	86	23	46	18	56
Australia	29	36	27	51	2	90	14	61
Austria	40	11	19	70	18	55	2	79
Belgium	12	65	3	94	8	75	20	54
Brazil	7	69	16	76	25	38	23	49
Canada	27	39	31	48	4	80	21	52
Chile	15	63	8	86	33	23	34	28
Colombia	10	67	14	80	39	13	11	64
Denmark	38	18	39	23	9	74	37	16
Finland	33	33	24	59	17	63	35	26
France	9	68	7	86	11	71	29	43
Germany	30	35	21	65	15	67	9	66
Great Britain	31	35	35	35	3	89	8	66
Greece	17	60	1	112	27	35	16	57
Hong Kong	8	68	37	29	32	25	17	57
India	4	77	34	40	21	48	19	56
Iran	18	58	23	59	24	41	28	43
Ireland	36	28	36	35	12	70	7	68
Israel	39	13	13	81	19	54	25	47
Italy	23	50	17	75	7	76	4	70
Japan	22	54	4	92	22	46	1	95
Mexico	2	81	12	82	29	30	6	69
Netherlands	28	38	26	53	5	80	38	14
New Zealand	37	22	30	49	6	79	15	58
Norway	34	31	28	50	13	69	39	8
Pakistan	21	55	18	70	38	14	22	50
Peru	13	64	7	87	37	16	31	42
Philippines	1	94	33	44	28	32	10	64
Portugal	16	63	2	104	30	27	33	31
Singapore	6	74	40	8	34	20	24	48
South Africa	24	49	29	49	16	65	12	63
Spain	20	57	9	86	20	51	30	42
Sweden	35	31	38	29	10	71	40	5
Switzerland	32	34	25	58	14	68	5	70
Taiwan	19	58	20	69	36	17	27	45
Thailand	14	64	22	64	35	20	32	34
Turkey	11	66	11	85	26	37	26	45
U. S. A.	26	40	32	46	1	91	13	62
Venezuela	3	81	15	76	40	12	3	73
Yugoslavia	5	76	5	88	31	27	36	21

*R - The lower the number, the higher the ranking on that dimension

societies, and cultures. Religion, on both the individual and cultural levels, appears to be the primary mediator of uncertainty. As cultures became abstract and scientific, laws and technology arose to take over much of this task. Perhaps the major question is, To what do you (or your culture) turn when facing a major crisis of uncertainty (AIDS, for example)?

Of the individualism dimension Hofstede says, "It describes the relationship between the individual and the collectivity which prevails in a given society. It is reflected in the way people live together—for example, in nuclear families, extended families, or tribes; and it has all kinds of value implications. In some cultures, individualism is seen as a blessing and a source of well-being; in others, it is seen as alienating" (p. 148). When compiling information on this dimension, one must be careful not to let family structures (nuclear, extended) interfere with (obscure) the role of the individual. In Costa Rica, for example, there is a close-knit extended family structure, and at the same time a strong individualistic tendency. It just depends on what type of behavior you are recording.

Sex roles have been studied extensively. Hofstede calls this value dimension masculinity and gives further evidence that, "The duality of the sexes is a fundamental fact with which different societies cope in different ways; the issue is whether the biological differences between the sexes should or should not have implications for their roles in social activities. The sex role distribution common in a particular society is transferred by socialization in families, schools, and peer groups, and through the media. The predominant socialization pattern is for men to be more assertive and for women to be more nurturing" (p. 176). This dimension is built around the most rapidly changing structure of beliefs and values. In every culture the inequality between the sexes is being challenged. The movement from biological differentiation to gender (psychological) differentiation is of major importance in most communication situations. How are the sex roles changing in your neighborhood?

TRANSITION

We have seen that values can cause problems in intercultural communication. It has been hinted that these problems may be more severe when encountered in business or political negotiations, but for the individual the results are just as devastating when negotiating on a personal basis. In each case the person's as well as the culture's values come into play and one may feel just as ethical or unethical with the outcome of negotiations on any level. Our values are connected intimately with the development of our cybernetic. We make our communication decisions based on them, for they let us know what the doables are. At times, when we are pulled between two values, we may feel that they are noise in the system. But in terms of an HCS they can be the strongest bonds, and they are an integral part of all three dimensions of cultural orientation.

As we look at Hofstede's four value dimensions in the next four chapters, you may find that your own values differ somewhat from those of your culture; that is to be expected. You may also find that you have some central primitive beliefs from which stem most of your higher order beliefs. Perhaps you will also see how these beliefs and values affect your communicative behavior. In the next chapter we will address the power distance dimension and show its role in the cultural orientation model.

INDEPENDENT STUDY

Our main goal in this chapter was to present the concept of values in general.

1. You will find many publications on values—in magazines, books, and journals. Look at some of these and compare them to what was said in this chapter. Are there differences that seem to be significant?

2. Every day the newspapers report another "deal" or event in which the ethics of the participants are questioned. Look into one of these in enough depth to decide what the value structures are of all sides in the issue. Draw a conclusion based on your own values.

3. Using the value systems of Rokeach, construct a questionnaire to elicit the values of the respondents. Give it to at least ten people in two cultures (or subcultures). Compare the results.

CHAPTER EIGHT
Power Distance

In 1980 I was asked to evaluate the effectiveness of La Universidad Estatal a Distancia of Costa Rica in their effort to reach the very poor (Borden and Tanner, 1980). In searching for a term to designate this group in the Spanish language questionnaires, I found that, although several terms described this group, all of them had negative connotations that made them unacceptable. The direct translation, muy pobre, was unacceptable as it refers to "beggars," "paupers," "poor in spirit," and the like. After some discussion with several researchers, we thought perhaps clase baja, (lower class) should be the term. Several days later we learned that this was not satisfactory, for it referred more to a social class of people and did not have the economic connotation we desired.

The search for the correct terminology was further hampered by the fact that proud people do not want to be considered lower class, poor, or impoverished. It was also found that there was no standard income level across the country below which a person was considered poor. The living standard of this class of people was dependent upon their rural or urban dwelling, area of the country, type of employment, etc. The class "very poor" is extremely relative to the area in which one lives. Thus, even the term ingreso bajo (low income) was not suitable for our purposes.

A search of the dictionary revealed several alternatives which might have been appropriate for the study. These were terms like empobrecitos (meaning impoverished with all its negative connotations), desgraciados (meaning unfortunate but with the connotation of a wretch), desventurados (meaning unfortunate or disadvantaged), menesterosos (meaning needy person), and necesitados (meaning poor or needy person). Unfortunately, none of these terms are commonly used in Costa Rica to refer to the class of people in which we were interested, and they would have been misunderstood. The term we finally found to be generally used in Costa Rica to refer to the very poor in any region was marginados (marginals—those who were not yet making it but had the potential to do so. Although everyone knew what this term meant, no one could define it objectively, nor were there any statistics to indicate its use in census data. However, it was used successfully in the interview material and in the final report to designate our target class.

In this chapter we will look at the first of Hofstede's dimensions of belief systems, power distance. In every culture there is an identifiable hierarchy of classes. These classes are defined and maintained by the labels given to them in everyday human communication. Thus, power distance is made visible by the language (verbal and nonverbal) we use. Many of these inequalities play an important role in operations of a culture, e.g., president, employers, employees, and all of the ranks of military organizations. There are both positive and negative inequalities in every society.

ON DEFINING POWER DISTANCE

As indicated in Chapter 7, power distance is one of the four components (subsystems) of our cultural belief system as identified by Hofstede (1980). He says that "The power distance between a boss B and a subordinate S in a hierarchy is the difference between the extent to which B can determine the behavior of S and the extent to which S can determine the behavior of B" (1984, p. 72). An important aspect of power distance so defined is that it is interactive and communication dependent. Both parties have some ability to control the behavior of the other; it is not a one-way process. An example in which power distance is obvious illustrates this point. In a family, the children are subordinate to the parents, but a child's behavior often controls the behavior of the parent (or the baby sitter!).

Hofstede continues by saying that "Power Distance is a measure of the interpersonal power or influence between B and S as perceived by the least powerful of the two, S" (p. 71). Usually, the superior perceives less distance between the two than does the subordinate, but for Hofstede the measure is from the bottom up, not from the top down.

> Subordinates as a group are accessary to the exercise of power in a hierarchical system: The way the system functions reflects their collective complicity and the role relationship to which both parties contribute. Authority only exists where it is matched by obedience. . . . On the psychological level, the need for independence in people is matched by a need for dependence, and the need for power by a need for security; dependence and security needs stem from early childhood and are common to all mankind; independence and power are only developed later in our lives, if they are developed at all (p. 70).

It is true that one cannot be a boss if one has no subordinates. When there exists a hierarchical ordering of roles, the focus of the construct power distance is on the style of decision-making by the superior. Does she or he demand obedience or negotiate solutions? Do both parties accept the inequalities in their positions or is it the fact that subordinates are constantly striving to reduce them? To answer this question one needs to know all of the various dimensions of power distance—economic, social, political, etc.—for without these one would not know upon which one the subordinates were striving for equality. Power distance has as many faces as there are reasons for being. It only exists because there is a relationship between the two roles in question, with one having some kind of power over the other.

Cultural Inequalities

Since Hofstede generalizes from his work with organizations to cultures, we may look at power distance as cultural inequalities and ask the question, "How does a culture deal with the inequalities found within it and between it and other cultures?" A long time ago the United States struck down the idea of separate but equal, giving voice to the idea that whenever there are divisions, there are inequalities. We pride ourselves on having a universalistic legal system under which all humans are created equal. But are they? No, but that is one of the myths upon which our culture is built. Those who blatantly disregard this axiom are caught and must pay the consequences: Nixon, Boesky, North. Although in most cases (at least in these cases) when someone of power, wealth, or status acts contrary to the law, the penalty does not match the crime in the eyes of the "average person." "Some pigs are more equal than others!" (Orwell, Animal Farm).

In every culture there are advantaged and disadvantaged groups. The question is, how are they treated? What is the structuring mechanism of the culture? What ways are provided for those of a lower class to climb up the status ladder? For example, is biology or environment or race destiny? In the strongly independent culture of the United States, we tend to think that anyone can become anything they really want to become. But is this true (even if you can give an example for each situation I might bring up)? What is the interaction of persons with society that enables one to succeed and another to fail in their quest to advance their place in life? We tend to put our hopes into three avenues to success (success being the realization of our most desired position of superiority): education, occupation, and income.

One of the primary characteristics of inequality is that the subordinates are continually trying to decrease the distance between themselves and their superiors, and the superiors are trying to maintain or increase the distance between themselves and their subordinates (inferiors). This is true whether the inequalities are within a culture or between cultures. It is not always a conscious act, but the mere use of the language by which different groups are defined and talked about (to one country the rebels are right-wing subversives, to another they are freedom fighters) automatically reinforces the stereotype (van Dijk, 1986). We reproduce our cognitive biases (values) in our talk. That is one of the reasons why, in the 1960s, the term Negro was exchanged for the term Black. A new identity was being forged and it needed a new label. In a lesser sense we are seeing the same type of transformation with the women's movement; man is becoming human, girl is becoming woman. As was brought out in other chapters, our language can have a stereotyping effect on our thinking and actions; it is the bridge between behavior and cognition.

Conflict Management

Wherever differences occur, there is the potential for disagreement, conflict, and hostilities. Conflict is often looked upon as a negative process leading to the dissolution of a relationship—the breakup of an HCS. However, with proper management, it can lead to a deepening of the relationship: better bonding, a decrease in entropy, and an increase in synergy. It should be looked upon as a natural phenomenon in any and all types of relationships (Roloff, 1987). In fact, some feel that a relationship without conflict is no relationship at all. Along with the more positive approach to conflict has come an attempt to manage them rather than resolve them at all costs. This is an important point, for, whereas conflict resolution often involved competition with winners and losers, conflict management stresses communication, negotiation, compromise, and equality.

Hocker and Wilmot (1985) suggest that when conflict is managed, both parties have a concern for themselves and a concern for the other. The various styles of conflict management differ in the weights given to these two concerns and can be considered as a positive or negative style depending on the goals of the participants. They discuss five different styles of conflict management:

Competing: characterized by aggressive and uncooperative behavior, pursuing your own concerns at the expense of another.

Collaborating: when high assertiveness aimed at reaching one's own goals integrates with a high concern for the other person.

Compromising: characterized by beliefs such as "You have to be satisfied with part of the pie."

Avoiding: The person does not openly pursue his own concerns or those of the other person, but effectively "goes weak," refusing to engage openly in the conflict.

Accommodating: the individual puts aside his or her own concerns in order to satisfy the concerns of the other person.

Each of these styles can be used by groups or governments as well as individuals. Consider the interactions between Russia and the United States in light of these approaches to conflict management.

The superpowers are more or less equal, but how does one manage the power distance (conflict) between the United States and Panamá, or one of the Central American countries? Surely, in most categories the United States would be seen as being superior to any of them, but what about in the categories of sovereignty and autonomy? Should all nations be considered equal in the sense of independence from the rule and/or wishes of another? The history of the interaction between the United States and Central America and Panamá is one of paternalism, as though they were our children and we had the right to intervene in their internal affairs (LaFeber). But how could the United States ever consider them to be equal? Our concept of power is force, not negotiation, so our approach to conflict resolution has been to use force or the show of force (Riesman, 1961)—a competitive style.

While in Costa Rica in 1984 I attended several gatherings where the U.S. ambassador to Costa Rica was questioned about how the problems in Nicaragua and Panamá might be solved. His stock answer was to send in the Marines. In contrast, President Oscar Arias of Costa Rica put forth a Peace Plan that was signed by the presidents of the five Central American countries, for which he received the Nobel Peace Prize in 1987. One of its major points was not only the sovereignty of each of the Central American countries but also of Central America itself. It involved continuous negotiations among equally autonomous nations, a collaborative or compromising style. This is a very difficult process to accomplish when the two superpowers are using the region as a playground to act out their differences.

Environmental Concerns

Since our primary concern in this text is to explicate the constructs that will help us understand intercultural communication, it is necessary to look at each of the value subsystems to see if the differences in national values will affect intercultural communication in various situations. Using Hofstede's work as the basis for our four value subsystems, and knowing that these four dimensions resulted from his work in multinational corporations, means that we must take particular care in generalizing them to other contexts. Three contexts seem appropriate for this process: the social/public/political, the organizational, and the personal. However, Hofstede has shown that these values are generalizable to the nation's middle-class norms.

Social/public/political   This is the most abstract, least organized context in which we must look for evidence of power distance. We immediately see that it is there. Societies are organized on many different plans, but they are all organized. The political structure may be open or closed, explicit or implicit, but there is always some form of hierarchy. The true commune does not exist. Thus, we can always find some form of power distance at work in any society (the lack of such would be just as important because it would give us a true base for comparison). Power seems to be a basic pursuit of human beings; some will want to lead, some will want to follow. The problem comes in when there are too many leaders and not enough followers, or when the followers do not agree with the directions of the leaders.

Organizational Hofstede gives us solid evidence that power distance exists in this context. He says that "An unequal distribution of power over members is the essence of organization" (p. 69). It is the judicious use of this power that reduces the entropy and increases the synergy of the organization. The value systems of bosses and employees may clash or be harmonious, but they are always evident in the power distance found in the organization. Each person is responsible to someone, if not in the organization, then to the clients or consumers. Each type of organization has its own style of behavior (Theories X, Y, and Z) and, indeed, its own culture (Deal and Kennedy, 1982).

Personal Although Hofstede says that the value dimensions are characteristics of societies and not individuals, we need to realize that the characteristics of a society are the norms of the people are living there. The data collected by Hofstede were the responses of thousands of individuals. His statistical operations produced the figures that tell us how various cultures differ. It should be obvious that individuals differ in the same way and on the same dimensions. On the power-distance dimension some individuals are authoritative, confrontational, submissive, or negotiatory. It's possible that a scale could be produced that would reveal the personality characteristics of individuals in much the same way as the Hofstede questionnaires revealed those of cultures.

Types of Power

Although Hofstede's research was within an organizational setting, in his analysis he shows that "the power distance thus defined, which is accepted by both B and S and supported by their social environment, is to a considerable extent determined by their national culture" (p. 72). As we have seen, our personal, organizational, and social belief systems are all related even though they may differ somewhat due to specific context. We all learned our value systems growing up in a culture. Thus, to some extent we all are a reflection of the culture's value systems. The same is true of our concept of power and how that power is operationalized.

King (1987) says "Much power is group power. Although power seems to be exercised by individuals, they often do so as agents or 'leaders' of their sponsoring groups. The power of the lone individual is an ideological and aesthetic creation" (p. 4). The role or office filled by an individual is usually the seat of power. The individual who fills the role may have arrived there in one of three different ways (Henley): *Dominance*—the office or role is taken by force (actual or implied) as in a coup. The office holder seeks to control with little or no input from the subordinates. *Authority*—the office or role is earned by filling the prerequisite for it such as education, longevity, skill, etc. This does not mean that the officeholder will be any different from the one who takes it by force, but it does mean that he or she has worked within the structure of the culture to obtain the role. *Status*—the office or role is bestowed upon the person because he or she has obtained a high popularity with the constituents. Again, he or she may be just as ruthless or benevolent as the other two types, the difference being that the role or office was a gift from the fans.

May (1972) gives us five types of power that are particularly well-defined for interpersonal relations. They are: *Exploitative*, which is the use of power with no regard for subordinates; they are there to do your bidding. It can be subtle, as in Machiavellianism, or flagrant, as in slavery. *Manipulative*, which is persuasion with a hidden agenda. The con artist is a good example. *Competitive*, which is power against another person. It can be either negative or positive: Negative in that only one may be able to win; positive in that it can heighten the efforts of each and raise them to heights they had not realized possible. *Nutrient*, which is the power to facilitate growth in another person. This often goes unperceived on the part of both people. *Integrative*, which is power to work with other people, thus reducing entropy and increasing synergy so that objectives are realized.

One could use all of these five types of power in social and organizational contexts, but they are best suited for the analysis of interpersonal systems. Power distance can be measured in systems using any of these types of power. The difficulty arises when one realizes that systems usually contain more than one type of power and that the types of power are not mutually exclusive. When looking at another culture, it is a plus if you can identify the principal type of power used on each of the three levels: social, organizational, and personal.

High and Low Power Distance

In developing the power-distance dimension, Hofstede found one question that seemed to best exemplify this subsystem of beliefs: "How frequently, in your experience, does the following problem occur: employees being afraid to express disagreement with their managers?" (p. 73). It is a simple matter to extend this concept to culture in general. What are the consequences of disagreeing with authority? We saw this situation played out rather dramatically in the '60s and '70s. Some would say that change occurs only when the status quo rebels. "The squeaking wheel gets the grease." But some cultures have ways of dealing with dissidents; just ask Amnesty International.

Fear of disagreement is a measure of power distance. Do you confront issue with your friends, lovers, spouse, boss, society, or do you wait for them to work themselves out? Low power distance (LPD) says there is little fear of confrontation; there is a higher level of the feeling of equality, and the cultural structure is such that this feeling is facilitated. High power distance (HPD) emphasizes authority and subordination, with little tolerance for individual freedom (especially to question the decisions of your superiors). You might equate the two extremes immediately with democracy (LPD) and communism (HPD). but consider the authoritarian father, schoolmaster, boss, or judge in a culture where all are equal under the law but power is translated as force, and in a culture where power is translated as negotiation (a contrast between the United States and Costa Rica, for example). This applies more to the distinction between conservative and liberal (as we use them in the United States) than between democracy and communism.

CULTURAL CHARACTERISTICS

Inequalities between cultures or among components of a culture can exist on many different dimensions: wealth, power, technology, human rights, among others. More basic than these types of equalities is how a culture treats these inequalities in the process of everyday living. If power distance is the fear of confronting those having power over us, then if we know the position of a culture on the Power Distance Index (PDI) scale relative to our own position, we will have a starting point from which to proceed in our understanding of that culture. Referring back to Table 3, we see that the United States ranks 26 out of 40 cultures on the PDI. The Philippines has the highest PDI (subordinates are extremely submissive) and Austria has the lowest PDI (subordinates are much more confrontational).

Just knowing where a country is ranked on the PDI does not tell us much unless we know more of the characteristics of a culture that correlate with this dimension. The societal norms for high and low PDIs are given in Table 4. We will discuss some of the implications of these findings to give you an idea of what they tell us. For example, it was found that high PDI cultures expect more initiating behavior on the part of authority figures that do low PDI cultures. Thus, if you were a consultant working in a high PDI culture, there might be a higher expectation for you to present them with the finished idea rather than work with them to develop it.

The fact that high PDI cultures feel that power holders are entitled to privileges while low PDI cultures feel that all should have equal rights poses a real problem for intercultural communication between the two. A friend of mine in Costa Rica who is a political scientist told me that the people there expect a person who is voted into office or receives an appointment to a prestigious office to use that office to accumulate the things necessary to remain in the standard of living to which they have become accustomed or to which they would like to become accustomed. We feel that this often happens in the United States but we do not accept it as the standard behavior pattern.

Looking at the characteristics of the high and low PDI countries indicates two diverse kinds of societies. The high PDIs tend toward a society that is highly structured, has rigid control, uses force or coercion, is intolerant, has individual freedom but little equality, and is elitist. The low PDIs tend toward a society that has less structure, more flexible control, negotiates, is tolerant of others, believes strongly in equality, and has less hierarchy. Of course, these are the extremes; most cultures have some of each of these characteristics.

Table 4:   The Power Distance Societal Norm (Hofstede, p. 94)

LOW PDI	HIGH PDI
1. Inequality in society should be minimized.	There should be an order of inequality in this world in which everyone has his rightful place; high and low are protected by this order.
2. All should be interdependent.	A few should be independent, most should be dependent.
3. Hierarchy means an inequality of roles established for convenience.	Hierarchy means existential inequality.
4. Subordinates are people like me.	Superiors consider subordinates as being of a different kind.
5. Superiors are people like me.	Subordinates consider superiors as being of a different kind.
6. The use of power should be legitimate and is subject to the judgment between good and evil.	Power is a basic fact of society which antedates good or evil; its legitimacy is irrelevant.
7. All should have equal rights.	Power holders are entitled to privileges.
8. Powerful people should try to look less powerful than they are.	Powerful people should look as powerful as possible.
9. Stress on reward, legitimate and expert power.	Stress on coercive and referent power.
10. The system is to blame.	The underdog is to blame.
11. The way to change a social system is by redistributing power.	The way to change a social system is by dethroning those in power.
12. People at various power levels feel less threatened and more prepared to trust people.	Other people are a potential threat to one's power and rarely can be trusted.
13. Latent harmony between the powerful and the powerless.	Latent conflict between powerful and powerless.
14. Cooperation among the powerless can be based on solidarity.	Cooperation among the powerless is difficult to bring about because of low faith in people norm.

However, if we know their tendency to behave one way or the other, we shouldn't embarrass ourselves on our first contact.

Another variable in power-distance dimension is that of sex. Do the different sexes behave differently with respect to this dimension or are they within the normal deviation of the country? The data indicate that there are little or no differences between the sexes. Differences between classes do occur within a culture, however, especially in less economically developed countries like Mexico and India (where there are also strong class differences). It was also found that education level affected the PDI. "We see that the lower-education, lower-status occupations tend to produce high PDI values and the higher-education, higher-status occupations tend to produce low PDI values. Education is by far the dominant factor. . . . Every additional year of formal school education needed for an occupation reduces the occupation's PDI score by about 18 points" (Hofstede, p. 77). Education level appears to be a good predictor of PDI level; the more education, the lower the PDI. In high PDI cultures the students are more dependent, do less questioning, and have more rote learning.

Three other variables can help us predict the PDI level of a country: geographic location (latitude), population size, and wealth. The usual evolutionary assumption was that the further you get from the equator, the more technology you needed to master to survive the changing seasons. This led to a more cohesive, interdependent society with a low PDI. The opposite was true for societies closer to the equator; they were more independent and required more organization and structure to maintain their society. So, the farther from the equator, the lower the PDI. Is this born out by Table 3? The second variable, population size, says that the greater the population, the higher the PDI (more structure is required). The third variable, wealth, says that the lower the GNP, the higher the PDI. For the last two variables it is an interesting exercise to find reasons for them being dependent or independent variables.

TRANSITION

In this chapter we have looked at a number of correlates of inequalities within cultures. The primary value correlated with high and low power distance is the fear of confronting authority. We have seen that this leads to different types of conflict management and different types of power manifestations. There are some dependencies on social, organizational, and personal contexts and on education, wealth, population, and location of the culture. The general cultural norms given in Table 4 should help you understand intercultural communication, remembering that any index of cultural differences is a good stereotype to begin with but not upon which to fashion policy.

This subsystem of cultural values can help us surmise the cultural orientation of a culture. High PDI cultures are more closed-minded and universalistic. Since higher education levels reduce the PDI, we would assume that they are also associative. Thus, low PDI cultures would be the opposite: more open-minded, particularistic, and abstractive. Do these assumptions agree with what you know about the countries in Table 3? In any negotiation situation, a government's PDI may be a source of noise in the HCS being developed. In the following chapter we will look at the cultural differences and similarities on the uncertainty-avoidance dimension.

INDEPENDENT STUDY

In this chapter you have been given a number of variables upon which cultures may differ.

1. Find an informant from a high- and a low-PDI country and discuss with them the characteristics given in Table 4. How closely do they fit with the perception of their cultures? Write a report.

2. Consider the three types of power and determine which types of governments would be representative of each. What types of conflict management might each one use, and how well could they communicate with each other? Report to the class.

3. Find two or more informants (at least one male and one female) from a culture and determine what its PDI is. A number of possible questions for this inquiry are given below, but you can probably think of others. Write a report.

TENTATIVE QUESTIONS

I. What is the hierarchy of power in society, family, politics, business, etc.?
  A. Are the levels of power generally accepted in families, society, organizations, etc.?
  B. Does power in one area carry over to another?
  C. Distribution of wealth/power (is it equal, are they equal)?
  D. Is it necessary to have inequality? What does this say about a large middle class?
II. How is power perceived—differently for different sexes, classes, organizations, etc.?
  A. What are the attributes of power—money, prestige, status, authority, etc.?
  B. What is the role of education in the power hierarchy?
  C. Is it important to "save face"? How is this done?
III. Can two people feel equal but be on different power levels?
  A. Can relationships cross power boundaries—classes, boss/employee, races, etc.? (marriages, friendships, etc.)
  B. Is the culture generally one of conformity or independence, and is this linked to their power structure?
  C. Is vertical movement easy, encouraged, accepted, etc.?
IV. Does the power structure lead to a "closed system"?
  A. The role of minorities, all types?
  B. How are power differences enforced, disciplined?
 V. Is power actively sought, built, maintained by individuals, organizations, etc.?
VI. How is the power structure taught to children?
VII. What is the work ethic?

You should not feel that you must limit your questions to these; they are only given as suggestions. What you must find out is how your culture handles inequalities.

CHAPTER NINE
Uncertainty Avoidance

Catholicism is the dominant religion in Costa Rica. While I was studying Spanish there in 1981, I was invited to go on the annual pilgrimage to the Basilica of our Lady of the Angels in the city of Cartago. On the 2nd of August each year, thousands make this pilgrimage as penance or in thanksgiving for a blessing attributed to *La Negrita*, the affection name for the Virgin Mary. From the nation's capital, San José, this is a 15-mile trip that is made on foot, with the last mile, half mile, block, or yards made on your knees, depending on your devoutness, offense, or blessing. Many people make much longer trips. When I told them I was not Catholic, they said that didn't matter; it was the experience that counted.

We made the pilgrimage, leaving San José early enough Saturday evening so we would arrive sometime very early Sunday morning. As we walked we found that many families had set up makeshift food stalls to feed the hungry pilgrims. There was an air of conviviality among the thousands—from small children to the very old—who wound their way to the Basilica. Having reached the shrine, where there was a continuous Mass, we paid our respects, toured the Basilica, and slept for a few hours on the grounds outside. Of the people there, perhaps 10 percent had an air of devotion; for the rest it was something to do and a time to enjoy.

As the sun began to show itself, the real "penance" began—trying to find a ride back to San José. Thousands waited for the buses; others had asked a friend or someone in the family to come and pick them up. We finally found a friend of a friend who had extra room in his car and were home by 10 o'clock, the time at which the real religious celebration began in Cartago. Those who felt obligated to go on the pilgrimage also felt they had fulfilled their *promesa* (vow) and would incur some blessing from it.

Though most Costa Ricans are Catholics, religion is not something to which they are really committed. One friend said that the church was only there for your baptismal, your wedding, and your funeral. Nevertheless, true to the Latin custom of going through a friend to obtain a job, cut through bureaucratic red tape, or get a favor, they have their own special saints to whom they pray (rather than to God) for day-to-day favors. *La Negrita* is the most special, and so there is a day each year to honor her. There is also an average of one saint's day each month for which the whole country has a holiday. And Costa Ricans take their holidays seriously—from Wednesday through Sunday of Easter Week you will scarcely find one person on the streets of the capital. Although they do not let religion "get in their way," neither do they want to anger the saints.

In this chapter we will look at the systems of beliefs contained in the dimension called uncertainty avoidance. We know that at best, life is uncertain and that reducing this uncertainty is a major facet of our lives. Somehow we have to have a structure in our lives that helps to alleviate this uncertainty. It may be religion, family, society, our job, or any number of other constructs. In each case we need to know where the control is. To be mature is to have developed schemas to handle the uncertainties in our life. Most schemas for handling uncertainties are culturally determined.

DEFINING UNCERTAINTY AVOIDANCE

In the preceding chapter we dealt with some of the problems of equality. In this chapter we will deal with some of the problems of its counterpart, freedom. Maximum personal freedom signifies minimum external control. Without external controls, the person must choose his or her every act. This is extremely difficult, for there is no way of predicting the outcome, or even setting up expectations, for human events. External controls can be subtle or written on tablets of stone. In either case they give us some type of direction in our life. Frankl believed that lack of external controls was a primary factor in the problems of U.S. society. He called it an existential vacuum and, using an evolution model, indicated that we had lost even our animal instincts (see quote on page 44.)

This loss of instinct coupled with that of tradition has been replaced with a system of law and order. The organization of our culture has become much more systemic with towns, municipalities, boroughs, cities, etc. all interdependent on each other and on society as a whole. Since we are all equal under the law, there has to be a seat of government to enforce these laws. Our lawyers are attempting to define every behavior from a legal perspective so that each offense has its just punishment. The fact that many offenses today did not exist in days gone by (youthful offenders were punished by their parents or given a good beating and sent home) is evidence that we are getting away from human relationships as a way of avoiding uncertainty and placing our trust in the organization of society with all of its legal implications. This dehumanization helps to transfer our locus of evaluation from within ourselves to society as a whole. Hardly anyone wants to be different as our mass media tell us what to wear, how to look, what to eat, and who to be. They have become our security blanket.

Our desire for security as an individual is no less than that for an organization or a culture. It is a basic need of human existence (Maslow). To bring structure into one's life is to bring a sense of security, i.e., to avoid some of the uncertainties. We know what to do, how to do it, and when to do it, or we know someone or something that will tell us. As Frankl says, tradition has been a primary source of security. It has been handed down to us through our families, our schools, and our religious institutions. But as we become more and more liberated from our traditions, we find many more choices are available to us and thus, many more decisions to make. The avoidance of uncertainty is only accomplished through structures that give us a sense of knowing what to expect. Isn't it paradoxical that we want to have the freedom to deviate form the norm, but we want others to behave as the norm (tradition) predicts? Freedom brings ambiguity.

Hofstede says that

> Extreme uncertainty creates intolerable anxiety, and human society has developed ways to cope with the inherent uncertainty of our living on the brink of an uncertain future. These ways belong to the domains of technology, law, and religion; I use the terms in a broad sense. Technology includes all human artifacts; law, all formal and informal rules that guide social behavior; religion, all revealed knowledge of the unknown. Technology has helped us to defend ourselves against uncertainties caused by nature; law, to defend against uncertainties in the behavior of others; religion, to accept the uncertainties we cannot defend ourselves against. The knowledge of a life after death is the ultimate certainty of the believer which allows him to face uncertainties in this life. The borderline between "defending against uncertainties" and "accepting them" is fluid; many of our defenses aiming at creating certainty are not really doing so in an objective sense, but they allow us to sleep in peace (p. 111).

As we shall see, different cultures solve their uncertainty problems in different ways. Tradition is still a strong source of values for many cultures and plays a role in the behavioral norms of all cultures—either in compliance or rebellion. It is seen in all three domains of uncertainty avoidance: Technology (as defined above) has given rise to all of industry, which not only gives us a stable means of maintaining our livelihood but also a means of combating the unknown consequences of "progress." U.S. culture has come to look to it to solve its deepest anxieties, namely, war, disease, famine. Law (the rules we live by) is firmly nested in tradition. New cases are argued from precedents, while old cases are revisited to change precedents. We look to rules to define the roles we will play in life and turn to laws to change traditional roles that are no longer acceptable. Of the three domains, religion may be the most rooted in tradition. Its primary strengths are its longevity, its traditional way of conducting its business (ritual), and its linkage to the supreme being. These three facets of religion comfort the person who realizes that death is the consequence of life and poses the ultimate uncertainty.

Uncertainty avoidance, then, is the normative behavior of a culture for the purpose of alleviating fears of the unknown and reducing anxiety in all areas of one's life. It takes form in three distinct domains: technology, law, and religion. Hofstede says that "On the cultural level, tendencies toward rigidity and dogmatism, intolerance of different opinions, traditionalism, superstition, racism, and ethnocentricism all relate to a norm" (p. 112) for uncertainty avoidance. Humans seek to control their environment either through actual physical control, as in power distance, or through the control of their own perceptions and cognitions in uncertainty avoidance.

Sources of Anxiety

What are the commonalities in human existence that will let us compare the way cultures address the problems of human uncertainty? As we have shown in past chapters, culture and the individual's development within it are both a function of communication. In every culture the human being must develop a cybernetic, or self-concept (see Chapter 2). The person's cybernetic is a dynamic, mediating subsystem of the human system (Markus & Wurf, 1987). The five subsystems of this self-concept are commonalities that cut across all cultures, though they may have different definitions and importance. If we consider their development as the development of schemas (McCall, 1987) for the mediating function of the subsystem, and the stress applied by different cultures to "fit in," we can find some of the sources of anxiety that will cut across cultures.

Bodily Self takes on notably different forms as we move from one culture to another. We are all familiar with examples from cultures who used to bind various parts of the body so they would take on a particular shape, and the humiliation of U.S. fathered Vietnamese children left behind when the United States pulled out. In the former case a child whose figure did not conform to the cultural norm brought shame upon itself and its family. In the latter the child was faced with a life without respect in its home culture. What types of anxiety do you think these people face?

One's physical appearance must meet the norms of its society to be fully integrated into that society. Besides this, one's beauty is relative to the culture which produced it. In Costa Rica, for example, a woman is *hermosa* (beautiful) only if she meets the criteria of the culture (having large hips and buttocks). Others may be *linda* or *bonita*, both lesser forms of praise for the female figure. The slender, curvaceous U.S. woman going to Costa Rica may be *linda* or *bonita* but never *hermosa*. The eyes of the beholder are conditioned by the culture in which they developed!

Self-Identity may be less obvious than bodily self until we find ourselves in another environment. We may seldom think of who we are until we find that people aren't responding to us the way we are used to. You are a child at home, a student at school, an employee at work, and a lover to your boyfriend or girlfriend. How would you react if your boss treated you like a lover and your boyfriend or girlfriend treated you like a child? We seldom realize how important the situation is to our identity. No one in any culture has a single identity, and multiple identities bring on all kinds of anxieties. If you are highly respected at school but are not shown the same respect at home, it may be difficult to attribute this to the differences in the role you have in each of these situations.

Each role we take has rules associated with it that define it within our specific culture. Seldom are all the rules the same from one culture to another, though at first glance they may seem to be. If you saw students on the campus of the University of Costa Rica, they would look pretty much like students on any campus in the United States. They dress as they please, carry books, study, and enjoy themselves. Although the general rules for the role of a student are about the same as in the United States, there are some major differences. All Costa Rican students live at home, or with a family if they are from another city; there is almost no campus social life. The major difference, however, is that the students study and write papers together; if one has a problem and can't get an assignment done, someone else will do it for him or her with no feelings of unethicalness. It is not unethical; it's the way it is done. I suspect it is done in the United States, too, but not without the attendant feeling of having cheated.

Self-Extension is risk taking to see what possible roles we may take. In risk taking there is always a high degree of anxiety; we are never quite sure what the outcome will be. The form that risk takes from one culture to another varies, just as it does from one social setting to another in the same culture. There may be no risk at all, felt or real, for a person to walk home late at night in a small town but a great deal in a large city. We may have some apprehension about going on for graduate studies in our own culture, but wouldn't even think of doing so in another culture where we had to learn another language as well. Think of those students in your university or college from other cultures and try to identify with the risk they are taking and the anxiety they may have.

Being a foreigner alone in another culture is a risk to your identity. Trying to find out if this extension of yourself is working is anxiety producing. Numerous uncertainties are connected with it. When I was stopped at an immigration checkpoint in Costa Rica just south of the Nicaraguan boarder, I was alone in my VW bug, just functional in Spanish, and had a research meeting to attend the next day. I had considerable anxiety. It increased when the young officer took my passport away from me, saying I had overstayed my visa. He gave me a receipt for my passport, however, and I continued on my way. I drove all over Costa Rica for the next three weeks without it, with little or no anxiety. Costa Ricans are extremely friendly people, and the Civil Guard is controlled by the people, not the other way around. You feel uncertain and anxious only when you don't know what to expect.

Self-Esteem is that subsystem of our cybernetic that is the measure of our worth, as we see it. Does it ever give us cause for anxiety? As we develop our self-concept, beginning in the formative years of our youth, our self-esteem may be the major facilitator of our development—negative or positive. If our culture is highly competitive and we are not, our self-esteem may be lowered. We will be urged by salient, significant others to extend ourselves, take a risk, don't be afraid to fail, etc. However, if we do so and fail, it is even more difficult for that other person to keep our failure from depressing our self-esteem.

Self-esteem is built on our successes and failures in the development of the first three subsystems. We need to feel good about our body, the roles we have perfected, and our ability to extend ourselves into other areas of life. The beautiful, liberated Anglo-American woman who extends herself by risking an extended stay in Costa Rica may find her self-esteem lowered when she is not praised for her beauty nor for the roles she takes in her new culture because neither her beauty nor her roles are praiseworthy in that culture. Our self-esteem subsystem is the major source of anxiety in our cybernetic, as it has the task of evaluating our behaviors in the other four subsystems.

Self-Image is the measurement of our behaviors in the other four subsystems against our ideal self. That means we must have some idea of where we should be at this stage in our life. As you can imagine, this ideal has strong cultural overtones. What are the possibilities, given who you are and the rules of your culture? Of course, there are always exceptions, but are you satisfied with your present state, or does your self-image tell you that you must try harder or take a different path? What kinds of anxiety does this subsystem generate? Did you really think you would be elected class president? Can you put up with the ambiguity of not knowing whether you will make it, or do you only try the sure thing? What kind of future does your culture teach you to expect?

Sometimes when we are outside our own culture we can do things that are not possible back home. A Japanese housewife with her husband in the United States was studying English and mathematics while he was getting his Ph.D. When asked how she would use this knowledge back in Japan, she said that she would probably never be able to use it because her culture and her husband did not allow housewives to work outside the home. She just felt that for her own self-image she had to learn as much as possible, given this opportunity. She said that some of her friends in the same position were just sitting at home. One's personal constructs affect his or her self-image perhaps as much as the culture does.

We develop our self-concept with its five subsystems as we interact with those around us. It is a continuous process from birth to death. Rogers (1971) tells us that as we mature, our locus of evaluation (where we look for confirmation when making our decisions) moves from internal to external to internal. That is, as a child we are our locus of evaluation, completely egocentric. One of the most difficult things our parents have to do is to get us to consider someone else's feelings or priorities when deciding to do or not to do something. When this is accomplished there is the possibility that our locus of control will take up permanent residence in our family, our peer group, or society in general, and we will never be our own person. As a person matures he or she begins to realize that one's relationships with others must be taken into consideration, but we must also consider our own priorities and feelings. Heath (1965) calls this dimension of maturity allocentrism—integrating the external with the internal considerations.

Perhaps you can see where uncertainty and anxiety might enter the process of maturation. Completely egocentric persons have little concern with ambiguity. Since they are the only consideration in their decision-making process, nothing else matters. But as we begin to consider others, we are never sure what their feelings and priorities are, and this ambiguity raises our anxiety level. Most of the information used in the process of integrating the external with the internal forces is not communicated to us but is collected through observation alone (see Chapter 1). This means that we interpret it without the aid of the other's dialogue. Thus, it takes on the meaning shaped by the norms of our culture and our own particular attitudinal frame of reference. How many times have you done something, thinking that it was what the other person or persons wanted, only to find out that you had misread the signals you had gathered? The perceptual skills we learn during this phase of maturation will be called upon throughout our lifetime.

Communication and Uncertainty

"Communication and uncertainty are inextricably intertwined" (Berger, 1987, p. 42). Any new situation brings this home quickly: your first visit with a friend's family, your first day at the university, or the first time you visited another culture are all examples where uncertainty was obvious, the need to communicate was felt, and your anxiety level was probably heightened. In all new situations the most apparent uncertainty is what to say. Most of us have developed schemas to deal with this situation—we talk about the weather! When we meet someone with whom we have to communicate or we want to communicate, we have our stereotypes to fall back on. This is a good use of stereotypes (they reduce some of the felt uncertainty) as long as we are consciously modifying them as we develop our understanding of this person. Reducing uncertainty through communication fits most easily into the need for rules and/or laws to give structure to our existence.

From a systems perspective, uncertainty reduction is equivalent to entropy reduction. When two people communicate they form a human communication system, and this reduces entropy (Chapter 1). The integration of the information received by the two people from each other restructures the cognitive structures of each. This restructuring has the added factor of a system's focus involving two people, thus developing an organization that has the potential for greater amounts of entropy reduction. If we extend this situation to ambassadors for two countries or corporations, one can see the potential for greater benefits than just uncertainty reduction between two persons.

Berger and Bradac (1982) propose two types of uncertainty: cognitive and behavioral. Cognitive uncertainty refers to our uncertainty about the beliefs, values, tacit knowledge, and schemas used by another person in his or her psychological creation of the immediate reality. Behavioral uncertainty refers to our inability to predict how another person will translate his or her understanding of the situation into overt behavior. Cognitive has to do with the way you perceive the situation, behavioral with how you respond to it.

For example, I was once in Panamá speaking with a matronly shopkeeper in Spanish. She paused in the conversation to ask if I were from a Nordic country. I said no, I was from the United States; she immediately switched to English, told me she was Jewish and had lived in Brooklyn for several years. Lots of uncertainty reduction; suppose I had been offended by her first guess of my citizenship? How might I have reacted? Could I have predicted her reaction to my disclosure? How did each of us integrate this information into our cognitive structures? I might add that she became a remarkably fruitful resource for the research project I was working on in Panamá.

For initial encounters, we all have rituals with which we cope with the uncertainty of the moment. In the above example I was talking to her about the merchandise she carried in her shop. As that was my sole purpose, she had been helpful in reducing my uncertainty about that particular subject before the above-mentioned incident occurred. It should be clear, then, that the purpose of the encounter affects the strategy used to initiate contact. Of course, there is also some uncertainty in whether the participants see the purpose of the interaction in the same way.

The rituals we use to initiate communication differ according to the level of the system of which we are a member (Berger and Bradac). If we are at the macroscopic cultural level, we need only be aware of cultural norms. This is also true when communicating across cultures. If you know the norms of the other culture, you can get past the initial interaction (do you bow, shake hands, or what?). At the next level, the sociological, you need to know the norms of specific groups and social roles within a culture (leadership, political, sales). Knowing the social norms, you can interact on a daily basis with little fear of ambiguous situations. On the psychological, or personal, level you must know the norms of the individual with whom you communicate. Knowing his or her normal behavior allows you to initiate the communication process and pursue it as deeply as the system allows.

Kelly says that we anticipate events and, as good scientists, we measure our perceptions of the event against our anticipation, adjusting our constructs to bring our future anticipations into closer agreement with our perceptions. Our waking hours are filled with anticipations of the events we are about to experience. Our expectations are based on our tacit knowledge of the system in which we are working at the moment. If someone in that system, whether it is cultural, sociological, or psychological, deviates from our expectation, we want to know why. If they do not deviate from our expectation, then we do not have to adjust the stereotype we carry for that person. Our tolerance for deviation determines whether we modify our stereotype of that person and thus reduce uncertainty. As we get to know a person, the more our image of that person agrees with our perceptions. Our tolerance for deviation is affected by our interest in, or reason for, communicating with the person.

It follows that in order to reduce uncertainty we must know more and more about the person with whom we are communicating. If we substitute a culture for the person in the above sentence, the truism remains. Berger and Bradac suggest three ways of gathering this information: passive, active, and interactive. Passive is merely observing the person or culture and abstracting "meaningful" behaviors from these observations—an etic activity. Of course, the "meaningfulness" of the abstraction is controlled by our own cognitive constructs and, therefore, may have little or no congruence with that of the observed.

Active gathering of information involves asking questions of others about themselves or the culture—an etic/emic activity. This gives us the benefit of meaningful constructions from another's point of view; when modified by our own cognitions, they may give a more accurate rendition of the person or culture. The consultant's level of knowledge will also bear on the final product.

Interactive gathering of information involves talking with the person or with representatives of the culture—an emic activity. When we experience the person or the culture, we have first hand knowledge and, depending upon our communication competence, we can be more or less assured that we know what we want to know about the person or the culture. In one sense this will reduce uncertainty, but in another sense it may increase it. We may be led into deeper levels of knowledge that will raise higher levels of uncertainty.

At each level of information gathering we attribute meaning to behaviors according to our likes and dislikes, i.e., our value systems. It is only at the interaction level that we can pursue a collaborative effort to true under-standing of a person or a culture. This may mean adjusting many of our preconceived notions about them. One means of increasing our ability to abstract meaningful information is to differentiate between the action, the person, and the situation or circumstances in which the action takes place. As one goes from passive to active to interactive, the differentiation process becomes more difficult as the level of analysis becomes more subjective.

The knowledge we create about a person or a culture while going through the above processes allows us to reduce the uncertainty we have about that person or culture. Berger and Bradac further tell us that this knowledge can be divided into three levels: descriptive, predictive, and ex-planatory. At the descriptive level we are only able to identify the person or culture. This level involves many of the nonverbal codes and is basically concerned with the physical dimension. At the predictive level we are con-cerned with the behaviors of the person or culture. These we must also be able to describe (recognize), but we have sufficient information to allow us to predict with some certainty what behaviors will take place in a given situation. On the explanatory level we attempt to construct the personal or cultural constructs of the observed and attribute the behaviors to psychological char-acteristics of the person or culture. As you can see, the three levels of informa-tion gathering coincide quite nicely with the three levels of knowledge.

It is obvious that communication is a means of reducing uncertainty on the dimension of rules/laws as they concern individuals and their interactions.

It is not so clear what role communication takes in reducing the uncertainty found in one's interaction with the environment and the unknown. However, two points should be made concerning the latter two dimensions. The first is that the uncertainty we have concerning these two facets of life will affect our communicative behavior, as they are two of our basic value systems. The second is that the only way we can get to know our own beliefs on these two dimensions is through the process of communication. This latter communication usually takes place in our families, schools, and religious institutions.

High and Low Uncertainty Avoidance

One of the items Hofstede used to define his Uncertainty Avoidance Index (UAI) had to do with obeying the rules of a company even if the employee would perform better for the company if he or she did not obey the rules. This type of question can be generalize to the cultural level by associating the rules with the laws of the land or cultural norms—a question of particularism vs universalism. Another question had to do with one's expectation of stable employment with his or her present company. This, too, can be generalized to the cultural level by associating one's stability with permanency of family dwelling and desire for traditional standards, behaviors, and morals. The third question specifically asked about the feeling of stress on the job, but it can easily be generalized to the cultural level by associating this with stress in general. A more objective measure might be the percentage of adults suffering from high blood pressure.

A high UAI score indicates that one needs structure in his or her life to help avoid the ambiguities of life: behaviors should be predictable; people should obey the rules; a more conservative, fundamental attitude should prevail. Thus, there is adherence to rules, long-term commitment, and high anxiety. A low UAI score indicates a culture that can tolerate ambiguity at all three levels: individuals make their own decisions on when rules should or should not be followed; behaviors are less predictable; and a more liberal atmosphere prevails in which ambiguity is tolerated. Thus, rules are not considered necessary, commitments are less binding, and there is less anxiety. In which category do you find yourself?

CULTURAL CHARACTERISTICS

The UAI gives us a measure of a culture's ability to tolerate ambiguity in its day-to-day interaction (1) with the environment, for the purpose of maintaining life; (2) with the social rules, norms, and institutions, for the purpose of maintaining workable relationships among its members; and (3) with the religious, philosophical, and scientific institutions, for the purpose of understanding the unknown. High scores mean low tolerance of ambiguity and high need for structure. Looking back at Table 3, you will see that Greece and

Portugal have the highest UAI scores and Denmark and Singapore have the lowest. The U.S. is in the lower 25 percent.

Some of the findings from Hofstede indicate that in high-UAI countries, company employees have less ambition for promotion, prefer larger companies, tend to avoid competition, prefer group decision-making, dislike foreign managers, and resist change. All of these indicate a need for certainty and intolerance for ambiguity. Employees in low-UAI countries tend to show the opposite needs. That these findings are generalizable is shown by the high correlations of the UAI scores with other measures of cultural anxiety, need achievement, and attitudes and values. In general, all of these scores mean that low-UAI cultures are more willing to take risks than high-UAI cultures.

Besides the characteristics of low- and high-UAI cultures given in Table 5, other generalizations can be made. High-UAI cultures tend to have:

Table 5:   The Uncertainty Avoidance Societal Norm (Hofstede, p. 140)

LOW UAI	HIGH UAI
1. The uncertainty inherent in life is more easily accepted; each day is taken as it comes.	The uncertainty inherent in life is felt as a continuous threat that must be fought.
2. Ease	Lower stress.
3. Time is free.	Time is money.
4. Hard work is not a virtue per se.	Inner urge to work hard.
5. Weaker superegos.	Strong superegos.
6. Aggressive behavior is frowned upon.	Aggressive behavior of self and others is accepted.
7. Less showing of emotions.	More showing of emotions.
8. Conflict and competition can be contained on the level of fair play and used constructively.	Conflict and competition can unleash aggression and should therefore be avoided.
9. More acceptance of dissent.	Strong need for consensus.
10. Deviance is not felt as threatening; greater tolerance.	Deviant persons and ideas are dangerous; intolerance.
11. Less nationalism.	Nationalism.
12. More positive toward younger people.	Younger people are suspect.
13. Less conservatism.	Conservatism, law, and order.
14. More willingness to take risks in life.	Concern with security in life.
15. Achievement determined in terms of recognition.	Achievement defined in terms of security.
16. Relativism, empiricism.	Search for ultimate, absolute truths and values.
17. There should be as few rules as possible.	Need for written rules and regulations.
18. If rules cannot be kept, we should change them.	If rules cannot be kept, we are sinners and should repent.
19. Belief in generalists and common sense.	Belief in experts and their knowledge.
20. The authorities are there to serve the citizens.	Ordinary citizens are incompetent versus the authorities.

1. more legislated rules and laws
2. a higher need for identification cards for its citizens
3. more "experts" in each occupation—stricter line between lay workers and experts
4. more formalized (structured) religions
5. more dogmatism in other ideologies, and, perhaps
6. fewer games of chance. The idea of risk is unacceptable.

TRANSITION

As we look back on the evolution of culture, we see that uncertainty was probably a major force in the organization of families, societies, and cultures. Religion, on both individual and cultural levels, appears to be the primary mediator of uncertainty. As cultures became abstract and scientific, laws and technology arose to take over this task. Perhaps the major question in uncertainty avoidance is, "To what do you (or your culture) turn when facing a major crisis (the greenhouse effect, corruption in politics or business)? Do you pray, call in a scientist, or pass another law?"

We have seen that communication plays a major role in reducing uncertainty. In intercultural communication the probability of reducing uncertainty is enhanced if we know the cultural orientation of the person with whom we are communicating. In terms of cultural orientation, high UAIs are more structured and resistant to change. This would suggest that they are on the closed-minded, universalistic end of these two continua. As for the associative/abstractive continuum, it is difficult to use the UAI for placement, although there is some indication that high UAIs would be more associative if the abstractive culture is more open and liberal (as it usually is). Rituals become a prominent way of avoiding uncertainty, and these are linked more with associative cultures than with abstractive ones.

As we grow up we develop our personal cybernetic (self-concept). Understanding the role of each of the five subsystems will help give stability to life. For intercultural communication we must know if the schemas we have created in the development of our self-concept are similar to those developed by our counterparts in the other culture. To reduce the uncertainty between us and others, we must know as much of their tacit knowledge as we can. The only way to do this is to communicate and negotiate a common ground of understanding. In the next chapter we will analyze the individualism component of Hofstede's four universal belief systems.

INDEPENDENT STUDY

We have seen that uncertainty reduction is achieved through communication. When working on the uncertainty avoidance dimension there are three major areas of uncertainty that we need to reduce across cultures:

stability in human existence, structure in human relationships, and approaches to the unknown.

1. Find an informant from a high- and a low-UAI country and discuss with him or her the characteristics given in Table 5. How closely does the person fit with the perception he or she has of his or her culture? Write a report.

2. With an informant from a high- and a low-UAI country, discuss the development of his or her cybernetic. How is it affected by the various sources of uncertainty? Report to class.

3. Find two or more informants (at least one male and one female) from a culture and determine what its UAI is. A number of possible questions for this inquiry are given below, but you can probably think of others. Write a report.

TENTATIVE QUESTIONS

I. What are the primary attributes of the five components of their self-concept?

II. What are their initial encounter rituals, and how do they reduce uncertainty?

III. What factors in the culture seem to breed stress?

   A. Is there much job movement, or do people stay with the same company for life?

   B. Does the culture give the appearance of hyperactivity or is it laid back?

   C. How do they feel about competition in sports, business, politics, etc.?

   D. How does the culture deal with ambiguity?

IV. Is there much risk taking? How does this behavior fit into the need for security?

   A. How is success measured—recognition, security, etc.?

   B. Are there opportunities for change?

V. Is it a law-and-order culture with clear-cut rules of behavior? What does this do to individualism?

   A. Does the culture have a tolerance for deviance, protest?

   B. What is the role of the elderly in this culture?

   C. How do they feel about the individual's ability to control her or his own life?

VI. What is the basic religion, and what does it teach about the future, day-to-day living, etc.?

   A. How do they feel about life after death?

   B. Is discrimination, prejudice, etc., obvious in the culture; does it exist at all?

VII. Is the general mood optimistic or pessimistic?

   A. How does the culture feel about uncertainty—accept it, ignore it, etc.?

   B. At what age do people choose a career, and do these follow family lines?

VIII. How do they feel about the role of technology in solving problems?

You should not feel that you must limit your questions to these. They are only given as suggestions. What you must find out is how your culture handles uncertainty.

CHAPTER TEN
Individualism/Collectivism

There is a bold paradox in the Costa Rican culture: on the one hand they are extremely individualistic, and on the other they are a decidedly group-oriented culture. Let me give you an example. In 1978 I was asked to analyze the communication systems within La Universidad Estatal a Distancia (UNED). When I arrived with two assistants, a small group of young Costa Rican males who had spearheaded positive changes in the high school educational system asked us to meet with them to explain why UNED should even exist. They were opposed to the government spending educational money on this new university.

We met one evening at the home of one of the members on a mountain overlooking San José. These young men were macho, and it was a major accomplishment for them to let one of my assistants, a young North American female, meet with them. However, the meeting went well, and I saw for the first time how well they worked in group negotiations. Around midnight the meeting broke up, and we went outside to ride back into San José. At that point they began discussing who would ride with whom. There were four jeeps and only three of us, so one host would be left without a North American. A half hour later (the three of us were freezing, as it was 50 degrees on the mountain!), all three of us broke off diplomatic relations and got into one jeep. That was what they were waiting for—some definitive action on our part so they could work around our pleasures! Costa Ricans are a very courteous people and will not knowingly offend anyone, particularly a foreigner.

In this chapter we will discuss the third dimension of belief systems, individualism vs. collectivism. It seeks to discover the source of the decision-making process because it is essential to human and societal growth. As cultures developed, different styles of decision making evolved. Some were more individualistic, others were collective. Today, although human beings seem to be naturally gregarious, humanity is culturally defined. Whereas individualism precipitates technology, collectivism is essential to the maintenance of the human race.

DEFINING INDIVIDUALISM/COLLECTIVISM

Hofstede calls this dimension individualism, but it may be easier to visualize it as the locus of the decision-making process on the individualism/collectivism continuum. Our life is a continuous series of decisions; some we make without thinking, others we labor over with or without help. Where is the locus of evaluation—do we make the decision based on our priorities or someone else's? Where is the locus of control—are we free to make our own decisions or is there a source of power outside of us with more control? Are these two loci primarily in the individual or in the group, society, or culture?

This dimension is closely related to uncertainty avoidance and power distance in that it seems to have definite ramifications for each of them. If you look back to Table 3, you will see that being high in individualism means being low in the other two. The United States has the highest individualism index; we are, without doubt, the most individualistic culture on earth. Perhaps, then, we do not need to tell you to what this dimension refers. You are all part of it, are taught how it works every day, and will undoubtedly teach your children the same beliefs and values. But what are the beliefs and values that underlie our strong individualism?

The United States was founded by adventurers and dissidents. Our history has continued to build on these quests for freedom and independence. If things don't suit us where we are, we move on to where we can do as we want. Our independence is seen in the strong isolationist policy followed up through the first half of this century. We neither wanted nor gave help until the last moment. Taking what we wanted from others, we became more feared than respected, for we knew no equal. Only *in* the United States were all men (sic) created equal; with our individualistic lust for freedom and power, however, that is also a falsehood (Rokeach, 1968).

What of the other countries of the Americas? Canada is much like the United States with respect to individualism. Their fourth-place finish may have been tempered by their French heritage. As for the rest of the countries, the only common thread is the role of the adventurers plundering the natives. The Europeans who colonized these countries were mainly from Spain and Portugal and brought with them the collectivism they shared with their homeland. These peoples today are much more affiliative than individualistic. They have great extended families to whom they look when they need to show their honorableness. It is not so much what the individual has done but the family name that counts. The singleness of the ethnic and religious backgrounds of the settlers for the first two or three hundred years reduced the need for one group to dominate, or prove itself to, another, thus reducing the internal individualistic drive for independence and recognition.

When we define individualism it must be juxtaposed with its counterpart, collectivism. Early societies in the United States were mostly collectivist, as they were built around some denomination of the Christian religion. One of the principles set forth in the New Testament was to have "all things in common" (Acts 2:44; 4:32), the truest form of communism! Individualism was looked down upon as disrespectful to God. However, the family proved to be a more basic unit than the church, and neither could claim to be a true collectivist unit. A collectivist unit moved in sync with its leader—what he or she believed and did, the unit believed and did. We can get some idea of this type of organization by looking at the cults of today, especially the tragedy of Jonestown. The Christian religion has always maintained that each individual is a free, moral agent and must make his or her own decisions. Thus, even the religious organizations in the United States had a form of individualism.

For those who moved away from the towns, farming and hunting were the way of life. Society was decentralized, and communication was slow and unreliable. You knew your neighbors and a few other people, but you were pretty much self-sufficient, independent, and isolated. The extended family was the basic building block of the nation. Then, when the industrial revolution came along, all of this changed. Men and women began to move to the centers of manufacturing and commerce. The nuclear family became the basic building block because it could move to the centers of action. You had to know more people, and your livelihood began to depend more and more on what others did, but not in the sense of a commune. The need for information in the shortest possible time and the mechanization of industry have resulted in a new day, the present, where information is the most important commodity we have, and its transport and management is the largest growth industry in the world (Dizard, 1982). Both information processing and industrial mechanization are being taken over by the electronic computer, and the individual has become the basic building block in our society.

Even in the tradition-driven segment of our population, the farmers, we have had a real sense of individualism, namely, their independence and self-sufficiency. When the farms were all small, the farmers would help each other during the harvest, but as technology grew, so did the size of the farms, and the collective spirit disappeared. Only in subcultures such as the Amish do we see the collective mind at work in the United States today. Here tradition and religion are the primary guiding lights. In tradition-directed societies "The parents train the child to succeed *them*, rather than 'succeed' by rising in the social system" (Riesman, p. 39; emphasis in the original). In the United States today few children follow their parents into occupations; the technological complexity of most occupations demands more training or education than the family can supply. This fact sharpens the focus on individualism.

We have mentioned before the assumption that we carry mental programs, scripts, schemas, and an attitudinal frame of reference which we use in our decision-making processes and by which we are known to our associates. This is true whether we are in a collectivist culture or an individualistic one. Tyler (1978) says, "Much of the programming is the same for all or most of the human race; much is imposed by the structure of particular cultures and subcultures. But in addition there are programs unique to individuals, and these are fundamental to psychological individuality" (p. 107). Thus, an individualistically oriented person may emerge from a collectivistic culture and vice versa. However, it would appear that it is easier to go from collectivism to individualism than the inverse.

Lidz (1976) reinforces the importance of the culture in the development of the individual.

> A culture, then, has become an essential part of the human endowment. To examine the influence of the culture upon personality development is not to continue an old conflict concerning the importance of cultural versus biological factors in personality formation, but simply to recognize that the biological nature of the human organism is such that it depends upon the assimilation of cultural instrumentalities to make possible survival and development into a person. The culture in which the child is raised serves as a mold to shape the rough outlines of the personality, delimit drives, and provide organization to the manifold ways of adapting to the environment permitted humans by their physical endowment. Although the repressive and limiting influences of society have been bemoaned, delimitation is essential to the realization of potential. A person cannot develop into a harmonious entity without it. Indeed, without the skills and customs provided by society, a child cannot become anyone at all (pp. 13–14).

In individualistic cultures, even the focus on the person, as opposed to the individual (Borden and Stone, 1976), stresses the importance of individualism. Psychologists ushering in the "me" generation did so in this manner. Bugental (1976) says,

> What is plain is that *I* am the center of my own life. . . . If I am fully to experience my life, I must experience it at its center—that is, I need to feel my 'I-ness.' That's what inner awareness is about. It's the experiencing of I-ness. . . I experience my I-ness when I know that I want something clearly and that I want it because *I* want it, not because somebody or something told me I should want it or that most people want it or that four out of five medical authorities recommend it. My consciousness of wanting it is immediate, beyond question, and unreasoned (pp. 4–5; emphasis in the original).

Bugental's "inner awareness"—the locus of evaluation resting solely within the individual—can lead to allocentrism in the mature person, but it more often leads to the egocentrism of the immature. All authors agree that individualism is inner-directed. As we have mentioned, our self-concept is developed around cultural norms and is the self-regulating (cybernetic) mechanism of the individual. When it is focused inward, it leads to egocentrism; when it is other-directed, it can have two different foci. One is the other-directedness of the caring person, which, when balanced by a natural internal locus of evaluation, leads to maturity. The other is the other-directedness of the person whose *locus of control* becomes the immediate situation, society, and culture; "the 'other-directed' American: a new kind of collectivist who takes his bearings from his peer group and from the mass media" (Hofstede, 1984, p. 150). This seems to be a contradiction in categories: a "me-ness" culture with an external locus of control. May (1969) refers to this as our "schizoid world."

Locus of Control

Locus of evaluation and locus of control, though closely related, are not the same construct. Locus of evaluation refers to the focus or center of the evaluation—the individual or someone else or the group or society, or the culture within which the individual functions. Is the considered action good for me (internal locus of evaluation) or for others (external locus of evaluation)? When we have made this distinction, there may or may not be a conflict between the two foci of evaluation. If not, we will not have to decide which party will prevail, but if there is a conflict (it is good for me, but bad for society), then we have the dilemma of choosing whose good shall prevail.

Some would call the result of our decision in the latter case our locus of control, because our decision was controlled by our desires to serve self or to serve others. This is not the meaning of locus of control, however, because in this case you had control over your decision-making process (you were able to discern the value of the action for each party and made your choice), so you were being governed by an internal locus of control. If you had been governed by an external locus of control, you would have felt that you had no control over the decision-making process and done what habit, tradition, norms, or others dictated you should do. Several characteristics go along with locus of control. When persons have an internal locus of control, they feel more or less in control of their own destiny (as in the poem *Invictus*). If they have an external locus of control, they are pushed and pulled by the powers that be with little or no say in what direction they should go (as with Ahab in *Moby Dick*).

Are you the "master of your fate" or are you merely "fate's lieutenant"? How do you see the world? Of course, these are the two extremes on the internal-external continuum, and most of us are somewhere toward the middle. Our position on this continuum may also vary depending on the domain of the action, e.g., we may feel that we are in control of our diet but have not control over our chances of getting cancer. The situation might also have some effect on one's locus of control orientation. Harari, Jones, and Sek (1988) compared the internal-external locus of control orientation of Polish and U.S. college students and found that the U.S. students revealed significantly more internal locus of control and the Polish students disclosed significantly more external locus of control. Although the Poles are traditionally individualistic, it was assumed that the present political climate might have affected their locus of control orientation.

An external locus of control is closely related to fatalism—feeling that you are in the hands of an all-powerful god, government, or situation. Lefcourt illustrates this with a story told by Manual Sanchez in Lewis (1961, p. 171).

> To me, one's destiny is controlled by a mysterious hand that moves all things. Only for the select, do things turn out as planned; to those of us who are born to be tamale eaters, heaven sends only tamales. We plan and plan and some little thing happens to wash it all away. Like once, I decided to try to save and I said to Paula, "Old girl, put away this money so that some day we'll have a little pile." When we had ninety pesos laid away, pum! my father got sick and I had to give

all to him for doctors and medicines. It was the only time I had helped him and the only time I had tried to save! I said to Paula, "There you are! Why should we save if someone gets sick and we have to spend it all!" Sometimes I even think that saving brings on illness! That's why I firmly believe that some of us are born to be poor and remain that way no matter how hard we struggle and pull this way and that. God gives us just enough to go on vegetating, no?

The other side of the coin is seen in Ayn Rand's *The Fountainhead.*

Lefcourt (1976) concludes,

> In general, it may be concluded that perceived control is positively associated with access to opportunity. Those who are able, through position and group member- ship, to attain more readily the valued outcomes that allow a person to feel personal satisfaction are more likely to hold internal control expectancies. Blacks, Spanish-Americans, Indians, and other minority groups who do not enjoy as much access to opportunity as do the predominant Caucasian groups in North American society are found to hold fatalistic, external control beliefs (p. 25).

If we took this from the subcultural to the cultural level, we would expect so-called Third World cultures to hold more external locus of control beliefs, i.e., be more on the collectivistic end of the individualism-collectivism con- tinuum. (Table 3 supports this prediction.)

Internal locus of control is seen as a defense against wholesale submis- sion to authority. "The degree to which man is capable of questioning his own assumptions, is in the habit of deliberating over his options, and is attentive to information relevant to his decision-making, to that degree will he be less assailable by forces directed against his integrity" (Lefcourt, p. 51). Research results show that "internals were not as easily duped for as long a period as were externals due to a greater readiness to recognize and cognitively come to terms with change" (p. 63). It was also found that those who feel they are at the mercy of an external force show little initiative toward achieving long-term goals, i.e., delayed gratification. It would appear, then, that abstractive, univer- salistic, open-minded cultures are the more progress oriented. Lefcourt gives a list of adjectives describing internals: "clever, efficient, egotistical, enthusias- tic, independent, self-confident, ambitious, assertive, boastful, conceited, hard headed, industrious, ingenious, insightful, organized, reasonable, and stub- born" (p. 134). No such list exists for externals.

Lifestyles

Since World War II we have witnessed an explosion of alternative lifestyles in the United States and perhaps in the world (Lande, 1976). Most of these have been pushed out of sight by society in general, but all of them have had an effect on that society. Mitchell (1984) has found that in the United States nine definable lifestyles are related to our value systems. These can be categorized into four groups: need-driven, outer-directed, inner-directed, and combined outer- and inner-directed.

Need-driven: This group is composed of the poverty class. They tend to be "despairing, depressed, withdrawn, mistrustful, rebellious about their situation, left out of things, and conservative" (p. 5).

Outer-directed: This group takes in the middle class and are usually "traditional, conforming, conservative, moral, nonexperimental, family-oriented, hard working, successful, self-reliant, and patriotic" (p. 5).

Inner-directed: This group includes those who are both "contrite and aggressive, demure and exhibitionistic, self-effacing and narcissistic, conforming and wildly innovative. They are very well educated and hold well-paying technical, professional jobs, and are socially conscious" (p. 6).

Combined outer- and inner-directed: "These are the people who have put together the decisiveness of outer direction with the penetration of inner direction. They are open, self-assured, self-expressive, and often possessed of a global perspective" (p. 6).

High and Low Individualism

The individualism-collectivism and internal-external locus of control continua both represent a bipolar categorization schema that pits the person against the community all the way from the family to the culture. As was stated in the last chapter, Rogers and Heath say that the mature person is allocentric, i.e., he or she takes the good of others into consideration when making his or her decisions, but the locus of evaluation for the decision is within the individual. That is, of course, a purely Anglo-American definition of maturity. In other cultures, e.g., Japan, this type of person would be considered immature because he or she would appear to be highly egocentric. For the Japanese, the group-concept, not the self-concept, is the cybernetic that regulates a person's decision-making process.

Hofstede (1984) tells us that the items that best represented a high individualism (IDV) were those that supported "a personal sense of accomplishment," "time for your personal or family life," and "freedom to adapt your own approach to the job," while those that represented low IDVs (collectivism) supported "good physical working conditions," "fully use your skills," and "have training opportunities" for advancement (p. 155). The first three clearly speak to the internal locus of control, while the last three are more externally focused. In collectivism more dependence is placed on the organization. It was also found that the level of individualism correlated positively with the economic level of the culture. One reason for this might be that the acceptance of new technology is much lower in collectivistic cultures than it is in individualistic cultures.

One of the primary differences between high-IDV and low-IDV cultures is how they answer the question, To what do you attribute success and failure? The answers in high-IDV cultures focus on the person, his or her responsibility, and the future; the answers in low-IDV cultures focus on the environment (cognitive and physical), the person's inadequacies, and the present. The research on the individualism-collectivism dimension found no differences attributable to sex, occupation, or age of the respondents. This may have been an artifact of the research subjects, since they were all employees of a large multinational corporation.

CULTURAL CHARACTERISTICS

The IDV scores give us a means of comparing cultures on their internal versus external locus of control. We would expect cultures that have high IDV scores to be more independent, autonomous, closed, and isolationistic, but with considerable individual freedom. Granted, this is generalizing from individual characteristics to cultural characteristics, but it is the accumulation of individuals' scores that create the norm for the culture. When communicating with someone from a culture for which we know the IDV, we can begin with the reverse process and assume that the person has the characteristics of the culture as a *first* attempt at understanding them. After that, we must observe and modify our perceptions of this person.

The cultural norms given in Table 6, as in the other tables, refer primarily to the middle classes of the countries studied. Thus, when using this table to find out what characteristics you might expect in say, Argentina, you would

Table 6:   The Individualism Societal Norm (Hofstede, p. 171)

LOW IDV	HIGH IDV
1. In society, people are born into extended families or clans which protect them in exchange for loyalty.	In society, everyone is supposed to take care of him or herself and his or her immediate family.
2. "We" consciousness.	"I" consciousness.
3. Collectivity-orientation.	Self-orientation.
4. Identity is based in the social system.	Identity is based in the individual.
5. Emotional dependence of individual on organizations and institutions.	Emotional independence of individual from organizations or institutions.
6. Emphasis on belonging to organization; membership ideal.	Emphasis on individual initiative and achievement; leadership ideal.
7. Private life is invaded by organizations and clans to which one belongs; opinions are predetermined.	Everyone has a right to a private life and opinion.
8. Expertise, order, duty, security provided by organization or clan.	Autonomy, variety, pleasure, individual financial security.
9. Friendships predetermined by stable social relationships; but need for prestige within these relationships.	Need for specific friendships.
10. Belief in group decisions.	Belief in individual decisions.
11. Value standards differ for ingroups and outgroups; particularism.	Value standards apply to all; universalism.

find that since Argentina is about in the middle of the 40 countries studied (Table 3), when going there you could use the categories listed above but you would have to be very careful *not* to assume the behaviors of either high or low IDV. The information given in Table 6 is meant to stimulate your thinking about these categories so you can investigate and assimilate the knowledge needed to understand intercultural communication.

TRANSITION

Hofstede's individualism dimension of beliefs is more easily viewed as the locus of control for the decision-making process. Are we controlled by our self-concept or by that of others—namely, family, society, culture? If we look at individualism in this way, we see that high individualism is correlated with highly independent, autonomous, freedom-loving, achievers. Low individualism, or collectivism, is correlated with group-dominated decision making, conformity among individuals, higher emphasis placed on equality, and more accepting of a person's present condition.

How does this subsystem of values fit into the cultural orientation model? High IDVs tend to be closed-minded and abstractive, but are they particularistic or universalistic? Although they need specific friendships, they still want the rules to outweigh the relationship. Therefore, they would be considered universalistic. At the same time, they would feel that they have the right to behave in a particularistic manner when their desires conflict with the rules or laws.

In the next chapter we will analyze Hofstede's masculinity dimension of values to see what it means and how we can apply it in our attempts to better understand intercultural communication.

INDEPENDENT STUDY

Specific studies on locus of control in cross-cultural decision-making processes are nonexistent. Thus, we must look to those studies of locus of control for individuals and assume that they are active in the decision-making process.

1. Look up Mirels, H. L. (1970). "Dimensions of Internal Versus External Control." (*Journal of Consulting and Clinical Psychology, 34*:226-228) and use the I-E scale he uses to investigate the differences between cultures. You should study a minimum of ten members of each culture to give you a passable sample. Check your results against the positions of the cultures in Table 3.

2. Do the same type of research as in (1) above with males and females. Is there a significant difference?

3. Choose informants from two cultures who are some distance apart on their IDV scores (Table 3) and interview them to see if you can determine which of the characteristics listed in Table 6 they have. The following questions can be used to give you some direction in your search for your culture's values on this dimension.

    1. What are the basic attitudes (beliefs) of the culture about individualism vs. collectivism?
        a. Does the culture allow freedom of individual expression? What does this mean?
        b. What is the role of the family in this culture—in relation to the individual?
        c. What happens if an individual has strong beliefs that are not in sync with society, family, business, etc.?
        d. What effect does your culture's position on individualism have on emotional ties in social, organizational, and family situations?
        e. What are the personal values of the individual in this culture?
        f. How much emphasis is placed on self-identity, self-extension, self-image, etc.?
        g. Does the emphasis on the individual change with age, sex?
        h. What is the strongest force against individualism—family, religion, society, etc.?
        i. How is the individual treated in their language?
    2. What are the constraints on their behavior—society, profession, family, religion, etc.?
        a. Is life a series of obligations or expressions?
        b. Do you have a right to a private life?
        c. What kind of a relationship does a person have with an organization?
        d. Which is stronger, individual or social ethics?
        e. Are social norms developed and taught to children?
        f. Does political policy favor the individual or the collective initiative?
    3. How are decisions made in their culture? Family? Business?
        a. What is their culture's attitude toward conformity?
        b. When you have a problem, do you try to solve it yourself or do you get group input?

You should not feel that you must limit your questions to these; they are only given as suggestions. What you must find out is how your culture handles individualism.

CHAPTER ELEVEN
Masculine/Feminine

In the mid-1970s my wife and I were in Puerto Rico, where she was researching the cultural history of the island. We were to drive around the island on a picture-taking trip, and she thought it might be interesting if we switched roles—she would do all of the driving, reserving hotel rooms, ordering in restaurants, etc. This was convenient for me since I spoke no Spanish at that time and she had taught it in high school before going on to graduate school. The role switch had another twist. My wife was an attractive blonde with eyes that danced with mischief. Puerto Rican men might not marry a blonde, but they do notice them!

We drove to Ponce on the south shore of the island, and she went into the hotel to ask for a room. I followed with the luggage. I heard her say something to the middle-aged man at the desk and saw his eyes, wide with admiration, shift to me as if to say, "Can I help you?" She was being ignored! I said nothing. She explained that we would like a room for the night. He kept looking at me! After several minutes of this, I said, "I'm with her," and he reluctantly let her sign the registry. This caused more problems because she had not taken my name, so our last names were different.

I began to feel sorry for both of them, but was unable to help because I couldn't understand a word they were saying except "no." There were a lot of words coming from both sides, which indicated a great deal of misunderstanding and/or confrontation. We were finally given a room, but both of us received strange looks from the hotel staff during our stay there. As our trip progressed we tried different tactics on the hotel clerks. We had no problems if I first said, in English, "We would like a room," and then my wife repeated it in Spanish. The clerk would talk to her in Spanish until we signed our two names; that always started a debate! *Machismo* is an exceedingly strong force in Latin cultures.

Sex-role stereotypes are held firmly by most cultures. In this chapter we are particularly interested in sex roles and sex traits as they pertain to the belief systems of different cultures. *Sex* is biological, with two categories: female and male. *Gender* is psychological, with three categories: masculine, feminine, and androgynous. We will find that there are cultural differences in both sex and gender. Although it is difficult to tell peoples' gender by looking at them, one can usually tell their sex, and their gender is usually stereotyped from this. The sexual dichotomy gives us the two most stable, universal subcultures.

DEFINING MASCULINE/FEMININE

Men are different from women; we all know that. Just what the differences are, however, most of us are still trying to find out! We know that an essential biological characteristic of males is that they produce sperm, and of females that they produce eggs. These biological differences are absolute and universally recognized. What men and women do with their lives besides procreate, however, is neither absolute nor essential to either sex. Other biological differences between men and women exist, but they are not absolute. Some women are taller, weigh more, and have more hair on their bodies than do some men, although the opposite is usually the case. Sex roles may also have strong biological antecedents, but biology is not destiny. Anything one sex can do, the other can do also; perhaps not as well or as fast, but it can be done. Thus, the biological component may only be considered an obvious perceptual marker, and sometimes that is even misconstrued!

If biology is not the essential component to sex-role differentiation (what is a masculine role, what is a feminine role), then perhaps the key lies in the psychological domain. When we recognize some behaviors as masculine and some as feminine, we are saying that, as a rule, the majority of people taking this role are male (for the former) or female (for the latter). Thus, most miners, construction workers, and truck drivers (and university presidents) are males, while most nurses, secretaries, and school teachers (but not principals) are females. To say the former roles are masculine and the latter are feminine is *not* to say that only that sex can fulfill this role, but rather that the characteristics of the person filling this role are associated with that particular sex. Strictly speaking, this is a differentiation on the basis of gender rather than sex.

The close association between gender and sex-based characteristics is reinforced by all of society. When a child is born, the most important information, after the welfare of the child, is its sex. Once that is known, much of his or her learning patterns is predestined. He or she will be treated like a boy or girl—and God forbid that these characteristics be reversed. The toys with which they are allowed to play and the activities in which they are allowed to partake are all culturally defined as boys' things or girls' things. One of the reasons given for girls being ahead of boys in verbal skills is that they play with dolls (with whom they talk), while boys are not allowed this type of toy or activity. The correlation between boys and masculine characteristics and girls and feminine characteristics is easy to see.

The problem arises when we try to separate the biological male from the psychological masculine (or the biological female from the psychological feminine) to see if the role taken requires either the biological or the psychological antecedents of either sex. Just because the biological male has been conditioned to display the psychological masculine characteristics, and he has traditionally taken a certain role in society, does not necessarily mean that he is the only sex that can do the job (although our nonconscious ideologies would say, "How else could it be?"). There are three variables in the equation for sex-role differentiation: biological characteristics, psychological characteristics, and cultural characteristics; or *sex*, *gender*, and *tradition*. All three of these must be considered when looking at this value dimension.

Hofstede (1984) tells us that the traditional masculine characteristic is "assertiveness" and the traditional feminine characteristic is "nurturance" (p. 178). However, in some cultures these two characteristics are reversed, and certainly they are reversed in many instances on the individual level. "The fact that an active feminist movement exists in a number of countries (albeit predominantly the wealthy ones) shows that some women, at least (and some men, too) no longer take the traditional patterns of male dominance for granted and try to develop alternative role distributions" (p. 179). The fact that sex roles are a social phenomena, however, means that this process must be started with the newborn baby. One does not merely adopt the psychological characteristics of one's sex in a particular culture. The androgynous person (one having high psychological characteristics of both sexes) may be the most logical solution. Coincidental with this focus may be the change in the cultural emphasis from *what* do you do, to *who* are you?

Many cultures already have this focus on the person. In Costa Rica, for example, who you are is extremely important. Others want to know your family tree, for it reduces the uncertainty connected to doing business with you or even being your friend. At the same time, Costa Ricans have a strongly male-dominated society, with a prominent sex role differentiation. They have not begun to develop the androgynous person. In the United States, we have tried to change by encouraging women to be more assertive rather than men to be more nurturing, and the movement on the female side is much more rapid than on the male side. Of course, many would ask if the sexes *should* be equal. "The economic systems of many countries are kept in balance only by women doing menial jobs and being paid less than men even if they do the same jobs" (Hofstede, 1984, p. 183). Your answer to the above question, then, may rest on where you place the values of equality and freedom in your value system, as well as your religious and cultural orientation.

When defining the sex-role differentiation, we might like to set up an ideal state by which to measure all others. But we can only use the information that is now available from the field research that has been done. From this we learn that men are concerned more with success in economics and power, and women are concerned more with caring and relationships. Hofstede (1984) says that "Women compared with men tend to score the interpersonal aspects, rendering service, and sometimes the physical environment as more important, and advancement, sometimes independence, responsibility, and earnings as less important" (p. 185). This may change drastically in the years to come, but as of now the most important job characteristics for men are "advancement, earnings, training, up-to-dateness," while for women they are "friendly atmosphere, position security, physical conditions, manager, cooperation" (p. 186). What types of jobs do these attributes provide for men and women?

Sex-Role Stereotypes

Williams, et al. (1982) define sex-role stereotypes as "beliefs concerning the general appropriateness of various roles and activities for men and women" (p. 16). Sex-role stereotypes are the first level of explanation given when we are asked why one sex is preferred over another for a particular job (it is more appropriate for men to be truck drivers than women, for instance). If we persist and ask why, then we go to the second-level explanations, which consist of sex-trait stereotypes (men are more independent, stronger, aggressive, etc., and therefore more suited to the job). We will consider sex-trait stereotypes in the next section; let's look now at some of the sex-role stereotypes.

Do you remember when it wasn't appropriate for women to run for public office (particularly offices of great importance like prime minister, president, or governor)? Some of the traditional male bastions are still "off limits," but in others women have established a remarkable record. Some of the largest, most advanced, and most troubled countries in the world (India, England, and Israel) have been run exceptionally well by women. How long will it take for the sex-role stereotypes of leaders to be changed? Many occupations have an entrenched tradition of employing one sex or the other. How would you find out if these are culture specific or universal sex-role stereotypes?

If we look at the statistics for the United States, we find some information on the sex roles of its inhabitants (National Data Book, 1987). The strength of the sex-role stereotype of each occupation is difficult to measure, but the percentage of males and females in each occupation is one indicator. Between 1950 and 1985 the percentage of women working rose from 37.7 to 54.5, while the percentage of men working dropped from 83.3 to 76.3. In 1950 women made up 33 percent of the total work force; in 1985 it was 44 percent. With these statistics as a background, we can look at some specific occupations to see what the male/female distribution is. For each occupation I will give what percentage were women (1985): managerial and professional, 42.7; engineers, 6.7; math and computer scientists, 31.1; doctors and dentists, 14.8; nurses and therapists, 85.6: college and university professors, 35.2; school teachers, 73.0; lawyers and judges, 18.2; technical, sales, and administrative support, 64.7; and service occupations, 60.6. This gives you some indication of the importance of the sex role to these types of occupations. They can be broken down into much finer categories, but perhaps this is sufficient to indicate how sex-role stereotypes are operationalized.

Sex-Trait Stereotypes

When we consider that sex, gender, and culture all have a part in shaping the roles that each sex will be pulled toward, we must be aware of the fact that in the United States all roles (including those of father and mother) appear to be moving in the direction of more objectivity/less subjectivity, more production oriented/less relation oriented, and more success (monetary) oriented/less caring oriented. As role characteristics move in these directions, we are moving away from feminine characteristics towards masculine ones. This is based on sex-trait stereotypes. Williams and Best (1982) define sex-trait stereotypes as "the constellations of psychological traits that are said to be more characteristic of one sex than the other. . . . A sex stereotype is usually considered to be cognitive, it is a set of beliefs, it deals with what men and women are like, and it is shared by the members of a particular group" (p. 15).

We have to remember that these are stereotypes, however, and treat them accordingly. As mentioned before, if we treat any one person as though he or she were this stereotype, then we are in trouble. Because these are gender differences (psychological), the variation within the sex group (male or female) may be as great as the variation between sex groups. Nevertheless, sex roles are usually explained by sex-trait stereotypes, e.g., men are too crude to teach in elementary schools and women are too emotional to be good managers. When these sex-trait stereotypes are used in this way, they affect the opportunities given to each sex and restrict the thinking of both the people in control and the people controlled. The general society or culture then takes on a particular focus in relation to the sexes. The consensus from all cultures is that male sex traits are instrumental, female sex traits are expressive.

The pervasiveness and strength of sex-trait stereotypes are seen in the fact that they are developed in children of all cultures at a very early age. Williams and Best say that

> there were differences in the ages at which the children became aware of various stereotype traits. At age 5, the children were aware that women are supposed to be gentle and affectionate and that men are supposed to be strong, aggressive, and dominant. By age 8, the children had learned, in addition, that females are considered weak, emotional, appreciative, excitable, gentle, softhearted, sophisticated, meek, and submissive, and that males are considered disorderly, cruel, coarse, adventurous, independent, ambitious, loud, and boastful. By age 11, the children had learned, in addition, that females are expected to be talkative, rattlebrained, and complaining, while males are expected to be confident, steady, and jolly. On the other hand, the analyses indicated that the learning of the stereotypes is not complete at age 11, since the children did not know that women are said to be flirtatious and men are said to be logical. Apparently, the learning of certain aspects of the male and female stereotypes continues into the adolescent years (p. 25).

Having been learned at such an early age, it is easy to see how these stereotypes work as self-fulfilling prophecies.

To elicit the sex-trait differences between males and females, Williams and Best used a 300-word adjective checklist. From the responses to this list they were able to develop a 100-word list that contained the most descriptive adjectives for male and female sex traits in 25 countries. This checklist is given in Table 7. It can be used as a general orientation to what is meant by masculinity and femininity in the remainder of this chapter. Some of the items on both lists are positive and some are negative; some are weak and some are strong; and some are active and some are passive. These three dimensions of affective meaning (Osgood, et al., 1975) can be used to discriminate among cultures on the basis of each dimension. Do cultures favor masculine over feminine sex-trait stereotypes? That is, are they masculine or feminine dominant? Does this dominance appear on all three dimensions, or do cultures differ depending upon the dimension used?

For the evaluative dimension (positive-negative) they found nearly an even split among the countries, with 12 favoring male stereotypes and 13 favoring

Table 7: The 100 Items of the Pancultural Adjective Checklist

MALE-ASSOCIATED		FEMALE-ASSOCIATED	
Active	Loud	Affected	Modest
Adventurous	Obnoxious	Affectionate	Nervous
Aggressive	Opinionated	Appreciative	Patient
Arrogant	Opportunistic	Cautious	Pleasant
Autocratic	Pleasure-seeking	Changeable	Prudish
Bossy	Precise	Charming	Self-pitying
Capable	Progressive	Complaining	Sensitive
Coarse	Quick	Complicated	Sentimental
Conceited	Rational	Confused	Sexy
Confident	Realistic	Curious	Shy
Courageous	Reckless	Dependent	Softhearted
Cruel	Resourceful	Dreamy	Sophisticated
Cynical	Rigid	Emotional	Submissive
Determined	Robust	Excitable	Suggestible
Disorderly	Serious	Fault-finding	Talkative
Enterprising	Sharp-witted	Fearful	Timid
Greedy	Show-off	Fickle	Touchy
Hardheaded	Steady	Foolish	Unambitious
Humorous	Stern	Forgiving	Unintelligent
Indifferent	Stingy	Frivolous	Unstable
Individualistic	Stolid	Fussy	Warm
Initiative	Tough	Gentle	Weak
Interests wide	Unfriendly	Imaginative	Worrying
Inventive	Unscrupulous	Kind	Understanding
Lazy	Witty	Mild	Superstitious

(Source: Williams and Best, 1982, p. 81)

female stereotypes. For both the activity (active-passive) and potency (strong-weak) dimensions, all countries favored the male stereotype (active and strong), although with considerable variation in the strength of their choice.

Other cultural characteristics were revealed by the data collected in the Williams and Best study. One important aspect of intercultural communication is the interpersonal behavior of the participants. A theory that speaks to this aspect of communication is that of Transactional Analysis (Berne, 1961, 1964). Its main premise is that, although people use all five ego-states in their communicative behavior, they develop a norm of behaving in only one or two of these ego-states. The five ego-states are: Parent, subdivided into Critical Parent and Nurturing Parent, Adult, and Child, subdivided into Free Child and Adapted Child. The critical parent is directive and controlling; the nurturing parent is instructive and caring; the adult is reasonable and mature; the free child is creative and rebellious; the adapted child is conforming and dependent. Each of these ego-states represents a behavior pattern and can be associated with masculine or feminine sex-trait stereotypes (see Table 8).

One's psychological needs also play an important role in one's behavior. Williams and Best were able to subject their data to a psychological needs analysis to see if needs would cluster on the basis of masculine or feminine sex-trait stereotypes (see Table 8). The needs that are associated with masculinity and femininity tell us something about the behavior patterns of those (persons or cultures) that load heavily on either of these dimensions. One sees a strong difference between the two sets of characteristics. One who is masculine needs to dominate and to be independent, aggressive, exhibitionistic, success oriented, and persistent in his or her pursuits. One who is feminine needs to display inferiority, subordination, a desire for affection, a caring disposition, a friendly personality, and a desire for friends of the opposite sex.

Table 8:   Pancultural Similarities in Sex-Trait Stereotypes

CHARACTERISTICS OF MEN		CHARACTERISTICS OF WOMEN
	Affective Meanings	
Active		Passive
Strong		Weak
	Ego States	
Critical Parent		Nurturing Parent
Adult		Adapted Child
	Psychological Needs	
Dominance		Abasement
Autonomy		Deference
Aggression		Succorance
Exhibition		Nurturance
Achievement		Affiliation
Endurance		Heterosexuality

(Source: Williams and Best, 1982, p. 229)

Stereotypical Communicative Behavior

The sex-trait stereotypes presented above lead us to wonder if the communicative behaviors of males and females stereotypically differ. At this point in our discussion we see the importance of differentiating between sex and gender. Although the different communicative behaviors are usually attributed to males and females (sex), it is more likely that they are characteristic of masculine and feminine (gender) sex-trait stereotypes. The behaviors are physical but the schemas that elicit them are psychological. As you will see in Tables 9 and 10, the characteristics of the two genders are almost opposites of each other, and there are few items that one might question. Although myth has it that women talk more than men, in mixed groups men do more talking, as they have the position of dominance. In touching behavior the same is true; opposite sex touching by women is considered sexual whereas for men it is considered dominance.

Table 9:   Masculine Communication Characteristics

GENERAL RULE: THE MALE IS USUALLY IN THE ROLE OF THE SUPERIOR

VERBAL: Masculine more than Feminine.

    A. Uses more familiar terms.
    B, Uses more commanding language.
    C. Interrupts more.
    D. Talks over others more.
    E. Talks more in mixed groups.
    F. Uses more expletives.
    G. Uses a speaking style that is more externally centered, factual, literal and direct.
    H. More argumentative.
    I. More competitive.
    J. Uses more humor.
    K. Talks down to women (like a child).
    L. Speaks louder.
    M. Finds it hard to use terms of tenderness.
    N. Is hurt more by opposite sex labels.
    O. Pro-acts—long bursts of speech aimed at solving problems.
    P. Truncates his words.

NONVERBAL:

    A. More expansive—sits with legs apart.
    B. More relaxed.
    C. More gestures.
    D. More pointing.
    E. Dislikes crowding more.
    F. Does more touching (in mixed groups).
    G. Touch is a sign of authority.
    H. Given high status seating.

(Source: Borden, 1985a, p. 119)

A few nonverbal communicative behaviors have been shown to be different across cultures for both masculine and feminine sex-trait stereotypes. The most famous is the distance between the communicators. In Latin and Arab cultures particularly, the distance is much less than in the United States. They also touch more and use more gestures. It all goes with their more personal mode of communication and the fact that relationships are more important than business.

Table 10:   Feminine Communication Characteristics

GENERAL RULE: THE FEMALE IS USUALLY IN THE ROLE OF THE SUBORDINATE

VERBAL: Feminine more than Masculine.

A.   Uses more formal terms.
B.   More self-disclosing.
C.   Is more agreeable.
D.   Asks for help more often.
E.   Uses more modifiers (adjectives, adverbs).
F.   Uses more relational type language.
G.   Uses subjective language.
H.   Uses more tag questions (don't they?).
I.   Uses more qualifiers.
J.   Is more tentative.
K.   Is more elaborative.
L.   Gives more support.
M.   Does more listening.
N.   Starts talking at an earlier age.
O.   Has better linguistic skills through college.
P.   Uses more correct speech.
Q.   Reacts to others more than pro-acts.
R.   Is addressed by more diminutive terms.

NONVERBAL:

A.   Is more responsive.
B.   Is more accurate in reading nonverbal cues.
C.   Looks more at others.
D.   More averting of the eyes.
E.   Reveals more emotion through facial expression.
F.   Smiles more.
G.   Preens more.
H.   Is approached closer by both sexes.
I.   Stands closer to both sexes.
J.   Is touched more.
K.   Touching men is seen as a gesture of intimacy.

(Source: Borden, 1985a, p. 120)

The obvious question that one must ask at this point is, Are these stereotypes relevant today? The answer is, only as a first approximation to understanding the communicatee, which is necessary because it gives us a base from which to work. But because it is only a base, we can move away from it very quickly. Since both sex-role and sex-trait characteristics are changing rapidly, our expectation of communicative behavior must be tentative at best. There are no norms for change.

Changing Stereotypes

The statistics on sex-role changes given above were for the United States only. Young people probably are not as aware of the changes as those of us who were around when it all started. But you should be aware of the optimism with which female undergraduate students face the job market today. As far as jobs are concerned, there seem to be few sex barriers; salaries are a different matter, however. If we look at the changing opportunities for women we see that the sex-role stereotype is changing rapidly in the United States. This may be the basis for the myth that, "women in advanced industrial societies are better off than those in less developed societies, and that the position of women automatically improves as a byproduct of modernization" (Holloman, 1982, p. 167). Consonant with this myth is the one given earlier that Western type progress is what everyone else desires. Both are bald ethnocentric speculations.

The dominance of Western style belief systems is also seen in the fact that many sex-role stereotypes are carried to other cultures either by missionaries with "sex-appropriate behavior" or technology consultants with their ideas of men's and women's work. Inequalities between the sexes exist in nearly all cultures in one form or another as they do between the ins and the outs of any type of grouping. Some cultures are working more on the problems these inequalities precipitate than are others, but looking at the problems from an etic perspective does not always reveal the "truth." For example, with the Sandanista regime in Nicaragua using as many women as men in their military—and many of the women distinguishing themselves in these roles—one might think that sexual equality had taken a major step forward in this culture. On the contrary, the Latin machismo still holds that women are inferior, a sex-trait stereotype. It takes a long time for a change in sex roles to change the sex-trait beliefs.

In 1968, Bernard stated that there were two roadblocks to equality between the sexes: one was the necessity for reproduction and family care, and the other was that female children were not being socialized to be career oriented. As mentioned above, we have seen great changes in the latter and some change in child care in the former. The bottleneck seems to be in the willingness of males to take an equal role in what has been traditionally labeled women's work. This may also be changing rather slowly, though these changes are seen most often in dual-career marriages without children. Education seems to be the key to the advancement of women in all areas of endeavor. Not much is said about women in rural areas but, "As their education increases, they are making substantial contributions to raising standards of living within their own nations and are already branching out, with interest, to take part in various kinds of international movements" (Lanier, 1968, p. 115). Great strides have been made in this area also in recent decades.

Fairhurst says that:

> In the past 25 years the large number of women entering organizations and assuming occupations and positions of authority once thought to be male domains has dramatically changed the work force of most organizations. Males take orders from females, females do physical labor right alongside males, and traditionally employed females such as office workers negotiate collectively with their male bosses. Males also enter nursing and office work, traditional female domains. Men and women fight, negotiate, exploit each other, perform tasks, form friendships, and fall in love on the job. They communicate differently and more often than their counterparts in the past; they are changing the social order at work (p. 83).

Communication is the key to change. Fairhurst goes on to say that "Stereotypes are sustained when there are limited opportunities for the sexes to communicate, and when nontraditionally employed persons act in ways that reinforce the stereotypes due to a lack of power or an inability to use that power" (p. 89). The changing of sex-role and sex-trait stereotypes is making great changes in cultural orientations.

High and Low Masculinity

The last three sections have given you some specific masculine and feminine characteristics. Except in an androgynous culture, these can be construed as high and low masculinity characteristics. Hofstede (1984) labels the masculine/feminine differences as ego/social, with ego characteristics being the need for challenge, advancement, recognition, and earnings, and the social characteristics being the need for a good manager, cooperation, desirable area, employment security, and a friendly atmosphere. These are practically identical to the characteristics developed above for masculine/feminine. The ego end of the continuum is high masculinity and the social end is low masculinity. All cultures can be placed somewhere on this continuum.

High masculinity can be seen in a number of different dimensions. For example, objective vs. subjective, success oriented vs. relational oriented, active vs. passive, etc. Cultural characteristics will likewise reflect these attributes—high stress, leaning toward the individual as decision-maker rather than the group, preferring large companies to small, and feeling that knowing people is more important than an ability to get ahead. Job satisfaction is correlated with the feeling of challenge and the satisfaction with earnings. In a sense, high-masculinity cultures "live to work" and low-masculinity cultures "work to live."

CULTURAL CHARACTERISTICS

The masculinity (MAS) scores and the sex-trait stereotype scores give us a means of comparing cultures on this all-important dimension. In comparing cultures we should be aware that these values are assumed to be those of the middle classes across occupations, ages, and education. The high- and low-cultural characteristics given in Table 11 reflect this type of generalization. They are presented here to help you establish a benchmark or beginning point for your intercultural communication. If you look back at Table 3 you will see that Japan is the most masculine and Sweden is the least; thus, you certainly wouldn't expect to communicate in the same way in these two countries.

From the information in Table 11, we can see that high-MAS cultures differ significantly from low-MAS cultures. High MASs operate on a rewards system wherein monetary or status success is preferred to benevolence and caring for people. Thankfully, there are no completely high-MAS cultures, for some people within every culture differ from the norm. High-MAS cultures distinguish between male and female roles through early socialization, educational goals, and occupational opportunities. Low-MAS cultures hold equality, as well as their relationships with each other and their environment, higher. They are more humanistic, while the high MAS are more behavioristic.

Table 11:   The Masculinity Societal Norm

LOW MAS	HIGH MAS
1. People orientation.	Money and things orientation.
2. Quality of life and environment are important.	Performance and growth are important.
3. Work to live.	Live to work.
4. Service ideal.	Achievement ideal.
5. Interdependence ideal.	Independence ideal.
6. Intuition.	Decisiveness.
7. Sympathy for the unfortunate.	Sympathy for the successful achiever.
8. Levelling: don't try to be better than others.	Excelling: try to be the best.
9. Small and slow are beautiful.	Big and fast are beautiful.
10. Men need not be assertive but can also take caring roles.	Men should behave assertively and women should care.
11. Sex roles in society should be fluid.	Sex roles in society should be clearly differentiated.
12. Differences in sex roles should not mean differences in power.	Men should dominate in all settings.
13. Unisex and androgyny ideal.	Machismo (ostentative manliness) ideal.

(Source: Hofstede, 1984, p. 205)

TRANSITION

In this chapter we have presented the fourth value dimension of Hofstede. When communicating with a person from another culture, it is not difficult to find out where they stand on the masculinity/femininity continuum. Because this is the most subjective and the most notorious of the value systems, it may also be the most difficult one to deal with. We do not like to have our masculinity stepped on nor our femininity taken advantage of. Most of us would like to behave as we idealize the role our sex *should* play in society. However, when in a foreign culture, this is a herculean task. As they say, "When in Rome do as the Romans do."

The masculine/feminine continuum should not be a continuum. Unfortunately, we are socialized into characteristics which are then defined as opposites. Where do they fit in the cultural orientation model? Masculine characteristics appear to be closed-minded, abstractive, and universalistic, while feminine ones (low MAS) appear to be on the opposite ends of these continua. The changes we see taking place in this area of values reinforces Kelly's emphasis on the ability of one to reconstrue his or her perceptions of reality by changing his or her personal constructs. When using the cultural orientation model, one must be particularly aware of the rapid change taking place in sex-role stereotypes and the more slowly changing sex-trait stereotypes.

Putting the four value systems of Hofstede together with the cultural orientation of Glenn and the personal constructs of Kelly allows us to approach an intercultural communication event with some real constructs to assist us in understanding the other culture and facilitating their understanding of us. As we develop an intercultural communication competence, we will learn how to read new cultures and increase our probability for effective communication. In the next chapter we will discuss the process of enculturation to see how we become what we are in terms of culture.

INDEPENDENT STUDY

In this chapter little was said about domestic roles. However, the 100-item adjective check list can be used to study any role you care to. Remember to randomize the mixing of the masculine and feminine attributes before giving it to your subjects.

1. Team up with some of your classmates and compare the masculine and feminine characteristics attributed to:

   a. A specific culture.
   b. Some specific sex-roles across cultures, e.g., fathers and mothers in several cultures.

   You should have at least ten of each sex from each culture. Each person in your group can take a culture, and you can pool your information for the final report.

2. Choose informants from two cultures that are some distance apart on their MAS scores (Table 3) and interview them to see if you can determine which of the characteristics listed in Table 11 they have. You should have at least one male and one female from each culture in your sample. The following questions can be used to give you some direction in your search for your culture's values on this dimension.

    1. What are the masculine and feminine characteristics?
        a. Is machismo apparent, accepted, expected, etc.?
        b. Can men show emotions in public?
        c. Can women work outside the home?
        d. Family roles—distinct, enforced, accepted?
        e. How is machismo expressed most often/obviously in your culture?
    2. Are the sex roles distinct, enforced, accepted, etc.?
        a. How are the sex roles established—family, society, religion, media, etc.?
    3. Proper dress for women? Men? Children?
    4. Are sex roles reflected in pay scales, job types, classifications, titles, language, etc.?
    5. What is the acculturation pattern—nursery rhymes, books, games, folk heros, movie stars, etc.?
    6. Are the sex roles reflected in the communication patterns?
    7. Are the sex roles the same in all situations—business, courtship, sex, family, etc.?
    8. What are the basic expectations of the male, the female, the male role, the female role?
    9. What motivates—success? Material things?
    10. How is success measured for men? For women?
    11. Are there organizations seeking equality for the sexes, or is there general satisfaction with the sex roles?
        a. Are role reversals accepted—dominant/female, submissive/male, female boss/male employee, etc.?
        b. Are there really equal opportunities in education, business, politics? By law?
        c. How are homosexuals of both sexes treated?

Remember, these are only suggested questions; you may find that you want to pursue a different line of questioning.

CHAPTER TWELVE
Culture and Enculturation

As we have seen, your culture depends on where and when you grew up. In the cultural revolution of the '60s and '70s in the United States, many young people tried (in vain) not to categorize (stereotype) people; everyone was to be "themselves" and be accepted as such. In the late '60s I grew a beard (it was the "in" thing for professors) and visited a class of a former student of mine at another university. I was introduced only by name as a friend oɩ the instructor. After class a young "hippie" (my category) whom I had never met and who had never heard of me said, "*Professor* Borden, will you be teaching here this summer?" I said, "No, I'm just visiting." In the course of conversation I asked her if the fact that I was wearing a beard made any difference in how she perceived me. She said, "No, I *never* make inferences about people. I just accept them as they are." Obviously, though, something about me had triggered her professor schema and placed me in it. When you've been enculturated into an abstractive culture (developed all the schemas to function in an acceptable manner), it is impossible to function at a purely associative level (accept things as they are without putting them into a previously abstracted category). You cannot *unlearn* the abstractive process.

In this chapter we will look at how we become enculturated, i.e., assimilate our culture's belief and disbelief systems and orientation. We will see that language and culture are inextricably interwoven. We will look at the psychological and physical natures of enculturation and show that enculturation is a cognitive process. But we are almost never aware of this enculturation process, most of our culture lying below our consciousness. Thus, it is difficult to know how our culture affects us until we are in a situation where it is contrasted with another culture.

AN ENCULTURATION MODEL

As we have seen, culture may be considered from both the psychological and the physical perspective. From the physical perspective it is something that we live within and that affects our lives in a way in which we are almost always unaware. When we are taken out of our culture and placed in another (for example, when you moved away from home for the first time), we become aware of its existence. The fact that we notice the change when moved from one culture to another indicates that culture is also psychological.

Kelly says that we construe our world psychologically to develop the cognitive constructs we need to live in it. Hofstede (1980) based his research on the assumption that we have mental programs that direct our behavior. Work that is now being done in cognitive science uses "scripts" as a basic unit of cognition. Datan, Rodeheaver, and Hughes (1987) say that

> Individuals experience events in their lives as "scenes"—organized wholes combining people, places, time, actions, and, in particular, affects that amplify these experiences and provide a sense of urgency about understanding them. Out of early scenes, the individual develops sets of rules for interpreting, evaluating, producing, predicting, or controlling future scenes. These rules—"scripts"—are initially innate but are supplemented and replaced by learned scripts. Higher-order scripts are created when scenes are combined and instilled with fresh affect—"psychological magnification". . . . The order in personality development, then, derives from the individual's need to impose order—the script—on the critical events, or scenes, in life. And, finally, scripts that initially arise from scenes begin to give rise to scenes instead, as the individual's construction of experience affects experience itself (p. 164).

In scenes there is only an associative relationship. Scripts are the abstractions we make from them, and the expectations that are part of the abstractions give us the schemas we need to anticipate events. Thus, the cognitive processes (schemas) we develop begin to feed forward into our daily experiences through our anticipation of events. Piaget (in Furth, 1969) tells us that we develop schemas through which we assimilate knowledge into our cognitive structures. Thus, in creating our reality (culture) we develop psychological constructs that reflect our physical environment, including people and their behaviors (culture).

Glenn (1981) gives us three general approaches to the study of culture.

a. The functionalistic approach: The rationale of functionalism is that all cultures must provide for a number of social needs, from child rearing to religion. Each such universal need provides an organizational dimension; the different ways in which the needs are met become the values of the dimension.

b. The values approach: The main thrust of this appraisal is the analysis of the value orientations which govern how given peoples judge various aspects of the human experience. For example, with respect to nature, the orientation of some cultures may be governed by the expectation that man can dominate nature and that any behavior which leads to such a domination should be valued positively. The feeling in other cultures may be that man should find a way to attain harmony with nature. In still other cultures, the main feeling is that man is likely to be dominated by nature and must take steps to propitiate nature or to learn to accept nature's decrees.

c. The cognitive approach, suggesting that different cultures structure knowledge differently and that these differences will largely determine many aspects of behavior and communication, e.g., the topics which are felt to be worth talking about, the organization of information during communication, the types of information which are accepted as evidence for any given opinion (pp. 1-2).

All of these approaches indicate that something in a culture, called values, functions as the anchor for our behavior. For many years culture has been studied from a values perspective with little consideration for the role these values play in the communication process. However, we know that two people can have similar values and beliefs but behave differently. Thus, it may not only be the beliefs and values that differentiate among cultures (*b* above) but also the way in which they are operationalized (*a* above). Thus, both *a* and *b* are necessary for an understanding of culture, but they are not sufficient. One must also understand the cognitive processes that control our behavior (*c* above). Figure 7 is a model representing our cognitive structure and the processes that occur in enculturation.

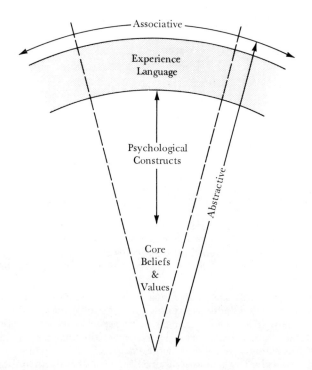

Figure 7: A Model for First Culture Enculturation

You are already familiar with the terms "associative" and "abstractive," so we will concentrate on the rest of the model at this time. Essentially, what we want to show is the interaction between experience and language; they are connected with our basic beliefs and values through what we call psychological constructs. The core of our cognitive structure is a set of "primitive beliefs" (Bem). He says that there are two levels of primitive beliefs: *zero order*, our beliefs in the credibility of our senses and external authority; and *first order*, our beliefs in what our senses and the authorities tell us. The difference between zero- and first-order beliefs is the difference between the source and the information presented by the source. As we mature, these core beliefs are elaborated into our values and higher order beliefs.

As discussed in Chapter 7, the resulting belief structure has been defined by Rokeach (1973) as having two basic components: *instrumental*—the preference for certain ways of behaving (honesty, ambition, open-minded), and *terminal*—the preference for certain end states of existence (security, peace, wisdom). These belief structures are thought to influence our behaviors and to result from our interactions with the environment (enculturation). Together they give us our world view and form our *attitudinal frame of reference* against which we measure experience and develop the evaluative attributes of our schemas. It should be obvious that there will be some commonalities among people of the same culture but also individual differences stemming from the personal nature of enculturation.

Bem further tells us that many, if not most, of the cognitive structures that regulate our behavior (including our beliefs and values) are below the conscious level. Using the example of male supremacy, he says that we have many *nonconscious ideologies* for which we can entertain no alternatives. One nonconscious ideology that seriously affects our intercultural communication is that we citizens of the United States refer to ourselves as Americans, as though we were the only ones. This was initiated by the fact that we were originally trying to differentiate ourselves from Europeans. However, the term has been assimilated into our cultural heritage, and we grow up referring to ourselves as Americans in every aspect of our culture. When we realize that we are only one of the many nations in North, Central, and South America, all of whom may be called Americans, it makes us appear rather ostentatious, ethnocentric, and egotistical. To those who ask, "But how else can it be?" the answer is, we can be called gringos, yankees, or *Estadounidenses* (the Latin American Spanish term for people from the United States) or Americans, *but* with the realization that we do not have exclusive right to this name.

FIRST CULTURE ENCULTURATION

Since language is an integral part of our culture, we will begin with a brief review of first language development. The constructs explicated here will help us understand what we mean by enculturation.

Language

We usually talk about learning a language. Even when talking about our first language, we refer to it as learning, e.g., "He is not learning his language very well" or "She is just learning her language." But it is not learning in the way we usually think of learning. If English is your first language, did you set about to "learn" it as a set of rules called grammar and syntax? Probably not! In the common sense of learning, we may put what we learn about a language in the following hierarchical pattern: vocabulary, syntax, grammar. Overriding all of these, however, is semantics; the other three constructs are meaningless without it. But how did you learn to use the first three constructs to achieve the last?

Whereas a number of theories of first language learning prevail, what we are interested in is the obvious truth that first language learning is more than sitting down and studying a language. We didn't do this until we had a considerable vocabulary and had been using rules of syntax and grammar in our speaking for several years. We might better characterize the first stages in this process as first language evolution. No one really knows what the learning mechanism is, but somehow it happens, and for the average person, once it starts it cannot be stopped. Something innate in human beings enables them— indeed compels them—to learn the language of their culture.

Semantics   The evolution or development of a language is semantically determined, i.e., language is structured to convey meaning; it is for communication and cannot be learned in the absence of it. Our first language is encountered in an associative mode; it is always associated with something in the immediate experiencing process (Figure 7). The learning or development of a language is an abstractive process and cannot be accomplished solely by association and reinforcement (Chomsky, 1959). Perhaps a primitive model will help illustrate the above concepts.

For many years meaning has been referred to as semantic space (Osgood, et al., 1957; Borden, 1963). We may view this as a sphere, with language as the tool by which we are able to apprehend specific areas of semantic space (see Figure 8). As language develops we are able to pack more and more information into fewer and fewer words, or concepts. We are able to move to higher and

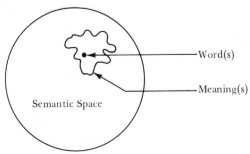

Figure 8:   Semantic Space

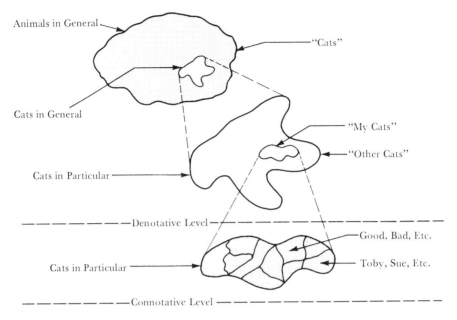

Figure 9: Language and Abstractions

higher levels of abstraction (Korzybski, 1948). Thus, with fewer and fewer words we are able to apprehend more and more semantic space. At the same time, we are able to move to deeper and deeper levels of convergence, i.e., to pinpoint exact meanings more precisely by using our vocabulary, grammar, and syntax more accurately.

An example may help illustrate the model. As a child you may have had a pet cat. You learned the word "cat." Before you learned through association and reinforcement that all other animals were not cats, this word apprehended (had the general meaning of) the semantic space for all animals. When you would see any animal you might point to it and say "cat." Soon you learned that there were other animals besides cats and this reduced the size of the semantic space being apprehended by this word. When you learned that there were other cats besides yours, you took another step in your abstractive process; you were able to differentiate between "my cat" and "someone else's cat." The category "my cat" is a much more personal area of semantic space than just cat, and so you began to personalize your abstractions, to separate connotative meaning from denotative meaning (see Figure 9).

If you had more than one cat, then you gave them names and further differentiated your personal semantic space. Simultaneously, you may have been learning that there were different kinds of cats,—good, bad, ugly, pretty, etc. Your semantic space for cats was being partitioned by modifiers that allowed you to apprehend a more precise area of semantic space. You were beginning to be able to differentiate among many different kinds of animals and cats. What we have illustrated here is designated as language evolution rather than language learning because it is accomplished primarily through associative methods—we associate these words with something in our immediate experience.

Abstraction   If you now find out that the many species of cats all belong to the genus Felis, you are learning the language that will allow you to specify precisely what breed of cat and type of animal you are talking about; you apprehend a more precise area of semantic space. When this happens you are using the abstractive nature of language to allow you to communicate effectively. The most basic levels of abstraction (often called "dead-level abstraction") are our most personal connotations. This is the associative end of the associative-abstractive continuum of semantic space.

Two very important constructs should be derived from the above discussion. One is that the deeper we go into semantic space, the more associative (personal) is the meaning of the language being used. The higher we go in semantic space, the more abstractive (nonpersonal) is the meaning of the language being used. The more associative (personal) the meaning, the fewer persons there are who share it (perhaps only two!). The more abstractive (nonpersonal) the meaning, the more persons there are who share it (perhaps a whole culture!). What does this say about intercultural communication? How can we let our communicatee know the connotative/denotative position a concept has for us?

The second point that must be made is that as we move from associative to abstractive, there must be more and more linguistic knowledge (information) available to build upon (Figure 10). Thus, what we are calling language learning (as opposed to language evolution) uses the vocabulary, grammar, and syntax already in the cognitive structure of the individual to construct new and more abstract concepts. A person must first develop linguistic associations at an experience level in order to have access to semantic space. She or he may then build more elaborate (precise or general) apprehenders (linguistic concepts) by developing the language system. The more abstract our language system becomes, the better we are able to express complex thoughts.

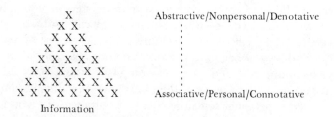

Figure 10:   The Associative-Abstractive Process

Enculturation

Each culture has a unique pattern of values and beliefs, and they are operationalized into culture-specific behaviors. Behaviors are either verbal (natural language) or nonverbal (proxemics, kinesics, oculemics, and the other codes given in Chapter 2). Our question now is, How does one acquire these behaviors? How does one develop the schemas that operationalize his or her values into behaviors that can distinguish one culture from another? How does one become enculturated? Glenn puts forth a theory that seems to me to be the most plausible. He takes a cognitive approach and bases his theory on the processes through which a person organizes his or her information into knowledge.

> The basic assumption underlying the model is that cognitive processes derive information from three separate sources. Each source provides certain limitations upon thought, and each provides a characteristic impetus to its development. Furthermore, each can be seen as conflicting to some degree with the two other ones. . . . The sources are:
>
> 1. The individual subject, characterized by the particularity of experiences, desires, wishes and dreams—and in slightly different terms, by the uniqueness of the way in which the conscious and subconscious are combined in every person.
> 2. The social group, characterized by public knowledge as opposed to private knowledge. The social group requires that its participants observe rules of mutual intelligibility—e.g., rules of logic as defined by the group.
> 3. The environment within which and upon which humans act. The main effect of the environment is to impose limits on the possibilities of action—of separating what can from what cannot be done (p. 27).

These three sources may be further explained in the language of this text as being determined by one's psycho-logic, socio-logic, and perceptions. Psycho-logic is the logic by which a person rationalizes his or her behaviors. It is a schema of one's cybernetic and is in a continuous state of development, although its primary development occurs during the formative years of one's life. It results from a person's attempt to maintain balance in his or her self-concept (Borden, 1985a). One's socio-logic is the rationality of society, often called logic or reason. It results from the enculturation of a person into a specific culture and affects the way a person views the world. In any situation one's behavior is constrained by what one perceives the situation to be. Perception is an abstracting process subject to one's personal and cultural orientation. Remember the three dimensions of communication decision making in Chapter 3?

The three sources detailed above can be linked to three epistemological styles and these to the development of the psychological constructs and processes that are our cognitive culture. Remember, culture is both psychological and physical: physical in that it is the milieu in which we carry on our daily existence, and psychological in that it is the reality of this milieu created in our cognitive structure. Glenn says the epistemological styles are:

1.   *The intuitive.* Knowledge is sought through private experience. The individual subject absorbs and transforms information at both the conscious and the subconscious levels, and in consequence, is not always aware of how he or she arrived at some beliefs. Items of knowledge which are and whose origins are unclear, are intuitions. . . .
2.   *The rational.* The rational approach seeks knowledge through the application of logical rules to an area of study.
3.   *The empirical.* The empirical approach seeks validation through demonstration. The usefulness of ideas must be tested by applying them in the environment (p. 28).

These three styles fall on the associative/abstractive dimension of the cultural orientation model. Glenn defines it as follows:

> Knowledge acquired through a largely spontaneous experience within an environment is *associative.* Such a knowledge fits closely with the feelings of individuals and the shared preoccupations of small or relatively small groups. The codification of thought into precise meanings and well-organized lexicons is carried out by *abstraction.* The results of abstraction do not reflect the spontaneous experience of small groups, but the specifically stated systems of knowledge of large groups—potentially of all mankind.
> Although differences along the associative-abstractive dimension are used in characterizing cultures, all cultures need and possess both types of elements (p. ii).

These definitions will help us explain the processes that occur as one becomes enculturated. Essentially, the model is one of developing communication competence and performance. If we assume that as a child grows she or he is enculturated into his or her culture, we may ask the question, why? The answer, of course, is to be able to communicate with other members of the culture and to become a responsible member of society. Communication has played a major role in any study of culture. Since we are looking at culture on a cognitive level, the role of language, and thus communication, is even more obvious. It is the process of becoming culturally literate, obtaining the tacit knowledge necessary to communicate with others in our culture.

With these thoughts in mind we can move on to the presentation of the model, which is an epistemological one that incorporates all three styles. Moreover, it gives an excellent explanation of the development of cultures as well as the enculturation of an individual (see Figure 11).

The extreme subjective apex consists of an individual and his or her perceptions. As soon as language is introduced, we know some abstraction has occurred, and as soon as there is communication, we have begun to move toward the co-subjective apex. Glenn says of this apex that it

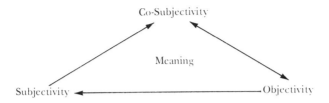

Figure 11:   An Enculturation Model

should be defined as the greatest possible communicative universality. A symbolic system shared by as many people as possible, both in space and in time, would have to be characterized by total symbol stability across subjects and in time; in other words the meanings attached to its symbols would have to be invariant, constant in time, and the same for all communicating subjects (p. 29).

We realize that this is impossible, and therein lies the problem of communication. Since language (verbal and nonverbal) is both connotative and denotative, we must realize that what someone says may mean many things to many people and, perhaps, none of these are the one the speaker had in mind. However, as we mature and become enculturated, we are expected to use symbol systems that reflect our culture's beliefs, values, and operational constructs.

To facilitate the development of co-subjectivity we must iterate between the objective and co-subjective apexes. The objective apex is as close as we can get to reality. As one abstracts from one's experiences to a higher conceptual plane and tries to communicate this experience, she or he may find it difficult, if not impossible. One then tends to adjust his or her perceptions and/or communicative style (both are variables at this apex) and to try again. This testing of constructs, revision, and testing again enables a person to adjust his or her psychological constructs to fit into his or her culture—to communicate. Glenn says that "at this apex identical events or situational constraints lead different subjects to identical nonverbal behaviors. This apex, therefore, stands for behavior which is marginally influenced by subjective considerations but reflects, to the extent of the possible, total objectivity" (p. 29).

Subjectivity   Whether we are tracing the development of a culture or the enculturation of an individual, we must begin at the subjectivity apex. An infant knows nothing else. Its knowledge is gained in an associative manner, associating experiences in time and space. It revolves around itself and its relationships with the environment. At this level one gathers knowledge through intuition—a subjective accumulation of personal "facts." It is egocentric. It is associative, attributing reasons to happenings in a narrowing process that focuses on the immediate without the benefit of predefined categories of significance.

On the associative level the obvious question is, What can be associated with what? One answer is that "One of the manners in which selections can be made is propinquity: Things which are experienced together either because they are perceived (or, more generally, sensed) together, or because they are remembered together, or again because the sight of one coincides with the memory of another" (Glenn, p. 9). As can be seen, associative processes are extremely limiting in their ability to organize information. Something else is needed to enable one to handle increases in either the amount or the complexity of information.

Glenn calls this something else *abstraction*. It is a method of organization that leads "to a selection of elements towards which attention should be directed, and elements which should be disregarded, at least within the context in which abstraction is carried out" (p. 9). It "consists in removing from existing associations elements which are deemed irrelevant: Furthermore, the progressive development of the abstractive part of a culture appears to be carried out by the additional removal of an increasing amount of associations" (p. 10). In associations, the question of relevance is disregarded; *everything* that occurs is part of the association. It is obvious that the "abstractive approach is capable of organizing much richer amounts of information (or the description of much broader environments) than the associative approach" (p. 11). Furthermore,

> This difference between associative and abstractive thought is related to the amount of information which can and needs to be incorporated into the cognitive structures, and to the organization of information connected with each style. Associative thought is marked by ill-defined relationships between elements. Only a relatively small amount of information can be remembered in an amorphous state. As the amount of information increases, it becomes necessary to organize knowledge, usually in hierarchical structures obtained through abstraction. Hierarchical structures are capable of incorporating new information into a relevant niche, while remaining stable in [their] other parts (p. 16).

This indicates a "direction of evolution: from less information to more information, from the weak structures of associative chains towards the stronger structures of hierarchies" (p. 16). As one is enculturated into his or her society, he or she abstracts the important behaviors and concepts of that society and develops the appropriate beliefs, values, and constructs to become a member of that culture. "The primary process for the acquisition of knowledge appears to be associative. Abstraction appears as the primary process for the organization of knowledge" (p. 57). As individuals develop the abstract concepts necessary for communication (language is an abstracting construct), they also develop a communicative style peculiar to their culture. This facilitates intracultural communication because of its co-subjective nature and tacit knowledge; members of that culture share these abstract concepts and communicative styles.

Co-Subjectivity   While the associative-abstractive dimension applies primarily to the collection and organization of information into knowledge, as young men and women develop language and the abstractive process, they move from a concern for persons (subjective) to the abstracted roles (co-subjective) that these persons may fill. Interpersonal structures based on personal relationships (kinships, friendships, memberships) are more important at the subjective end of the continuum, while social structures based on roles or categories (construction worker, sales person, college student) are more important at the abstractive end.

As the amount of information increases, it is necessary to organize knowledge. We have shown that this organization process is an abstractive one in which one chooses what to include and what to exclude from her or his cognitive structures. This moves one toward the abstractive end of the continuum, and she or he develops uniform practices that are often translated into rules and roles for human behavior. As was shown in the explication of co-subjectivity, this is necessary to ensure reasonable communication. In structuring knowledge we solidify rules for acceptable and unacceptable behavior. These rules and roles then become guidelines for the behavior that is preferred (or required) by the culture. If it is a highly abstractive culture, the rules may even be preferred to the continuation of personal relationships. They are made for roles, not people, as they must be objective—able to cover all situations—and not subject to the personal biases of the participants. A culture that is abstractive follows the law (both written and unwritten) rather than the interpersonal feelings of its members.

Objectivity   The third apex of this triangular model is that of objectivity. A person who has reached the objectivity stage is one who has built up his or her knowledge base through abstraction (reasoning) and is now proceeding to verify its behavioral schemas and theories by testing them against the particulars of his or her environment. Objectivity is the stage at which you put your hypotheses about your culture to the test. Most of these tests go unnoticed because they are an integral part of your communication behavior. The hypotheses are conceived through the regularity of your culture, and most of them are at a subconscious level. They are the expectations you have built up from the schemas you have developed as you increased your cultural literacy. A trivial example will illustrate this point. You are introduced to a stranger, and upon finding out that her name is Susan, you are struck with the feeling, "But you don't look like a Susan," and you may even say this. The point is that all of the Susans you have known have developed in your mind the schema for "Susan," and the person before you does not fit the pattern (expectations, hypothesis) of your schema.

An important point to make at this time is that this is a subjective, associative experience just like one you might have had at the subjective stage (the first time you ever met a Susan). But you've added the ingredient of theoretical constructs around which your knowledge is organized, which produces schemas of how things should be. At the subjective stage this experience would have been purely associative and would have been deposited in your memory as such, without any attempt to abstract to a "Susan" pattern. The objective and the subjective stages are alike in that they deal with the particulars of your culture. The former deals with them from the vantage point of theory, categories, and hypotheses (the abstractive end of the continuum), while the latter has no vantage point at all.

TRANSITION

We have used a great number of concepts to describe the enculturation of an individual. It has been suggested that we evolve from subjective to co-subjective to objective participants in our culture. Each of these stages have other characteristics that help in identifying them, but from different perspectives. The particularistic-universalistic dimension is a behavioral perspective. The associative-abstractive dimension is a cognitive perspective. Perhaps it will help to differentiate the stages of enculturation by putting all of the concepts that describe each stage together. These are displayed in Table 12.

One aspect of the co-subjectivity apex of our enculturation is that it is where we become culturally literate, i.e., we are developing the cognitive structures and processes that allow us to behave normatively in our culture. Intracultural communication becomes easier, our bonding processes are facilitated, entropy decreases, and synergy increases. We develop our cybernetic (self-concept), learn the cultural rituals, and develop our personal constructs for

Table 12:   Constructs in First Culture Enculturation

SUBJECTIVE	CO-SUBJECTIVE	OBJECTIVE
Associative	Abstractive	Empiricism
Particularism	Universalism	Scientific
Personal	Consensual	Nonpersonal
Immediate	Mediate	Observational
Relationships	Information	Function
Experiential	Reasonable	Supportable
Interpersonal	Rules/Roles	Causal
Psycho-logic	Socio-logic	Formal Logic

dealing with life and the value and belief systems that give us a cultural orientation.

As we grow up in a culture, we assimilate the behaviors and beliefs of that culture through the abstraction process, acting on the information we have gained from our experiences. This is necessary for communication with our fellow citizens. Nonetheless, the knowledge that is gained through this process must be verified before we can use it to become literate in our culture. Some of us evolve faster than others, but probably none of us are aware of the evolutionary process. That is why we call it enculturation instead of learning. In the next chapter we will discuss the notion of cultural literacy and its role in understanding intercultural communication.

INDEPENDENT STUDY

Can you remember any of the incidences that indicated you were becoming enculturated into your native culture?

1. Search your memory for an incident that helped you understand your culture. Perhaps you broke a rule that you didn't know existed. Perhaps you discovered a second meaning of a word that you had been using, thinking it only had one meaning. What were the implications for future communication?

2. In a group, choose a concept and explore all of the subjective and abstractive terms associated with it. Try to organize these hierarchically. (Check out your thesaurus for some help!)

3. To check the co-subjectivity of your schemas, choose a concept like "foreigner" and detail all of the attributes you have for this concept. Now ask members of your group, fraternity, family, or class to do the same. How co-subjective are you?

CHAPTER THIRTEEN
Cultural Literacy

I have a watercolor hanging on the wall in my study that was given to me by a Costa Rican in whose home I had just eaten dinner. Six of us gringos had been invited to share an evening with a Costa Rican cultural leader, and after dinner we sat in his living room exchanging gossip about our two governments. This house contained many antiques, including a number of exciting watercolors of typical Latin American scenes. Though I spoke no Spanish, I did know that a guest did not admire one of the host's possessions, for tradition demanded that it be given to him or her. However, I did not know that the nonverbal act of looking at the paintings would be taken as such an act.

My host must have seen the admiration in my eyes; he asked (he spoke some English), "What do you think of my paintings?" I replied, "Oh, did you paint these?" A colleague translated this into Spanish and the host replied, "No, no, *un amigo mío*. Which one do you like best?" At that moment I knew I was trapped, and tried in vain to extricate myself. My Spanish colleague whispered to me to make my choice or the evening would be ruined. So, with great embarrassment, I chose the one that now hangs in my study.

What could I have done to avoid this embarrassment? Most Latin Americans do not hold to this tradition today, but the old families feel honor bound to uphold the tradition. Of course, they can also tell if someone is trying to con them out of a treasure. In this chapter we will look at what a person must know to be culturally literate and one theory of how this is accomplished. Since cultural norms define acceptable and unacceptable behavior in given situations, it is important that we know where these norms come from.

DEFINITIONS

As early as 1952 (Kroeber and Kluckhohn) there were more than 100 definitions of culture. One would think that today we would be working with a well-defined concept of it, but this is not the case. As we have seen in preceding chapters, the anthropologists are still arguing over what they study. However, most writers now use a definition similar to that of Rosengren (1986, p. 19). "The culture of human society is a set of abstract, man-made patterns of and for behavior, action, and artifacts" (p. 19). Triandis and Albert (1987) elaborate, "If that broad definition is used, it is helpful to distinguish objective culture (tools, roads, gardens) from subjective culture (norms, roles, belief systems, laws, values)" (p. 266).

The material we have presented indicates that there are at least two valid approaches to the definition of culture. One is the environmentalist/behaviorist perspective, which is physical, etic, and measurable (objective). It has three subdimensions: the natural environment, the man-made environment, and observable human behavior. The other is the cognitivist perspective, which is psychological, emic, and inferential (subjective). It has two subdimensions, content and process, with content further divided into knowledge and belief systems and process subdivided into as yet an undetermined number of processes.

It would appear that we can translate these two perspectives into the physical and psychological dimensions of culture with little or no distortion. However, a third dimension must be accounted for, namely, languages (verbal and nonverbal). They are a part of the man-made environment and human behavior on the physical dimension and of both content and process on the psychological dimension. The primary cultural role of language is communication through which social systems are established, propagated, and maintained. This schema is given in Figure 12.

These three dimensions of culture are inextricably interdependent; one cannot exist without the other. Except for perhaps the natural environment, none of them came first. By developing in harmony with each other, they have developed to the point where we no longer need to look for first

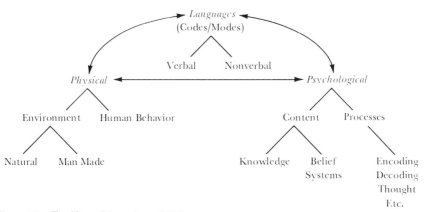

Figure 12: The Three Dimensions of Culture

causes. Certainly, this is irrelevant to a child growing up in any culture; it acquires and develops all three dimensions as part of its life cycle. None of the three are arbitrary for this child, so in that sense we are all products of our culture. But because we have the ability to make decisions (choices), we can alter our lifestyle by altering any one or all three of these dimensions. Regardless of the evolutionary level of individual cultures, all cultures remain equivalent to all others (Wagner), in the sense that they are all human systems developed to ensure the survival of their members. We must first discover our own before we can compare it to another. As we said in the beginning, culture is cognitive. We now add to that statement, *but not determined by any one of the three dimensions.* It is only through their interaction that we have a culture.

Perhaps we should quickly explain the three dimensions shown in this schema of culture. The physical dimension we take primarily from cultural materialism, as it focuses on the environment and the human's reaction to it as the basis of culture. Biological and social evolution are also of importance to this dimension. All of these approaches say that the human is environmentally determined; all behaviors are conditioned by the environment in which he or she develops. It is a behavioristic approach based on the need to be able to observe and measure *all* of the variables in the investigation of human behavior. The natural parts of the environment are all those entities ascribed to nature—geographical, geological, zoological, biological, etc. The man-made parts of the environment are all those entities (both essential and optional) created by the human being for survival. Human behavior is all observable human activity.

The psychological dimension is the subject matter of this book. Although we have seen some of the manifestations of this dimension from a theoretical perspective in the preceding chapters, much more is to be revealed. We will talk about the need to make visible our subjective culture. To some extent this is part of the cognitive content we are talking about now. It lies more in the belief systems part of content than in the knowledge part. The processes part of the psychological dimension is the most important aspect of human behavior for the understanding of intercultural communication; it is the core of the cultural orientation model. We looked into some of these processes in Chapters 5 and 6, and we will present more later.

On the language dimension we have seen that at least 14 nonverbal codes are used to communicate various purposeful messages and meanings; there may be 300 times more verbal codes. There are many important aspects of this dimension. These codes are the glue that holds a culture together, facilitates identity on both the personal and cultural levels, and has an effect on our knowledge and belief systems and the way we acquire and maintain them. They are a crucial construct in our understanding of intercultural communication. And yet the codes, too, are dependent upon the other two dimensions. We cannot stress enough the interdependency of these three dimensions.

LANGUAGE COMPETENCE

A basic background in verbal and nonverbal codes was given in Chapter 2. To help us understand the role language plays as a dimension of culture, we will now look deeper into the use of these codes. Linguists have made "a fundamental distinction between *competence* (the speaker-hearer's knowledge of his language) and *performance* (the actual use of language in concrete situations)" (Chomsky, 1965, p. 4). Although these linguists were concerned only with verbal codes, we will extend this definition to include nonverbal codes as well. This will allow us to consider both aspects of communicative behavior.

Verbal

Competency in a verbal code has three aspects: one is the ability to "invent an infinite number of sentences" (Deese, 1970, p. 35); another, the knowledge of when a specific sentence is correct; the third, an understanding of the basic message encoded into the sentence. Thus, competency involves the cognitive structures that encode and decode the signal, but from an idealistic, theoretical perspective. You are competent in English, Spanish, Chinese, etc., to the extent that you can generate all the utterances of a native speaker, know when someone is not speaking correctly, and understand what they are saying.

Competence develops with the maturation of the person and is more or less immune to the social conditions in which a person matures. Thus, we have the different dialects and speech patterns of various parts of the United States (performance), but in general the same level of verbal competency (Andersen, et al., 1987). Competence is our knowledge of the relationships between our language and its referents in the environment. This knowledge necessarily includes our vocabulary, the grammatical and syntactical rules, and their relationships to the meaning encoded into and decoded from our language (semantics). The study of meaning must involve the discourse of at least two people, as meaning is created in social space (Jacobs, 1985). A code (language) must be shared if its symbols are to have meaning (language exists for the purpose of communication). When meaning is coded into a signal, a certain amount of redundancy is coded into the signal to help clarify its meaning. For this reason it is said that a competent native speaker of English can fill in the blanks if every fifth word were omitted from a script (Motley and Borden, 1974). Thus, a basic assumption about human communication is that when a person is actively involved, she or he is anticipating events, even the signals that will be transmitted.

Nonverbal

While verbal languages are primarily informative, nonverbal languages are usually relational or meta-communicational (telling us something about the communication situation). Competence in nonverbal languages is equivalent to that in verbal language; it is the user's knowledge of the codes and when they are appropriately used. The three aspects of competency in a nonverbal code are: the ability to understand the significance of your relationship with the communicatee, the knowledge of when a specific behavior is correct, and an understanding of the basic message encoded into the signal. Thus, competency involves the cognitive structures that encode and decode the signal, but from an associative, particularistic perspective. You are competent in kinesics, haptics, proxemics, etc., to the extent that you: 1) know what behaviors are appropriate for a given relationship; 2) know when someone is not behaving correctly; and 3) understand the message encoded into a particular behavior.

Whereas we may speak only one verbal language, we all use many nonverbal languages to interact with other human beings each day. Although considerable work has been done attempting to develop both grammatical and syntactical rules for the nonverbal codes (Birdwhistell, 1952), there has not been sufficient success for nonverbal communication to be taught from this perspective. Because of their relational significance, individuals are the most important unit in understanding and using nonverbal codes. Even though there may be cultural norms for some codes, e.g., kinesics, haptics, and proxemics, the combination of individual variations and relational contexts makes it impossible to specify how one should behave in a given situation. Again, one must use the cultural orientation only as a first approximation to the behavior of the person with whom he or she is communicating.

As with verbal communication, we develop expectations in nonverbal communication as well. The traditional views of northeasterners being cool and southwesterners being warm in their first interpersonal encounters may be normative behavior, but we must be aware of these expectations when we make personal contact. When someone violates our expectations of nonverbal behavior, we are quick to evaluate this behavior and react accordingly. Deviations from expected cues may be positive or negative and precipitate vastly different reactions (Burgoon and Hale, 1988), but this evaluation may only be known to the participants.

In terms of the cultural orientation model, competency in nonverbal communication is associative and particularistic while competency in verbal communication is abstractive and universalistic.

KNOWLEDGE

Hall (1988) introduces the idea of "context" as an attribute of communication, which may help us develop our concept of culture. He says, "A high-context (HC) communication or message is one in which most of the information is either in the physical context or internalized in the person, while very little is in the coded, explicit, transmitted part of the message. A low-context (LC) communication is just the opposite; i.e., the mass of the information is vested in the explicit code" (p. 47). How much information must you encode into your signal for the communicatee to understand you? We know that we can communicate better with someone with whom we have many things in common: background, language, experiences, family, etc. This defines a high context situation. Most of the information is in the context of the situation. Thus, one needs to use few symbols to evoke the desired message in the mind of the communicatee.

Examples of a high-context situation might be a quarterback in the huddle or a mathematician giving a lecture (in both cases the criterial attribute is familiarity with the code being used); answering questions on an oral exam or helping someone in an emergency (in both cases the criterial attribute is background information); and fighting or making up with your lover (in both cases the criterial attribute is the experiences you have shared). The better you know the communicatee, the less background information you need to give when explaining an event. In fact, if you try to give more than is needed to understand you, he or she will probably cut you off.

The other side of the coin is the low-context situation, wherein little past knowledge is shared with the communicatee. Thus, the majority of the information must be encoded into the signal so the communicatee can understand what you are trying to say. Ever try to make conversation with a stranger? What is your first content area? The weather? The environment? Politics? When you tell about an experience you had, how much background do you feel you have to give to bring your audience up to where they will understand the story you are going to tell? When you are telling a story, how much information do you feel you have to give? This is one of the criterial attributes of a good comedian; he or she knows how much to tell. Such entertainers have to be able to judge the context within which the communication is taking place. A low context-situation means that you must supply most of the information in the signal you are sending.

The "Tonight Show" with Johnny Carson is a good example of high and low context. Occasionally in his monologue he will get involved in a content area in which the audience does not have sufficient background (context) for the joke and it flops. Sometimes he will try to give hints at what they should have known for the joke to have been successful. His writers must anticipate the background of the audience. This in itself is also an example of high and low context: those of you who are familiar with what I have just described are in the high-context group, and those of you who have never heard of Carson (perhaps some foreign students or those who go to bed early) are in the low-context group.

The context construct may be used with cultures, businesses, groups, families, etc. The higher the context, the less information you need encode into the signal you send; the lower the context, the more information you must send. In many ways this is similar to the restricted code/elaborated code distinctions of Bernstein (1966). Restricted codes are for those who know you and/or your subject matter. Elaborated codes are for strangers and those for whom the information must be explicit. Think of when you are learning a foreign language. You (and, you hope, your teacher and others you speak with) would use an elaborated code, i.e., give as many cues to the message encoded as possible. In Spanish, for example, it helps you pick out the verb if others use the first person pronoun when speaking to you. Later, you realize that in Spanish (and some other languages) you do not need to use the first person pronoun because the verb form is unique for that person. In fact, if you use it in some instances, you may be sending the wrong message (namely, you are egotistical). If you are with a group of native speakers of your new language, you may be able to detect a switch in their speech when they are talking to those who know the language intimately or to you. They usually elaborate much more for you—in vocabulary, syntax, and enunciation.

Cultural Symbols

Context is only one kind of knowledge a communicator must have to be effective. He or she must also know how to use the symbols of his or her society. Duncan (1968) gives us two propositions that are important to this understanding. He says, "Society arises in, and continues to exist through, the communication of significant symbols. . . . we say that the significant symbol, like all spoken symbols, is an expression experienced as a form of address to the self when it is addressed to another" (p. 44). One of the reasons why sending flowers to your lover or mother is so meaningful is that it carries an unmistakable message and meaning to each, and it evokes the same feeling in you. Of course, words are significant symbols also. Just think of some that evoke strong emotions: Jesus Christ, war, communism, mother, abortion.

The second proposition is "Man creates the significant symbols he uses in communication. . . . Machines signal through built-in message tracks, animals communicate through gesture and sound, but man, and man alone, *creates* the symbols he uses in communication. He is able not only to communicate, but to communicate about communication" (p. 46). The flexibility of language—the ease with which we are able to use it reflexively (language about language), and its ability to conjure up past experiences, to compare them with present experiences, and to project them into the future—gives us the ability to make choices and so impose structure on our perceptions and maintain or change the course of our culture. This would indicate that we should ever be in control of our language rather than vice versa. One piece of knowledge that we must have is that we create our symbols, and "Culture is acquired and transmitted by means of meaningful symbols" (Rosengren, p. 19).

A second kind of social symbol is the metaphor. Listen to men and women talk for awhile and you will be able to tell where they learned their culture. When you try to explain something, you invariably use metaphors and similes that arise out of the experiences most meaningful to you. Your best friend may be the "cream in your coffee" or the "garlic in your stew," your final decision becomes "the bottom line." Or you may use similes like it's "heaven" or "hell" or "the best thing that's ever happened to me." Reading the poetry of a culture often reveals the nature of the culture through the metaphors, similes, and other allusions to a meaning more abstract than the present situation. Abstract allusions are at least a second-level message encoded into the verbal signal. The frequency with which a culture's writers use allusions to specific environmental artifacts may be an index of the important symbols of that culture. We need to be mindful of the metaphors we use because they may be unintelligible to someone from another culture. For example, young women in Costa Rica call their boyfriends *mi media naranja*, my half of the orange. That doesn't translate into English!

A third type of knowledge that is important to cultural understanding is that of cultural myths. Whenever we speak of cultural myths, we usually think of the myths of "primitive tribes" (a myth in itself). Even with this primitive notion about myths we still should be able to realize that they form a subtle, sometimes insidious, basis for our communicative behavior. We may feel that enlightened cultures do not need myths to guide their behaviors, but it seems the myth is one of the primary ways of maintaining order (structure) in any culture. Myths are usually nonconscious; i.e., we are not consciously aware of them and their influences on the assumptions we make in our communicative behaviors. Knowing the myths operating in our culture may facilitate our communication with other cultures. Since they are probably not aware of their myths either, and they probably do not have the same myths as we do, you can see how confounding this one type of knowledge might be to intercultural understanding.

Foglesang (1982) details a number of cultural myths found in U.S. culture:

1. "The myth of Logical Necessity" says that our logic is the only correct one, when in reality it is an arbitrary rule.
2. "The myth of Technology" says that technology is not only necessary, but everyone desires it because it can only be beneficial to humankind.
3. "The myth of Development" is that the only possible direction for "good" social and economic growth is in the direction of the modern Western consumer society.
4. "The myth of Social Institutions" makes these institutions necessary to developed societies and representative of all that is good for society.
5. "The myths of the Educational System" are such that we believe that, *in terms of formal education*, the more educated you are, the better you are. Illiteracy equals poverty, and only the educated know what is best for those who are not educated (pp. 20-27).

Did any of these ring a bell?

Myths are value laden. The good-bad continuum is ever present. Because of this it is difficult not to let them affect our communicative behavior. They give us an ethnocentric world view. Extreme cases end up like the Ugly American; others are just obnoxious, frustrated, or misunderstood. We must cultivate a respect for the world view of others; learn their cultural myths; and find out what progress and development mean to them, and what their system of logic is. If increased technology means decreased humanity, is that progress?

Some cultures don't think so. Others feel that it is necessary because no one can be satisfied with the conditions in which they are now living if they are not like ours. Ethnocentrism is the basic problem in intercultural understanding.

If you firmly believe any of the above myths (after reading it you probably said, "But that's true," or "How else could it be?"), how would it affect your communicative behavior? For example, if we look at the role of formal education in U.S. culture, we can see these myths at work everyday; they are basic to the structure of our culture. Now if you try to transfer this thinking to a culture that is not constructed on these myths, you are not only destroying a culture but creating chaos in its place. Good examples of this situation can be seen in the films "The Gods Must Be Crazy" and "Out of Africa." However, we do not have to limit our examples to those of isolated tribes. Many blame the problems of the so-called Third World countries on their educational systems—they are not like ours!

Cultural Knowledge

Why do we have education systems? What is their purpose within a culture? Notice, we said systems. A paradox in U.S. culture is that we heap tremendous praise on individual creativity and success but make all of our young people submit to the same humdrum educational system. Why is this? Are we trying to make them all think alike, act alike, have the same basic knowledge, be adherents to the same political system, or propagate the myth that all persons are created equal? You may be able to come up with some more goals, but one thing the system is not doing is giving everyone the same basic knowledge. This is especially true in terms of spacial and temporal information. Every year we hear reports that the majority of high school graduates do not know the location of many of the 50 states and most of the countries of the world. Historical events are even less well known. But is this a problem? Who cares when Columbus discovered America, because he actually never set foot on "America." He only discovered some islands in the Caribbean and the coast of Costa Rica. Of course, I am being facetious, but if our educational system is supposed to make us all literate adults, what is the basis of literacy?

In other parts of this book we talk about the development of communication literacy from the original definition of literacy, viz., it involves only reading and writing. Cultural literacy is something quite different because it does not involve a skill as much as it does a knowledge. To be considered culturally literate one must have the basic background knowledge necessary to carry on general discourse in that culture without the need of supplemental information. In his preface to *Cultural Literacy*, Hirsch (1988) says, "To be culturally literate is to possess the basic information needed to thrive in the modern world. The breadth of that information is great, extending over the major domains of human activity from sports to science. It is by no means confined to 'culture' narrowly understood as an acquaintance with the arts. Nor is it confined to one social class" (p. xiii). That means that to be culturally literate we must be a high-context communicator in our culture.

Although that is a rather nebulous definition of cultural literacy, in practical terms it means that we are able to step into most conversations and understand what's being talked about. Obviously, cultural literacy is relative to the situation you are in. If you have played the game "Trivia," you know how relative knowledge can be: it may fluctuate with age, sex, social class, geographical location, and content area. But in general none of these variables are pertinent to the definition of cultural literacy. If we look at U.S. culture in general, what must we know to be considered culturally literate? One might think that with the general coverage of the United States by television networks, cable networks, newspapers, and magazines, everyone would be culturally literate whether they could read or not. However, most of our mass media give us information from the present, while much of our communication is built on information from the past. Nor is our "uniform" educational system able to impart the knowledge necessary for a high level of cultural literacy, which may be the reason why much of the material of the mass media is targeted for such a low level of literacy.

Those of you reading this text should realize that your being in post high school education gives you a leg up on cultural literacy (where does that metaphor come from and what message does it contain?). You are striving to obtain more of the shared information that will make you a member of the "educated" class of your culture. Theoretically, this means that you should be able to communicate more effectively across all classes of society because you have more information to share with prospective communicatees. "Only by accumulating shared symbols, and the shared information that the symbols represent, can we learn to communicate effectively with one another in our national community" (Hirsch, p. xvii). What does this say for intercultural communication?

Let's pursue the idea of shared information a little further. Hirsch sets the idea of cultural literacy in the context of reading. In doing so he defines it as, "the network of information that all competent readers possess. It is the background information, stored in their minds, that enables them to take up a newspaper and read it with an adequate level of comprehension, getting the point, grasping the implications, relating what they read to the unstated context which alone gives meaning to what they read" (p. 2). This means that we need to know the standard language of our culture, but more than this, we need to know the context of the symbols used in our language. This is one aspect of what Polanyi (1969) calls "tacit knowledge," the indwelling knowledge that allows us to function in our culture. Have you ever told a joke that no one caught and then tried to explain it? That's what we mean by context. You may understand all of the words but not get the point of the joke. Parents realize their children are becoming literate when they begin to catch linguistically complex jokes. Catching linguistically complex jokes in your second language also indicates a level of literacy in that language. If the joke is particular to a certain culture, then understanding it is a measure of literacy in that culture.

Table 13:   Partial Vocabulary of the Culturally Literate

abortion	Bach, Johann S.	calculus
Damascus	easier said than done	fair-weather friend
Gallup Poll	Hague, The	Ibsen, Henrik
Jackson, Jesse	Kansas City, MO	La Cucaracha (song)
macroeconomics	narcissism	O brave new worldl!
Pakistan	quark	radiation damage
Sade, Marquis de	Taj Mahal	ulcer
Valley Forge	Walkie talkie	xylem (only 4)
yellow press	Zimbabwe	1914–1918

Hirsch reports on research that developed a national vocabulary of the culturally literate. It has over 5,000 terms. To give you an idea of what type of knowledge is on this list, the seventh item of each letter of the alphabet is included in Table 13.

Are you familiar with all of these items?

Cultural Processes

Culturally literate persons have a second level of knowledge besides background knowledge. They must be able to take the limited information given in a linguistic statement (a phrase, sentence, joke) and relate it to the cultural expectations necessary to understand it. Researchers call this a schema, and it "functions as a unified system of background relationships whose visible parts stand for the rest of the schema" (Hirsch, p. 54). A schema is the prototype (most frequently occurring member) of the category of culturally expected behaviors attached to the visible parts (Quinn and Holland, 1987). Effective communication depends on how well the schemas of the communicator match the schemas of the communicatee. Perhaps this construct puts us into a low-context communication situation. If so, the following discussion should help give you the necessary background knowledge needed to understand it. If not, you can skip the next paragraph.

You meet a friend and he says, "I've got to talk to you about my roommate." What goes through your mind? What are you inclined to do, and why? The visible parts are: friend (same or opposite sex, casual, good, best, physical appearance, etc.); got (urgency, time constraints, tone of voice, personality factors, etc.); to talk (time, place, gossip, information, etc.); to you (relationship, emotions, why me, etc.); about my roommate (domain—explicit, implicit—history, relationship, etc.). With each visible point more information is called up to your quick-access memory. As you discuss this issue the information in your quick-access memory changes, as there is limited space for storage. When he says roommate, you may remember that they are having difficulties, or that he is always doing crazy things, etc., etc. However, you may not remember anything that is pertinent to this issue, so your friend may have to remind you so you can recall the proper schema. Without some background knowledge about roommates, your friend, what is involved in talking, why he wants to talk to you, and the context in general, this becomes a low-context situation, and he will have to give you a lot of background information for you to understand what is happening. The more background information you have, the higher the context and the less information is needed.

The above example comprises at least three culturally relevant concepts. One is the concept of friend. This concept covers fewer persons in Germany than it does in the United States, and fewer in the United States than in Costa Rica. Interculturally, it can be an ambiguous concept, but what schemas does it call forth? What kinds of behavior are culturally appropriate when dealing with a friend? The second is the concept of roommate. Unless you have attended a boarding school or college, you may have no background information on this concept. In some cultures this experience is reserved for only the elite. Again, what schemas does roommate call forth? Do you treat them like a friend? The third is the idea of talking to someone else about your problems. This is indefensible in some cultures, so the implications for intercultural communication problems are obvious. What is your typical reaction to this situation?

Although there may be some individual variations on the behavioral expectation for friends in the above example, the schemas for this experience are shared by the U.S. culture in general. Friends talk to friends about their roommates. Friends listen to friends when they are having a problem or success. Thus, we can call this a "cultural model." D'Andrade (1987) defines a cultural model explicitly as "a cognitive schema that is intersubjectively shared by a social group" (p. 112). Cultural models, then, are clusters of prototypical behaviors or processes that members of a culture associate with the visible concepts we use in our attempts to communicate. If the person with whom we are trying to communicate does not share these schemas, then effective communication will be much more difficult to attain. Cultural processes—the schemas associated with concepts—are one part of subjective culture and must be made visible when we attempt to communicate across cultures.

SYMBOLIC INTERACTION

We have looked at three different types of cultural knowledge, all of which can be contained under the term "tacit knowledge." One might ask how we obtain this knowledge (an extension of Chapter 12). Hertzler (1965) tell us that "knowledge is a social-cultural product, and that certain social factors influence (even determine) the mental productions of individuals, groups, and societies" (p. 132). What we know depends upon the culture and the society in which we were raised and upon the one within which we are presently living. But both of these statements make it sound like we are an object upon which society and culture act. On the contrary, neither society nor culture exists without us. You are culture and you are society. The cumulative effect of many of us with similar cultural and societal perspectives yields societal and cultural norms that are interpreted as a society and a culture for communicative purposes only.

Maines (1984) tells us that "consciousness and society are inseparable and that both are embedded in temporal ontologies. Those ontologies require that culture be viewed as meaning and that cultural activity be seen as occurring in social worlds whose boundaries are defined by the limits of effective communication" (p. 77). Communication becomes the primary ingredient in the definition of culture. Temporal ontologies say that "Human activity is always temporally located, produced, and referenced. To be human is to be in an interactional field of experience in which pasts and futures blend into the present" (p. 80). We cannot separate ourselves from the concept of culture nor the concept of time. We only exist in them, *but* they only exist in us. If we do not take a holistic (systemic) approach to life, we end up with the need to place ultimate control in the individual or the environment, but neither can stand alone.

Symbolic interactionists view culture as the perspective (world view) that allows us to share meaning (communicate, be bonded into an HCS). Culture is a human communication system, a high-level associative system as we defined them in Chapter 1. These systems only exist because humans share, are bonded together by, similar perspectives on life. There are many implications of this definition of culture. Since humans are dynamic, this means that cultures are also. The interaction we have with objects within our culture creates meaning for us (we are changed), but it also creates (changes) the culture with which we interact, and this process is continuous. Each reflects the other in a dynamic interaction through the symbols we create. This can only happen through what we call communication. With it we create common cultural symbols—the Statue of Liberty, the flag, Xerox, McDonald's, Kleenex, the "$" sign—with which our culture is communicated within the suprasystem of all cultures.

The symbolic interaction perspective rests on four constructs: "negotiation, process, emergence, and holism" (Faules and Alexander, 1978, p. 4). Communication is a constant attempt to *negotiate* the meaning of relevant cultural objects (both natural and human). As stated above, we are locked into the river of time, and this means that our communicative behavior is dynamic, changing over time. Thus, the construct, *process*. With process comes change in the meanings that *emerge* from our ongoing negotiations. This complex process of ongoing negotiations of meaning must be located within the *holistic* perspective of human behavior since a change in one component of the system affects all other components. Changes in the meaning of an object (say, marriage) are reflected in changes in cultural behavior (and vice versa). The inverse concept indicates both the complexity of the negotiations and the interaction of culture and persons.

TRANSITION

We have seen that there is no "good" definition of culture. Rather, culture results from the symbolic interactions of persons within the boundaries of effective communication. It is both objective and subjective, as it evolves from the negotiations we carry on over the meaning of salient objects in our environment, both natural and human. Most of these negotiations are performed through the use of language—the construct that bridges the two approaches to the study of culture. This leads to the realization that culture has three dimensions (physical, psychological, and linguistic), all inextricably interwoven.

Hall's concept of communication context is crucial to the development of effective intercultural communication, as all of the dimensions of knowledge are subordinate to it. We must discover the significant symbols in the other culture as well as in our own. Knowing our own significant symbols makes us culturally literate. But most of us are unaware of the symbols and the cultural processes that are associated with them. Symbols, metaphors, and myths all play a major role in structuring our culture. These are what we learn as we are enculturated into our culture.

To be culturally literate requires a background in historical and current events, but of even more importance is the understanding of the cultural processes that frame the behavioral expectations associated with the symbols of a culture. Both the cultural symbols and the cultural processes are developed through the symbolic interactions in which their meanings are negotiated. A most important aspect of this approach to culture is the realization that these negotiations take place within a human communication system and thus, the negotiated meanings affect both the persons and the system (culture); this change is then reflected into the continuing negotiation process.

Cultural literacy entails knowing much of what we have presented thus far on human communication and the personal and cultural orientation. Our personal orientation affects the schemas we develop to address the various situations in which we find ourselves. The cultural orientation will tell us something about the cultural processes most prominent in that culture. For example, if we take the concept friend, we know that a particularistic culture would choose friendship over obeying social norms, while a universalistic culture would do the opposite. In the next chapter we will look at acculturation—the process of developing cultural literacy in a second culture.

INDEPENDENT STUDY

If you found an idea in this chapter that intrigues you, check with your professor to see if you can do some research on it for your independent study. Here are some other ideas.

1. Look into the origins of some of our myths and metaphors and indicate how they might affect intercultural communication. Do other cultures have the same myths or metaphors?

2. Try translating a joke or metaphor from your first language into your second language. Check it with a native speaker of your second language. What, if any, errors did you make? Were they significant? Maybe they have a similar one but not a direct translation of yours.

3. Choose a culture and see if they have the same expectations for various relationships—friends, parents, enemies, boss/secretary, etc.—as you do.

CHAPTER FOURTEEN
Second Culture Acculturation

When learning a second language one first learns some vocabulary. The examples of first language vocabulary interfering with learning a second language vocabulary are legion. Sometimes this interference takes some strange twists. In English we are embarrassed; in Spanish, *tenemos vergüenza*. However, there is a Spanish word that sounds like embarrassed: *embarazar*—to make or become pregnant. Often when an English-speaking person learning Spanish suffers embarrassment he or she says, *estoy embarazada* (I am pregnant!). Everyone is amused except the person who said it, and she or he is even more embarrassed. Sometimes, however, this can work in reverse.

A young female college student on a trip to Costa Rica developed severe stomach pains while visiting one of the outlying cities. A Costa Rican male friend took her to a clinic where a Costa Rican doctor, who had studied in England and spoke English, examined her. Since her Spanish was not the best, her male friend accompanied her into the examination room. As the doctor was pulling down her jeans and pushing on her stomach to see where the pain was located he said (in English), "Are you embarrassed?" She said, "Yes," since there were two men in the room, she was being stripped, and her face was crimson. He responded, "Four or five months?" She immediately realized that he had reversed the usual English/Spanish language interference problem (she wasn't pregnant) and corrected the misunderstanding. Effective intercultural communication is sometimes difficult!

To understand intercultural communication, it is not enough to know the other person's language; one must also know the schemas for the concepts encoded into it. Since intercultural communication occurs between two people from different cultures, unless they are both literate in the other person's culture, the cultural dimension of communication will interfere with effective communication. Although our enculturation into our first culture evolved through a process of assimilation, cultures can be learned and literacy in a second culture can be achieved. As with first culture enculturation, communication is the primary vehicle through which one is acculturated into a second culture.

SECOND CULTURE COMMUNICATION

Communicating in a second culture (language) may lead one into some embarrassing situations. This can happen even if the language of that culture is the same as your own. For example, if you travel to England where the custom is to knock on your door to wake you up in the morning, it is not uncommon to be asked, before retiring, at what time you would like to be knocked up in the morning. In North American slang, of course, that has an entirely different meaning! How, then, can we learn another culture?

When you first arrive in another culture you will be hit with a psychological situation in which you feel you have lost control. We call this culture shock, "Psychological reactions to unfamiliar environments (Furnham and Bochner, 1986). One goes through four phases in coping with a new culture: The Tourist phase—everything is new and exciting; The Crisis phase—when you become disenchanted with the new culture and realize the many differences between yours (good) and theirs (bad); The Adjustment phase—when you accept the cultural differences and begin to construct an identity within the new culture: and the Back-to-Normal phase—when you feel at home in your new culture (Copeland and Griggs, 1985). This doesn't mean that you have adopted the new culture, but you have adapted to it (Kohls, 1979; Casse, 1979; Kim and Gudykunst, 1987).

Overcoming culture shock (adapting to your new culture) requires extensive communication. Kim (1979) says "the more the immigrant interpersonally communicates and the more he uses the mass media, the greater will be the refinement of his perception of the host society" (p. 437). It is through communication that we make visible each other's culture; we develop the context needed for understanding the schemas of each culture. We must also develop a new self-concept within the dimensions of the new culture. To do this we must reevaluate all five of the subsystems of our cybernetic (see Chapter 1). We must recreate the constructs with which we construe our sense of reality. Kelly (1963) says, "Man looks at his world through transparent patterns or templates which he creates and then attempts to fit over the realities of which the world is composed. The fit is not always very good. Yet without such patterns the world appears to be such an undifferentiated homogeneity that man is unable to make any sense out of it. Even a poor fit is more helpful to him than nothing at all" (pp. 8-9). We become acutely aware of how poor the fit is when adapting to a new culture, for our first culture's constructs continually interfere.

SECOND CULTURE LEARNING

The term "learning" has a connotation of detachment, like a culture is some-thing you can sit down and learn from a book, movies, etc. We usually approach it this way in our courses in intercultural communication. This is only learning *about* a culture, however. Learning about something may help us when we become involved with that something, but it cannot take the place of experiencing that something, e.g., love, sex, marriage. Thus, we must find a way not only to learn about a culture but also to experience the culture so we can assimilate its nuances into the psychological constructs developed in our second culture acculturation.

Language

As we have seen, language is a decidedly important part of culture, for it is the tool by which we both organize our cognitive structure (knowledge) and communicate. Thus, when we are thinking of becoming acculturated into another culture, the first thing we should think about is its language. Can you imagine being culturally erudite without knowing the language? That's like being a jetsetter without any money! So, the first step is to learn the language. We will not spend much time on this aspect, as there are hundreds of books on the subject, but one should always seek to learn the language and the culture at the same time (Levine, et al., 1987). Several points can be made about second language learning that will help us understand the relatively un-charted waters of second culture learning.

Anyone who has tried to learn a second language knows the frustrations that occur before fluency is realized. Even those programs that teach the second language from a communication perspective and emphasize complete saturation in the second culture are not able to overcome the frustration of first language interference. Why is this? We had no problems like this with our first language! But, what did we have with our first language? We had innate processes that assimilated our experiences with the first language into schemas that allowed us to expand our communicativeness exponentially once it was triggered. Once these processes accomplish their purpose, our first language becomes dominant, and everything we learn thereafter is in some way as-sociated with that language (either we learn it through our language or we use this language to talk about it). Since our first language dominates the psychological constructs of our cognitive structure, it permits the structure of our first language to dominate the acquisition process of the second language. The episode given at the beginning of this chapter is an example of the dominance of first language vocabulary.

Syntax also gives one problems. In English, adjectives almost always precede the noun. Those familiar with Spanish realize that adjectives may be placed before or after the noun and that their position gives different meanings to the phrase. Would you rather be *las grandes mujeres* (the great women) or *las mujeres grandes* (the big women)?; *el hombre medio* (the average man) or *medio hombre* (half a man)? It should be obvious that each language has its own peculiar syntax.

Since Spanish is a gender-based language (and English is not), it requires rules of grammar that English does not. One is that articles and adjectives agree in number and gender with their nouns. *El buen profesor* (the good professor—male) or *la buena profesora* (the good professor—female). If you let English grammar interfere you sound like a poorly educated person.

Yet another native language characteristic interferes with second language learning and usage. As our native language evolves our ears grow accustomed to the flow of sound we call speech. We are unaware that there are no words in normal speech—only sounds. A colleague used this example. Two friends meet on the street around noon and one says, "Jeet?" and the other answers, "No, jew?" How would a non-native speaker of English ever know that they were saying "Did you eat?" and "No. Did you?" It is easy to tell a non-native speaker of a language (until they are really fluent) by the way they enunciate their words when they speak. All of this goes along with the speed at which we speak. The language learner always feels that native speakers talk too fast. Of course, it is really that the second language learner listens too slowly. She or he is continually listening for *words*, hearing some sounds that sound like their native language and trying to block out the sound pattern interference from their first language.

As was indicated in earlier chapters, language is learned to communicate. Thus, the semantic component is essential to language learning. Words, phrases, concepts are used to apprehend portions of semantic space. We are seldom aware of the semanticality of words during first language development (unless we consciously try to learn a new word each day—or something like that). However, when we learn a second language we are constantly aware of this because we almost always define the new words in terms of our first language. This, of course, takes away from the richness of the new language, and until we realize that there is almost never a one-to-one translation of meaning from one language to another, we will never lose the constraints placed upon our second language by our first. We may write or speak words in the second language but will continue to use the structure of our first.

Culture

As in the learning of a second language one must ignore the structuring vocabulary, grammar, and syntax of the native language and replace it with that of the second language to be fluent in that language, so, too, in the learning of a second culture one must ignore the structuring values and schemas of his or her native culture and replace them with those of the second culture to be literate in the second culture.

When one is called upon to translate between two languages, one takes the meaning found in the first language and creates a congruent meaning in the second language using the structures of the two languages only as facilitators of meaning. Thus, bilingualism is a matter of semantics, not algorithms. One way of illustrating this is to find an equivalent idiom in the two languages. For example: Still water runs deep = *Del agua mansa me libre Dios* (literally, God keeps me from still water).

Analogously, understanding the behavior of a second culture means putting aside the values and schemas of one's native culture and replacing them with those of the second culture. There is no word analogous to semantics to use in second culture acculturation. The concept is that of transforming one's values into one's behavior, operationalizing one's values. This assumes that one's behavior emanates from one's value structure through various operationalization schemas. However, just as it is not possible to translate from one language to another by using linguistic algorithms, neither is it possible to translate from one culture to another by using transformations of behavioral schemas. An example may help make this clear.

In the United States it is customary for females to shake hands when being introduced. An informant told us that the same was true in Costa Rica. However, our informant, being male, was not bicultural in the male and female subcultures of his native culture. In 1979 a young U.S. female in Costa Rica for the first time was introduced to several women of different socioeconomic classes. She dutifully applied the schema she had been given. It wasn't until shaking hands with the maid who came in to clean her room that she learned (to her horror!) that to "shake hands" with another woman was the sign of a lesbian in her socioeconomic class (and, the maid thought, in others also). Non-lesbians grasp forearms. How could our North American female have known this Costa Rican operationalization of values?

What does it mean to learn another culture? Is there a vocabulary, syntax, grammar, and semantic? Partly yes, as learning the language of the culture is part of learning the culture. But, although language may reflect some of the values of a culture, it does not reflect all of the dimensions that must be considered in differentiating among cultures. If we go back to the models presented in Chapter 12, we realize that learning itself is an experience. Thus, it is associative and subjective. Although we cannot duplicate an experience with language, we can talk about it, associate words with it. For example, how would you characterize the last meal you had in a restaurant? What did you have? Where and when did you have it? If you now think about your thought processes as you were answering these questions, you realize that the first answer required abstraction, the second necessitated the association of names with foods, and the third made you probe your sense of space and time (nonverbal codes) for images with which you could associate a verbal code.

Now try the same exercise in your second language. Did you have to translate from one to the other (remember the association between the names of foods in the two languages)? Could you translate the name of the restaurant from your first language into your second language? (McDonald's is the same in every language, both verbally and nonverbally!) The fact that our first language is so dominant in the learning process makes it almost impossible to learn a second culture. Let's use another model to help us visualize this process.

The best way to understand this model is to let your mind go blank and see what mental pictures or words occur. As your mind moves through its meanderings, you will experience associations. On the language level we have probably all taken psychological exams where they ask you to write down the first word that comes to mind as you read a list of words. Word association has been used to map the mind much like a thesaurus. But other memories are associated with words besides other words (remember the schemas in Chapter 13). The main point is that a number of other things are associated with every experience—for instance, other experiences immediately preceding and succeeding this one, other experiences in the same location (and if it is a place you frequent, there may be a lot of these), and all of the sensations gathered by our senses (emotions, language, people, behaviors, evaluations, expectations). When you recall this experience, depending on your memory, you may be able to recall most of these associations by choosing the correct psychological cue. By choosing another cue you may be able to associate this experience with another experience in another place, at another time.

Now let's put you in another culture into which you are trying to become acculturated. You have started to learn the language, so you know some words, syntax, and grammar, but you are still using your first culture's semantic space to figure out what everything means. You are in San Pedro, Costa Rica, and you are starving (that sensation is probably the same in every culture). You have a copy of the *Tico Times* (an English newspaper) with you, and you know there are a lot of restaurants advertised in it. You open it and find an ad that reads:

RESTAURANT
La Galería
125m Oeste de ICE, San Pedro

What goes through your mind? The word *Oeste* looks familiar—does it mean east or west? Oh, yes. It means west. Which way is west? What does *m* mean—miles? No, meters. How far is a meter? I think *de* means "of" but what is *ICE*? It doesn't freeze in Costa Rica; how can they have ice? But it is a restaurant and it is in San Pedro! You close the newspaper and walk home, frustrated by your experience. Now let's analyze this example to see some of the first culture interferences that are affecting your second culture acculturation.

One is irresistibly drawn to information in their first language—thus, the English newspaper. This may help you know what is going on in the world around you, but it will give you very little indoctrination into your new culture. Fortunately for you, you hit upon an ad that did have some of the culture contained in it. The mixture of English and Spanish is quite prevalent in the larger cities and may be a good way to ease into the culture. Nevertheless, you have to remember (or learn) some of the English/Spanish equivalents. For example, most of the world is on the metric system; consequently, you must either learn the conversions or carry a converter with you.

In this instance a converter wouldn't do you much good because you have to know what the measurement means in this culture. Instead of using *cuadras* (blocks) as a unit of measure in the cities, they use 100 meters. The distance in the ad is about a block and a quarter. In actuality, if you were to measure 125m you would still be in the first block, for these two blocks are very long. The fact that you were able to come up with the English equivalent for *oeste* is to your credit, but since we are not used to giving directions by east or west, it doesn't do you much good. Perhaps this culture is more associative (tied closer to natural phenomena) than we are; they use the most basic directors—north, south, east, west—to orientate themselves.

The use of the term "means" in the above example gets to the heart of the problems of second language and culture learning. When we say "What does that mean," what we *mean* is, What is its English equivalent, for if we can find that, then we can use it to apprehend our old familiar semantic space (except that in the case of meters we have just seen that our old semantic space is not reliable!). Mistaking *ICE* for ice is another nearly irresistible urge. Anything that looks like English should be! In this case *ICE*, which should be written *I.C.E.* but usually isn't, stands for *Instituto Costarricense de Electricidad* (the electric company), and it is housed in a huge building that can be seen from anywhere in San Pedro. That is why it is used as the anchor for most directions.

Would it not be much simpler, you say, just to use the street number of the restaurant? Then you could buy a map of the city and find everything you wanted. Probably, but in many cultures this would be impossible because there are no house numbers and, in smaller towns and suburbs, no street names. The point being that if you do not know the territory, you can't get there! Why? There are probably lots of reasons, but two that might help you understand the culture are: being closer to the associative/subjective end of the continuum, this is a relational culture. They like to meet and talk with people. Giving directions can lead to 30 minutes of conversation and a feeling of interpersonal pleasure. A second reason may be one of security. You will always know who the strangers are! In a family-oriented culture this is important. This point is highlighted by the fact that sometimes the anchor used in their directions no longer exists—a huge tree which has long since died and been cut down or a church that burned 50 years ago. This is a nonmobile society!

The fact that this experience made you frustrated and tied you to your new home (perhaps with a Costa Rican family who spoke no English, so you felt isolated) indicates that you are developing feelings about this culture—probably negative. Back home we have street signs, house numbers, etc., etc., etc., and the comparisons with the first culture are constantly with us. Though we may be able to laugh about our frustrations, they still affect the way we feel about our second culture, and this affects the acculturation process. But how can we not compare the new with the old, the unknown with the known? We must have an anchor for our cognitive structure or we will go crazy. It is extremely difficult to ignore our old culture and let that void be filled with the new. Unfortunately, that is what must be done. Saturation in a new culture will help, but it is not easy.

A SECOND CULTURE ACCULTURATION MODEL

One could give examples of cultural interference for nearly every aspect of acculturation. But it would appear to be more useful to look at second culture acculturation from a more cognitive perspective to try and find some of the constructs that may lend some structure to the acculturation process and relieve some of the pain. Again we turn to Glenn's theories. Since contact with a culture must be subjective, we can assume that it is also associative (see Table 12). This is the nature of the subjective apex of the acculturation model. Because most cultural contact takes place in a communication situation, it is also co-subjective, and we can assume it is abstractive. Perhaps we can use these dimensions as an anchor for our second culture acculturation.

We have shown that it is extremely difficult, if not impossible, to approach second culture acculturation in the way in which we were enculturated into our first culture. True, our experiences are subjective and associative, as all experiences are, but the problem is that we already have psychological constructs from our first culture that we apply to these experiences. Thus, we are using the objectivity schemas (testing our hypotheses) of enculturation rather than the abstractive schemas (developing simple psychological constructs), which lead to the co-subjective stage. Remember that in the objective phase we are trying to support hypotheses developed from the co-subjective phase. In our present predicament we are trying to interpret abstractions from one culture using psychological constructs from another culture.

If we were even open-minded enough to test our hypotheses (drawn from our first culture), we would be ahead of the game. But we are usually only applying them as regulative rules and being frustrated when they do not fit the experiences we are having. Or worse, thinking they fit when they do not, but not knowing the culture well enough to know the difference. Somehow we must see associations among behaviors and be able to abstract constructs that we can use to understand and communicate with the new culture. This means that we must be actively engaged in all three apexes of the model.

Cognitive Processes

Perhaps a modification of Glenn's model for meaning (Figure 11) will help us reason through this dilemma. Figure 13 is an attempt to model how meaning is developed during second culture acculturation. The term quasi-

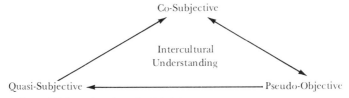

Figure 13: A Second Culture Acculturation Model

subjective is used as the primary perception apex to indicate that the associations we make with experiences in a new culture are never as open, innocent, and purely subjective as experiences were when we were children in our first culture (although the younger you are when entering a second culture the more closely they will approximate them). These associations are necessarily subjective, but they are also affected by the constructs of our first culture and the information picked up through communication with the second culture specifically about that culture.

In your first culture you may have been a child who always asked "why?". It is doubtful, however, that you ever got the cultural answer. Now you have authorities with whom you can discuss similarities and differences you have observed between your first culture and your new culture. From these experiences and the other information available to us, we must abstract the correct information and develop psychological constructs that will enable us to understand the behaviors of the new culture and to be able to communicate effectively and authentically with its members. This means developing an understanding of their values and beliefs, perhaps seeing some of their schemas, but most certainly developing a cognitive map of their attitudinal frame of reference. In short, learning their cultural orientation. With these tools we can both communicate with them and communicate about them to members of both cultures.

As we move from quasi-subjectivity to co-subjectivity, we are developing the understanding of the new culture to the extent that we can communicate with them *as one of them* (with the same tacit knowledge). This can be done on two levels: We can *play the role* of the culture, or we can *take the role* of the culture. In the former we know and understand the cultural orientation (cognitively) of the new culture but do not adopt it as our own, as we do in the latter.

Role playing is an important part of the pseudo-objective phase of our second culture acculturation. As we move from the quasi-subjective to the co-subjective and find constructs that appear to explain the second culture's behaviors, we must check these constructs against reality. In the second culture acculturation model we call this pseudo-objectivity. It is called "pseudo" because at this point in our acculturation, we will have constructs from our first culture competing with the development of constructs from our second culture so that the simple objectivity of our first culture will be impossible.

One important point to remember is, as we do not know our culture, so, too, they probably do not know theirs. Thus, asking them if this is why they do such and so will probably not get a legitimate answer. The process must be more psychological (revealing their psycho-logic) and unobtrusive. This is one reason why it is called role playing. We project ourselves into the position of a native and try to let the beliefs and values we have found in this culture direct our behavior. If our hypotheses are supported and the resulting communication is successful, we may continue to use these values, beliefs, and the cognitive constructs we have developed to function in this culture. If they are not supported, we must go back to the drawing board, do more investigation, and try again. The continuation of this process will enable us to be bicultural because we will develop a competency in the culture just as we develop a competency in the language. Developing a proficiency in either takes much longer, as it involves developing the cognitive structures that operationalize the beliefs and values.*

A number of different constructs must be taken into account as we attempt to become competent in another culture. In trying to establish these for any given culture, one must be extremely careful that they are not made into stereotypes and thus rigidify the thinking of the communicators. Perhaps the single most important concept in intercultural communication is that the communicators have an open mind. This does not mean that they have no standards, principles, or goals, but rather that they are able to use the abstraction process effectively by selecting the important aspects of the culture to include in their constructs while rejecting the superfluous. The other contributions of General Semantics given in Chapter 2 can also help us obtain more verifiable cognitive constructs of our second culture: Awareness, Indexing, Labeling, and Words as Maps (Johnson, 1946; Hayakawa, 1939; and Weinberg, 1959).

Visualizing Acculturation

Talking about the acculturation process can help you develop images in your mind of how it takes place and can point out some of the problem areas. But using an example with a visual model usually makes it clearer. This is dangerous, however, as it necessarily involves the abstraction process and, therefore, only gives you selected information. To get the full picture you must involve yourself in the acculturation process, using what you have learned as a guide and developing your own strategies for operationalizing this knowledge. We will use the concept of time (the nonverbal code, chronemics)

---

*We will not attempt to develop the behavioral model for second culture acculturation. One of the underlying assumptions of this theory is that when the mind develops the cognitive structures to use a given belief or value as the source of one's behavior, it will also create the appropriate cognitive structures to operationalize this belief or value. We are explicating an epistemological model, not a behavioral one.

to illustrate the acculturation process. The schema in Figure 14 may help you visualize it.

As we have noted elsewhere, after we learn our first language, the experiences we have had with the concepts associated with that language become transparent and our involvement with these concepts is abstracted to the language level. Unless we are called upon to recall a specific incident, the channels involved with subsequent experiences are most often verbal. When we begin to learn Spanish, or any second language, whether it is in a classroom or in a culture, the experiences associated with the construct "time" go directly to the language level after passing through our first language structures. Although we may have occasion to experience some of the differences in the concept of time between the two cultures, these experiences will be minimal compared to the multitude of experiences we have had in our first culture.

As seen in Figure 14, three major terms in Spanish deal with the concept for which we use the term time. We say, "What time is it?"; they say, *¿Qué hora es?* We say, "from time to time"; they say, *de vez en cuando.* We say, "Do you have the time?"; they say, *¿Tiene el tiempo?* In none of these cases can the other Spanish words for time be substituted for the one used. This is further complicated by the fact that *tiempo* also signifies the weather. Thus, we have to compartmentalize our understanding of time into at least three different areas, and even then there is probably not a perfect fit between what we mean by time in English and what is meant in Spanish.

If we take time to study the concept of time, we find that our construct has several demarcations. There is *formal time*—the time marked by calendars, birthdays, and seasons; *technical time*—that which is marked by stop watches, countdowns, and schedules; and *informal time*—that which is open to our interpretation, like appointments, sleeping hours, and leisure time (Hall, 1959). Unfortunately, not many cultures interpret these types of time in the same way

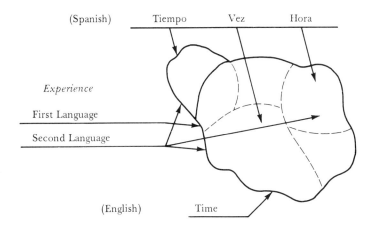

Figure 14:   Latino/Anglo Intercultural Time

(Ruhly, 1976). We in the United States have tried to take appointments out of informal time and put them into technical time; we are a displaced-point time culture. Others have taken schedules out of technical time and put them into informal time; they are diffused-point time cultures. When members of these two cultures try to communicate, there are usually misunderstandings.

Latin American countries have the stigma (for *estadounidenses*) of being *mañana* cultures. However, if you were to go to Costa Rica you would not get that feeling immediately. In the business and education sectors, most people wear watches, there are clocks in strategic places (though not as many as we have), formal time is made obvious by the large number of holidays, and most technical and informal time is reasonably close to ours. Differences begin to surface when you try to catch your favorite show on television, though; some of these schedules tend to slip a little! Costa Ricans have not yet moved personal appointments into technical time (although there is definitely movement in that direction), and so they may slip a lot. Nonetheless, the urgency with which the Ticos get on and off buses would make you believe that they were in a bigger rush than we are.

Another example is notable. When we refer to using time for some purpose, we talk about "spending" time as though it were money and we had only a limited amount. Asimov (1983) gives the perfect example: "You can replace money if you lose a wallet; buy a new typewriter or word-processor if your house is burglarized; marry again if a divorce overtakes you—but the hour that has vanished unnecessarily will never return" (p. 43). In opposition to this psychological construct for time, Latin Americans talk about *pasar tiempo* (passing time), but never *gastar tiempo* (spending time). To make this point even more pronounced, we ask, "Is your watch running?"; they say ¿*camina su reloj?* (Is your watch walking?); while both cultures say, "Is your watch working?" (¿*trabaja su reloj?*). This is also an example of the language of a culture reflecting its values and beliefs.

TRANSITION

It seems that we must struggle to separate the psychological constructs of our first culture from those of our second while not building emotional constructs that will interfere with our future acculturation. In second culture acculturation we have the advantage of being able to use outside sources to help us with this struggle. As we become more and more deeply involved with our second culture, we may begin to sense that this struggle may never end, for individual differences in the culture tend to make any generalizations suspect. This means that, as in any interpersonal communication situation, the person you are communicating with must be considered unique and that the cultural constructs you have developed can only be used as guidelines in your negotiations. However, these constructs—if they are valid—can speed the process of understanding and enhance the possibility of effective communication.

One of the major contributors to an efficient second culture acculturation is to find out its cultural orientation. Much of this can be done by reading about the culture with a specific focus on its behavior patterns (particularistic-universalistic), its educational process (associative-abstractive), and its treatment of subcultures (closed-minded/open-minded). Using an etic and an emic approach can enhance your chances for success. Your own cultural orientation (are you open, aware, accepting?) will help you gain a reciprocal response from them. Remember, a lot of what you see and hear will be noise in your system because you will be interpreting it from your first culture's frame of reference.

In this chapter we have gone through a series of examples to try and make the acculturation process more understandable. The interference between the psychological constructs of the first and the second culture is nearly insurmountable, as we must have some anchor for our thought processes. Approaching a second culture subjectively may help us make our cultural schemas visible at the same time we are discovering theirs. This should enhance our ability to communicate effectively with another culture. We will look more deeply into the processes of understanding intercultural communication in the next chapter.

INDEPENDENT STUDY

How can you gain knowledge about second culture acculturation without actually going through the process? Here are some suggestions.

1. Many of the movies you see have aspects of culture that play a role in the plot. Films about aliens, foreigners, and subcultures can all be analyzed from a cultural orientation point of view. Choose one and do an analysis of the interferences between the psychological constructs of the two cultures.

2. We have all moved from one place to another—moving to a new town, going to a new school, coming to college—and in this way experienced something of a culture shock. Using the four phases of coping with a new culture, analyze your own feelings and behaviors in one such move. When did you feel at home?

3. Using the four phases of coping with a new culture, interview several foreign students on your campus to see if they went through these phases. Can you see ways in which your culture could have made it easier on them?

CHAPTER FIFTEEN
Developing Intercultural Understanding

I am a rather nonsocial person—friendly, but detached—and thus, I have probably missed out on a lot of human experiences. Vicarious subjectivity just doesn't do it; it's like reading a sex manual and saying you have lost your virginity. To understand a culture's communicative behavior, you must be involved both physically and psychologically in its behavioral patterns. This was brought home to me one night in a disco in San José, Costa Rica.

I was taking intensive Spanish, and the teachers invited all of the students to a typical disco to celebrate something. I usually do not dance, but I love the music. I arrived late and sat with another male wallflower listening to a great band. At midnight two of the teachers (female) decided that we had sat long enough and literally dragged the two of us onto the dance floor. I have never had such an experience, before or since. By the end of the first song, I was into the music and dance, and when the second song was a slow one, I was into the culture! Costa Ricans are great dancers and their styles do not let you remain objective very long—especially when slow dancing. I never knew two bodies could fit together so snugly on a dance floor!

To complete the subjectivity of this experience, we discussed its implications to intercultural communication (a rather objective maneuver) for some time. It led to a much deeper understanding of the Costa Rican culture and the woman with whom I had danced. When we communicate, we create the reality of the moment, with each communicator building this reality on the constructs of his or her own cultural literacy (in both cultures). By attributing meaning to another's communiqué, we are construing his or her personal constructs but from our own cultural perspective. Understanding occurs when the construal of another's personal constructs is congruent with his or her construal of them. In this chapter we will look at a number of sets of constructs that will enable us to understand intercultural communication better.

CREATING CULTURE

One might use many approaches to argue the merits of cultural materialism and cognitive anthropology. If we use an evolutionary model, asking how different cultures develop, we can assume one of the two perspectives we mentioned in Chapter 6: culture is the reaction of humans to the environment, or culture is the cognitive constructs that allows humans to live in an environment. For the former, cognitive constructs are incidental to the process of creating culture, and for the latter, the environment is incidental to the creation of culture. The same can be said of these two approaches when we, through our lifetime, create our culture, or become enculturated. (Ontogeny recapitulates phylogeny.) But in this chapter our focus is on a third time frame, that of the intercultural communication event. How does one create (make visible) his or her culture in the process of creating (making visible) the culture of a person with whom he or she is communicating?

We mentioned in Chapter 6 that one indicator of our understanding of another culture is our ability to know what behaviors are acceptable in that culture and how they differ from normal behavior in our own culture. We are free to choose the behaviors that will characterize us in the host culture, but we should know the consequences of normal and deviant behavior in that culture. To have this understanding means that we have made visible the underlying cultural constructs of both the host culture and our own. But how do we find these constructs? Do we create them on the spot? Are they merely rules we have learned in our childhood? Are they abstract or concrete? Are they universal or particular to each event and each culture?

Human communication consists of many cognitive processes: the encoding, transmission, reception, and decoding of messages and meanings contained in verbal and nonverbal signals. We know that many times we respond to a signal that we have just received based on our perception of the signal and of the context in which it was sent. At other times we create the stimulus for someone else. In either case our cognitive constructs are shaping a part of the communication event, viz., the decoding or the encoding of the communiqué.

We know that we behave: we react to stimuli, and we also produce stimuli. Acts of life are observable, and we can see how different cultures conduct themselves in similar situations. For example, eating; fingers were made before forks, and so were chopsticks. There are different types of foods, different times of the day for eating, different ways of preparing food, and different protocols for invited guests. How do you react to any of these when they are different from what you are used to in your culture? Your family? How do you manage these aspects of eating when you are host to someone from another culture? to someone from another family? Are you sensitive to the other person's lack of knowledge of your norms and perhaps of his or her own norms?

We all have cultural constructs: i.e., knowledge of our way of life (content) and cognitive constructs (belief systems and preferred patterns of thought). Thus, we make choices; choices as to whether we will call our friends on the telephone, talk to them face to face, write a letter, or talk to them at all, even if we have just received a message encoded in the signal "please keep in touch" (a haptic metaphor that could have many meanings but bears the normative message of maintaining communicative contact). So we can choose to respond to stimuli or we can create stimuli of our own.

Cultural behaviors and their consequences (architecture, arts, social structures) are visible; cultural constructs (knowledge, belief systems, thought patterns) are not. The common element between these two aspects of culture is language, both verbal and nonverbal. Cultural materialism says that language was neither the result of the infrastructure nor did it create the infrastructure. At one point in time the cognitivists believed that it (language) played both roles (Burk, 1974). It was felt that language reflects the aspects of the infrastructure that are important to a culture and determines the perceptual and organizational patterns found in the cognitive constructs of a culture. Seems like a nice arrangement, doesn't it? Unfortunately, when language began to be studied with these ideas in mind, the researchers quickly forgot about the reflection and concentrated on trying to discover the cognitive constructs determined by the language.

THE SAPIR-WHORF HYPOTHESIS

Since language has been mentioned as the link between cultural behavior and cultural constructs, we must take a closer look at the work that has been done to define the nature of this connection. I think you will find that the theories presented here will raise your interest in language and give you an awareness that will help you focus on the language used by the other culture when you are engaged in intercultural communication.

Noted linguist Edward Sapir was one of the first scholars to consider the connection between language and culture. In his first major writing on the subject, he concluded that, "Language and our thought-grooves are inextricably interrelated, are, in a sense, one and the same. . . . it follows that the infinite variability of linguistic form, (is) another name for the infinite variability of the actual process of thought" (1921, pp. 217-18). By equating language and thought you would think Sapir would equate language and culture. But he concludes by saying,

> Nor can I believe that culture and language are in any true sense causally related. . . . It can be shown that culture has an innate form, a series of contours, quite apart from subject-matter of any description whatsoever, we have a something in culture that may serve as a term of comparison with and possibly a means of relating it to language. But until such purely formal patterns of culture are discovered and laid bare, we shall do well to hold the drifts of language and of

culture to be non-comparable and unrelated processes. From this it follows that all attempts to connect particular types of linguistic morphology with certain correlated stages of cultural development are vain (pp. 218-19).

So one's thought patterns and language were one and the same, but they had no causal relationship with culture in either direction, i.e., caused by the infrastructure or causing the infrastructure. The only connection Sapir found, at this time, was, "It goes without saying that the mere content of language is intimately related to culture. . . . In the sense that the vocabulary of a language more or less faithfully reflects the culture whose purposes it serves it is perfectly true that the history of language and the history of culture move along parallel lines" (p. 219). I think we would all agree with this statement. We need only look at American English (a good class project) to see that our vocabulary changes with the times—sputnik, glasnost, perestroika.

Aside from vocabulary it would appear that Sapir did not believe that language and culture had any great effect on each other. However, in his later writings he came down much harder on the notion that language and culture were inextricably interwoven. In a paper in 1928 he wrote,

> Human beings do not live in the objective world alone, nor alone in the world of social activity as ordinarily understood, but are very much at the mercy of the particular language which has become the medium of expression for their society. It is quite an illusion to imagine that one adjusts to reality essentially without the use of language and that language is merely an incidental means of solving specific problems of communication or reflection. The fact of the matter is that the "real world" is to a large extent unconsciously built up on the language habits of the group. . . . We see and hear and otherwise experience very largely as we do because the language habits of our community predispose certain choices of interpretation (Sapir in Landar, 1966, p. 223).

This statement seems to be the beginning of the Sapir-Whorf hypothesis concerning the role of language in perception and other cognitive processes.

Whorf raises some questions about the whole system of language and culture when he says,

> How does such a network of language, culture, and behavior come about historically? Which was first: the language patterns or the cultural norms? In main they have grown up together, constantly influencing each other. But in this partnership the nature of the language is the factor that limits free plasticity and rigidifies channels of development in the more autocratic way. This is so because a language is a system, not just an assemblage of norms. . . . There are connections but not correlations or diagnostic correspondences between cultural norms and linguistic patterns (Whorf, 1956a, pp. 156, 159).

What do you think about this? Does your language affect your thinking? Perception? Knowledge? If you know another language well, does it help or hinder your reflection on a topic, concept, or signal? Whorf spells out rather clearly how he feels about this.

> We dissect nature along lines laid down by our native languages. The categories and types that we isolate from the world of phenomena we do not find there because they stare every observer in the face; on the contrary, the world is presented in a kaleidoscopic flux of impressions which has to be organized by our minds—and this means largely by the linguistic systems in our minds. We cut nature up, organize it into concepts, and ascribe significance as we do, largely because we are parties to an agreement to organize it in this way—an agreement that holds throughout our speech community and is codified in the patterns of our language. The agreement is, of course, an implicit and unstated one, BUT ITS TERMS ARE ABSOLUTELY OBLIGATORY; we cannot talk at all except by subscribing to the organization and classification of data which the agreement decrees. . . . We are thus introduced to a new principle of relativity, which holds that all observers are not led by the same physical evidence to the same picture of the universe, unless their linguistic backgrounds are similar, or can in some way be calibrated (Whorf, 1956b, pp. 213-14).

One of the important aspects of this brief review of the Sapir-Whorf hypothesis is the truism stated above. It is absolutely necessary that we adhere to the conventions of our language if we expect to communicate with anyone. Communication operates on the basis of a shared code, meaning the vocabulary, grammar, and syntax by which a message is encoded into a signal. If, for example, you encode a message using English rules of grammar and syntax and a direct translation of the English words into a Spanish equivalent, it will be nearly impossible for a monolingual Spanish speaker to understand you. We usually do this when we are first learning the language, and call it Spanglish. If you are aware of the systemic nature of language, you will realize at this stage that you do not have a good command of the language yet (the native speaker will surely be aware of this).

There are other implications of this hypothesis about the role of language. Hoijer (1954) sums up the important aspects of this perspective on the role of language:

> The central idea of the Sapir-Whorf hypothesis is that language functions, not simply as a device for reporting experience, but also, and more significantly, as a way of defining experience for its speakers. . . . language plays a large and significant role in the totality of culture. Far from being simply a technique of communication, it is itself a way of directing the perceptions of its speakers and it provides for them habitual modes of analyzing experience into significant categories. And to the extent that languages differ markedly from each other, so should we expect to find significant and formidable barriers to cross-cultural communication and understanding (pp. 93, 94).

Unfortunately, most of the control attributed to language is beneath our conscious awareness. So, what has this look at the Sapir-Whorf hypothesis generated for us in terms of creating culture in the immediate time frame? According to this hypothesis, "linguistic structure predisposes the individual to pay attention to some things more than others, or to perceive things in one mode rather than in others, even though with respect to his general perceptual capacities he is no different, on average, from users of other languages"

(Carroll, 1963, p. 289). Because all languages have grammars, and in all languages one can create categories of things, one becomes habituated into seeing the world as he or she can describe it in his or her language. That does not change the "shape of reality" to someone else. If two people from two different cultures with two different languages can take the time to create each other's culture, then they will have a good chance at understanding each other. Usually, we assume the other person sees the world the way we do.

One aspect of this hypothesis that was touched on but not resolved is the connection between language and thought. If language affects our conceptualization, does it not also affect our thinking? Burk (1974) says that "A relationship between language and thought is believed to exist but the relationship is not DIRECT. The human cognitive structure is not directly available to study" (p. 33). We know that we can and do think without language, but to make our thoughts communicable they must be put into a verbal or nonverbal code that can be transmitted. Vygotsky (1962) explains it this way.

> Schematically, we may imagine thought and speech as two intersecting circles. In their overlapping parts, thought and speech coincide to produce what is called verbal thought. Verbal thought, however, does not by any means include all forms of thought or all forms of speech. There is a vast area of thought that has no direct relation to speech. The thinking manifested in the use of tools belongs in this area, as does practical intellect in general (p. 47).

Now, if we put the information we have just supplied into our systems theoretic perspective, knowing that the function of communication is to bond two or more components into an HCS and that one of the characteristics to be shared is the language used, what does this tell us about the ease or difficulty of communicating across cultures? When the Reagan administration tried to communicate with the Noriega regime (Any bias in my language? Can I interchange the words administration and regime?), do you think they tried to create each other's culture? When the Panamanians spoke in English to the U.S. diplomats, were they speaking from the U.S. cultural perspective? And vice versa? A few career diplomats have taken their job seriously enough to learn both the language and the culture of the country with which they are working. However, our system tends to move people around so often that they cannot become that much of an expert. And if they do become an expert and tell their less adept superiors that they are sending signals that will not be interpreted as they expect, then these diplomats must deal with the overriding concern of political policy. You cannot separate the two, and unfortunately, policy is usually built around our cultural constructs, not those of the country we are dealing with.

Notice that two transformations take place in the communication process in which our language has a decided effect on the outcome—decoding and encoding. A third process is also affected by our cultural orientation; when we decode a signal and obtain the message, we must then interpret it in terms of our cultural constructs. At this stage we have the opportunity to create (make visible) the other's culture (and our own) and evaluate the message in light of the similarities and differences between the two cultures. We usually don't do this (for one reason, it takes time). But we still must create a response and encode it into a signal to the other party, generally by using our cultural orientation rather than theirs.

SUBJECTIVE CULTURE

Creating cultural constructs in the immediate time frame with the linguistic relativity we have just discussed is no easy matter. It is not impossible, however, and if we stop and think for a moment, we will realize that something like this goes on every time we communicate with anyone. No two people have the same cultural constructs, at least subjectively, including their cognitive constructs. But we seem to be able to communicate our thoughts fairly well, some better than others. Why is this so? What is it about humans or communication or both, that allows us to at least on some levels communicate with each other?

Getting to know someone means getting to know how they interact with their culture—the "man-made part of the human environment. Subjective culture is the subjective reaction to the man-made part of the human environment which is typically found among members of a cultural group. A cultural group here is defined very narrowly as people who utilize a mutually understandable dialect and are in face-to-face contact with each other" (Triandis, 1974, p. 17). So, a cultural group is one in which its members react in similar ways to their human environment. Kelly (1963) would say that these people construe their environment similarly. The commonality corollary says, "To the extent that one person employs a construction of experience which is similar to that employed by another, his psychological processes are similar to those of the other person" (p. 104). This would mean that they are sharing a common view of experience and would enhance the bonding process. Singer (1987) discusses these processes in terms of perceptions. "A number of people who perceive some aspect of the external world more or less similarly and recognize and communicate this similarity of perception form an identity group" (p. 40). We can see, then, that similarities in subjective culture create culture groups that are bonded together by common perceptions of their human environment. Effective communication should increase as we become more aware of the way others perceive their environment and how this perception is similar to, or different from, our own.

Another way of saying man-made environment is to say "social environment." Subjective culture then becomes "a cultural group's characteristic way of perceiving its social environment" and this "refers to variables that are attributes of the cognitive structures of groups of people" (Triandis, 1972, p. 3). One aspect of cognitive structures is the formation of categories. For each category there must be "criterial attributes"; cultural groups have similar criterial attributes for the categories they share. "The perception of rules and the group's norms, roles, and values are aspects of subjective culture"(p. 4). The major attributes of categories, or concepts, both intra- and intercultural, are the evaluative, activity, and potency dimensions of Osgood's semantic differential (Osgood, et al., 1957; Osgood, et al., 1975).

According to Littlejohn (1983), the primary concern of Attribution Theory is "the way people infer the causes of behavior" (p. 185). He says that there are three basic assumptions. 1) "people attempt to determine the causes of behavior." Most people either assume that other people have the same reasons for their behavior as they do or they want to know why they are behaving as they do. 2) "People assign causes systematically." Some people have one reason for everything, but most will look at several causes before settling on one reason. 3) "The attributed cause has impact on the perceiver's own feelings and behavior. The communicator's attributions determine in large part the meaning for the situation" (p. 185). Most attributions are made to create a sense of balance in the mind of the attributor. They fit in with his or her psychologic so that he or she can make sense out of experiences. Thus, attribution is a way of keeping our view of reality intact. If we can give a reason for the behavior of another person that fits in with our cognitive structure, then we do not have to change it.

Although attribution theory was developed around the need to assign reasons for behavior, we have seen that it is also applicable to subjective culture in that we assign attributes to all our categories/concepts in the process of defining them. For example, what are the attributes you assign to the category/concept "friend"? Honest, cheerful, independent? How about the category/concept "father" or "mother"? These systems of attributes are a major part of our subjective culture; to enhance our intercultural communication we must find out where they are different from or similar to those of the communicatee. As Kelly (1963) says, "To the extent that one person construes the construction processes of another, he may play a role in a social process involving the other person" (p. 104). Our major social process is communication, and it should be obvious that if there are no similarities in our subjective cultures, we will find it exceedingly difficult to understand each other. We must be able to construe the world as the other person does if we expect to communicate effectively. That means making visible each other's subjective cultures.

COMMUNICATING CULTURE

What is the message in this subheading? Is it that when we communicate we are somehow putting forth, displaying, or demonstrating our culture? Or is it saying that culture itself is communicating with us? Another way of putting this question is, does culture determine how we communicate (and thus, when we communicate one can tell what culture we are from), or does our communicative behavior determine our culture (Atwood, 1984)? Another chicken-or-the-egg routine! You have already seen this type of problem, so how should we answer it? If you look at this problem from an evolutionary perspective it is difficult to imagine anything other than that the two processes are interactive; both are present in any communication event. It may be easier to see culture communicated to a child as she or he is growing up, but again, since a child is surrounded by his or her culture the opposite interpretation is also possible.

In the immediate time frame when two people of different cultures are trying to communicate, most often their cultures are determining how they will do so, and the languages used are only part of it. This is true unless they have somehow managed to transcend their individual cultures. The opposite is also true. As we have said before, communication creates reality by revealing our cultural constructs. One facet of this revelation is assigning attributes to the behaviors and concepts of the other person. We may or may not be aware of doing this, just as we may or may not be aware of the attributes we have assigned to our own behavior and concepts. For example, probably the most famous difference between U.S. culture and most others is our deification of time. We know this intellectually, but can we deal with it physically?

The first time I was kept waiting for two hours to see an executive in Costa Rica, I kept telling myself that this was normal behavior for them, but I don't think I believed it. What attributes was I assigning to this behavior? Inefficient? Disrespectful? Culturally unsophisticated? And what attributes was he assigning to my obvious irritation at being kept waiting? Egotistical? Disrespectful? Culturally unsophisticated? But what did we say when I was ushered into his office? He said (in English) he was very sorry to have kept me waiting and gave several reasons for it. I said (in Spanish) that it was no problem. We later became friends and discussed the false impressions we tried to make on each other—both being aware of the other's cultural construct of time but unable to create an authentic immediate culture. Now we are able to joke about this construct when either of us let it interfere with effective communication.

Several different theoretical approaches to human communication can help us understand what is going on in the communication process; attribution theory is just one of them. It gives us evidence that we do indeed communicate culture when we make visible the attributes we assign to behaviors or concepts. We may do this verbally or nonverbally; you might say, "I don't like that" or you might make a sour face. Both assign a negative attribute to the behavior or concept. Unfortunately, when diplomats are trying to solve international problems, their language is usually "diplomatic" and the attributes political.

Communication is a form of human behavior that creates, maintains, and reveals our cultural constructs. One approach to understanding and investigating human communication is called a Rules Theory (Cushman, et al., 1982). It is based on the assumption that:

> human behavior can be divided into two classes of activity: stimulus-response activities governed by causal necessity, and intentional and choice-oriented responses governed by practical necessity. The former behaviors are habitual and are termed *movements*, while the latter are evaluative and are termed *actions*. Action theorists restrict their domain of inquiry to those realms of human behavior in which persons have some degree of choice among alternatives, are able to critique their performance, can exercise self-monitoring capacities, and can respond to practical or normative forces (pp. 91-2).

We should note that all of these behaviors are possibilities; how many of them do we do?

This approach suggests that the individual processes information that affects his or her perceptions, thoughts, and actions, but it is only through communication that two or more persons can coordinate their efforts to achieve a goal. Thus, we create a system of rules by which we interact in order to attain the objectives of the group. "The *structure* of human communication is the content and procedural rules involved in regulating consensus. The *process* of human communication entails the adaptation of the rules involved in regulating consensus to the task at hand" (p. 94). The research in this area is with standardized situations in which the rules can be specified and expectations delimited. For example, rules of protocol in negotiations, formal dinner parties, and military discipline.

What are the rules for intercultural communication? Some of them are formal and the protocol is exact. Most of the intercultural communication that we will be doing, however, will involve the generation of rules as we go along. This means that one cannot investigate such behavior objectively, and it becomes part of one's subject culture. The crucial element in intercultural communication from a rules perspective is (again) making the cultural constructs visible. How do I know what rules you are operating under if we are not open about the process and disclose our rules? Even if we do find a means of determining what rules persons from another culture might use, we still may not know which ones take precedence. For example, in responses to the MACH IV test of Machiavellianism, Costa Ricans replied yes to both "The best way to handle people is to tell them what they want to hear" and "Honesty is the best policy in all cases." Can you solve this paradox?

Still another approach to human communication helps explain subjective culture and our need to create cultural constructs in the immediate time frame. The constructivist approach is based on the idea that humans are continually interpreting the world around them according to their own schemes.

> Behavior is organized through the application of interpretive schemes as well as strategies that translate intentions into behavioral displays. Human interaction is a process in which individual lines of action are coordinated through reciprocal recognition of communicative intent and in which actions are organized by

communicative strategies; both the reciprocal recognition of communicative intent and the employment of communicative strategies depend centrally on the interpretive schemes interactants bring to bear on the world (Delia, et al., p. 151).

You can already see where the problems arise in cross-cultural communication. Interpretive schemes must be a part of our cultural constructs and therefore, different cultures will use different interpretive schemes. These are one aspect of the particularistic-universalistic dimension of the cultural orientation model.

An interpretive scheme is "any classification device persons use to make sense of their world" (p. 152). The two most basic are the attributes we assign to behaviors and concepts and the personal constructs of Kelly. He makes two basic points: one is that meaning is not carried on the back of concepts or behaviors. Instead, the only meaning any event will have is what we ascribe to it. The second is that humans anticipate events. If their perception of the event does not match their anticipation, then they must change their construct system. For example, you have a date with your main squeeze and you anticipate the usual good time. But something goes wrong, and it ends up being a miserable night. How do you reinterpret the events to give them a positive perspective? You have to alter some of your personal constructs—those cognitive constructs that give meaning to experience.

"Because individuals are born into a human community, they enter a world that is already defined, interpreted, organized, and meaningful. The world the individual faces is a world of preconstituted meaning, and it is to this meaningful world that the individual must accommodate" (Delia, et al., p. 154). A child learns to interpret meaningful behavior as it is enculturated into its culture; it develops cultural constructs that work for it. Even though we are unaware of most of these constructs, they become part of the schemes we develop to coordinate our behavior with others. Two people with similar organizing schemes will have greater success in coordinating their activities. This is true on a cognitive as well as a behavioral level, and the implications to intercultural communication are obvious.

TRANSITION

"Even if one has a perfect knowledge of all the rules that one must know to act like a native—that is, even if one has been brought up as a native, a privilege all human beings enjoy with respect to at least one culture—predictions based on a knowledge of those rules alone cannot in principle predict the great bulk of behavior stream events" (Harris, p. 269). That humans have the ability to make choices is a given. That we often make the wrong choice is also a given, particularly in the field of intercultural communication. That these wrong choices do not always bring disaster is another given. That they may cause embarrassment, frustration, and poor relationships is also a given.

In this chapter we have seen that by making visible our subjective culture, we may create an immediate culture with the one with whom we are communicating, if that person is also making his or her subjective culture visible. Of course, regardless of what the other person does, we will be creating their subjective culture for them in our mind. It will probably be from the language they use, but it will be constructed on the basis of our cultural constructs, as it will be construed from information gathered rather than growing out of mutual disclosure. In either case we need to be especially mindful of the attributes we assign to any behavior or concept. This brings us back to the cultural orientation model.Intercultural communication is low context, for we usually know little of the semantic space of the communicatee. The bonding process is activated because we both intend to communicate, but the reduction in entropy and the increase in synergy may be very small. This is especially true if we are communicating with someone in a different sector of the cultural orientation model than we are. Through the language used and the communicative behavior displayed we may be able to project where the communicatee is on the closed-minded/open-minded dimension and the particularistic-universalistic dimension. If we keep in mind that this is only a guess as to their cultural orientation, and that it is subject to change as we communicate, we will have a better chance of understanding intercultural communication. In the next chapter we will pull together the main points of the Cultural Orientation Model and show how it may be used to foster interpersonal/intercultural relationships.

INDEPENDENT STUDY

A number of areas of subjective culture can be researched in your library. Here are a few examples.

1. Look into the changes in language use in the United States either over time or space. What can you find out about the different meanings of the same word in different locations of the country?

2. Conduct a survey to find out how many different words we have in our language (including slang expressions) for some popular concept (for example, males, females, cars, etc.). Tie this into the Sapir-Whorf hypothesis.

3. Conduct a survey to find out how many attributes we ascribe to some popular concept (for example, males, females, cars, etc.). Can you find a pattern that helps you see what our subjective culture is?

CHAPTER SIXTEEN
Constructs for Understanding Intercultural Communication

The late Professor Edmund S. Glenn's understanding of intercultural communication is at the heart of the present work. His unique background gave him insights into the mysteries of cultures that few can equal. Born in Lodz, Poland, he received most of his education in France. He served in the armies of Poland, France, and the United States in World War II. He then joined the U.S. State Department from which he retired after 20 years as the Chief of Interpretation and Special Assistant for Intercultural Research. His basic languages were Polish, French, Russian, and English, though he spoke many more. During his time with the State Department he was the personal interpreter for Presidents Truman, Eisenhower, Kennedy, and Johnson and for Secretaries of State Acheson, Dulles, Herter, and Rusk. His heart and soul were dedicated to understanding among nations.

I once had dinner with him in Chicago, where he was giving a paper on the cognitive approach to intercultural communication at the International Communication Conference. The young woman who waited on us was obviously not an Anglo-American. As she left with our drink orders, a number of us at the table were speculating about her native culture. She had a definite accent, dark olive complexion, dark brown eyes, and long black hair. We all put her somewhere in Europe. Edmund said she was from Poland, so we suggested he speak to her in Polish when she returned to see if she would understand. He did, and as he spoke I watched her face. Her eyes widened, almost as with fear, and then the tears started sliding down her checks. He had been speaking to her in the dialect of *his* native province in Poland, and it happened to be hers also! She had not heard the dialect for six years, and was nearly overwhelmed.

Why do we communicate the way we do? We know that human communication is constrained by the boundaries of an HCS, i.e., on the personal, situational, and cultural dimensions. Since one's cognitive style affects the doables one can entertain in an intercultural communication event, it is imperative that we know ourselves. Having an open mind may enhance one's ability to take the correct perspective when communicating in an intercultural situation. But the most difficult part of understanding intercultural communication comes with knowing the correct cultural orientation of the communicatee. To do this one must be culturally literate in his or her culture.

RECAPITULATION

Intent to communicate is an important concept because it highlights the fact that much of the information we process is not intended and therefore, can only be interpreted within our own personal constructs. These are almost always based on our first culture's perspective. Thus, much of what we think we know about a culture, based on our perception of it, is really only the etic constructs we have created out of our first culture's psychological constructs. The interference of our first culture's cognitions with the development of our second culture's cognitions is the primary noise in the intercultural communication process.

Construct #1. *The degree to which we can understand intercultural communication depends upon the degree to which we are aware that our intent to communicate, either as communicator or communicatee, may result in only expressive behavior or information gathering respectively.* Thus, we must understand that although things are happening, no communication may be occurring.

The development of the person's cybernetic (self-concept) in his or her first culture is closely related to the degree of literacy achieved in that culture. Since both of these processes are predominantly subconscious, we are seldom aware of the balance among the subsystems in our cybernetic (though we may feel the need for more psychological stability) or the depth of understanding we have of our culture (though we get some idea from the grades we receive in school and how well we can "hold our own" with various factions of our culture). It is the person's cybernetic that controls his or her behavior (both physical and psychological), and so it plays a major role in the enculturation process. Second culture acculturation suffers from the noise of the first culture's constructs, and it is nearly impossible to acquire all of the tacit knowledge of a second culture that would make one fully bicultural.

Construct #2. *The degree to which we can understand intercultural communication depends upon the degree to which our cybernetic in one culture can operates independently of our cybernetic in the other culture.* Thus, we must build identity in our second culture much like we did in our first culture.

Languages (both verbal and nonverbal) play a major role in all developmental processes—e.g., the cybernetic, enculturation, acculturation, and cultural literacy. With them we are able to describe the physical environment, and through the process of abstraction, we develop the concepts and schemas of our psychological constructs. Language is the medium through which we create the bonds of our HCSs. With proper use we can apprehend the most precise area of semantic space or the most general, but if it is not shared equally by the communicatee (co-subjectivity), we will not be able to communicate effectively. Knowing the rituals in the language of a second culture often hides the fact that we are not competent in the language of that culture.

Construct #3. *The degree to which we can understand intercultural communication depends upon the degree to which we are competent in the language of each culture.* It is only through competence in the language of our second culture that we can be successfully acculturated into it.

Human communication is constrained by the boundaries of the three dimensions of decision making: personal, situational, and cultural. Personal constraints are seen in the doables one is permitted by one's cybernetic and the cognitive style one has developed to deal with incoming information. Situational constraints depend upon our perception of the communication situation and our ability to take the perspective of the other person (meta-perspective). The better we can do this, the better we understand the situation and can be realistic about its demands (exigences). Both personal and situational boundaries are interdependent with our knowledge of the norms of our culture and those of another culture. Cultural constraints, particularly at the level of tacit knowledge, are a major problem in intercultural communication.

Construct #4. *The degree to which we can understand intercultural communication depends upon the degree to which we are able to work within the constraints (personal, situational, and cultural) of the HCS established by the communication from the two cultures.* Knowing the doables, exigences, and norms of both cultures is essential to intercultural understanding.

Human communication functions to bond two or more people into a Human Communication System (HCS). Thus, two cognitive level systems are bonded together into an associative level system. The more similar the personal constructs of the two subsystems, the stronger the bond and the less information needs to be carried in the signal to assure effective communication (high/low context). Cultural context includes one's knowledge of the environment (both natural and human made), human behavior, tacit knowledge of the two cultures (facts, beliefs, values, symbols, and schemas), and the languages of the two cultures.

Construct #5. *The degree to which we can understand intercultural communication depends upon the degree to which we are culturally literate in our own and the other's culture.* Although much of first culture literacy comes from nonconscious assimilation of information as we are growing up in the culture, we can learn enough about a second culture to achieve an adequate level of literacy that allows us to understand intercultural communication with that culture.

It was shown that communication plays a major role in the development of the four universal value dimensions. One communicates from some position on the power distance continuum. Communication helps alleviate uncertainty and is a major facet of all cultural schemas for uncertainty avoidance. It was shown that cultures can be placed on a continuum from individual to collective in the decision-making process depending on the locus of control for that culture. The way that cultures address sex-role stereotypes and attribute their behavior to sex-trait stereotypes is revealed by their position on the masculine-feminine values continuum. All of these were shown to contribute to an understanding of the cultural orientation model.

Construct #6. *The degree to which we can understand intercultural communication depends on the degree to which we know the position of our culture and the other's culture on the four universal values dimensions and their interaction with the cultural orientation model.* It is the interaction of our belief systems and our cognitive style that produces the personal constructs through which we view the world. When raised to the cultural level, these become the four dimensions of belief systems and the cultural orientation model with which we can develop cultural constructs that will allow understanding in intercultural communication.

Human communication is a cognitive process involving the generation of a message(s) from the meaning(s) in the mind of the communicator, the intentional encoding of the message(s) into a signal (using a limitless combination of verbal and nonverbal codes), its transmission through a channel(s), reception by the communicatee, the intentional decoding into a message(s), and the subsequent creation of a meaning(s) in the mind of the communicatee. In intercultural communication the focus is on the role culture plays in the above process. The cultural orientation model says that cultures may vary on three dimensions: the particularistic-universalistic continuum, the associative-abstractive continuum, and the closed-minded/open-minded continuum.

Construct #7. *The degree to which we can understand intercultural communication depends upon the degree to which we know the cultural orientation of our culture and the other's culture on the associative-abstractive, particularistic-universalistic, and closed-minded/open-minded dimensions and can use it as the first approximation of the cognitive style of the communicants.*

Summarizing the book into the seven constructs given above allows us to focus on the important facets of intercultural communication. It assumes that you have developed the tacit knowledge (through readings and exercises) necessary to understand each of these constructs. The summary is the result of my abstracting those points I felt most pertinent to understanding intercultural communication. A further abstraction leads to the concepts found in Table 14. You can see what abstraction does and all of the knowledge that underlies the tip of the iceberg. These concepts are like index terms to open up our files of knowledge and bring to mind all of the information that supports each of the seven constructs.

Table 14:   Competency Concepts for Intercultural Communication

---

1. Intent to Communicate.
2. Independent Cybernetics.
3. Language Competence.
4. System Constraints.
5. Cultural Literacy.
6. Universal Belief Systems.
7. Cultural Orientation.

INTERCULTURAL COMMUNICATION COMPETENCE

When we are actively involved in a communication situation, we are taking turns being speaker and listener, *but* our communicative behavior is continuous. It may be easier to grasp the fact that we send and receive signals at the same time (as we may be taking in the signals from our audience through any or all of our senses while we speak) than it is to grasp that while we are listening we are also sending signals to the communicator. Many of us are predominantly listeners (quiet people), while others of us tend to be speakers (talkative). Regardless of whether you emphasize communicator or communicatee, we know that the process of communication is continuous, and both of the traditional phases are of equal importance for effective communication.

In previous chapters we have seen that in the communicator phase of the process we tend to act on the basis of stereotypes. Since we construe our reality based on the norms of our culture and our upbringing, these stereotypes tend to be both ethno- and egocentric. As long as we use these stereotypes solely for introductory purposes they will probably serve us well, but as we get acquainted with our communicatee, we will soon realize that she or he is more of an individual than a stereotype and we must adjust our communication to this fact. Initiating and adjusting communication strategies to fit the situation means that we must have a reasonable command of the verbal and nonverbal codes common to both of us.

Collier (1986) states that in terms of communication competence "Persons are ethnically/culturally competent to the extent that they share perceptions as to appropriate ways of behaving and prefer the same outcomes from behavior" (p. 578). This definition is equivalent to saying that two persons are interculturally competent communicators when their personal and situational constraints are congruent. The cultural dimension is included in her remarks that "when rules of appropriate behavior are not shared, are not known, or are simply violated, meaning is less likely to be shared and the interaction more likely to be dissatisfying in terms of goal attainment, and less likely to be perceived as affirming of the self-concept" (p. 579). Knowing the rules is part of cultural literacy, and affirming the self-concept facilitates the development of independent cybernetics. The constraints of the three dimensions of decision making, then, help us to define the competent intercultural communicator.

Another definition of communication competence is constructed by Diez (1984). She says that "communicative competence is situational, interactional, functional, and developmental" (p. 57). We have spent considerable time on the situational component. Interactional (ongoing negotiations between two or more people) was mentioned in Chapter 1 and is assumed to be an integral part of the definition of communication. Functional refers to the effective use of codes, modes, rituals, etc., and developmental indicates that competence is an ongoing, learned communication characteristic. The time it takes to become reasonably competent varies with the individual, but no one can do it overnight. Those who are most suited to developing this characteristic are those who have grown up being bilingual and bicultural. One then needs only to develop the awareness and perceptual skills of a competent communicator. Experiencing more than one culture is absolutely essential to understanding intercultural communication.

Other researchers have been able to show that other concepts are important to the concept of competency. For example, Wiseman and Abe (1986) suggest that "a competent communicator must be able to recognize and sustain the other's perspective on the situation in order to see how the other defines it (and thus, what code is appropriate), to see how the other expects the conversation to progress (and thus, what utterances and topics are appropriate), and to see how the other sees himself (and thus, what title or name is appropriate)" (p. 613). This focuses directly on the role of perspective taking in defining the competent intercultural communicator. One who is able to put oneself in the role of the other person is obviously better able to adapt to the requirements of the situation, all other things being equal.

We have mentioned that the cognitive style of the communicator affected his or her ability to enter into effective negotiations with another person. Wiseman and Abe (1986) further say that "cognitively complex persons form more accurate perceptions of the other, are able to empathize better with another person, and better adapt their communication to the listener" (p. 614). However, they do not perceive themselves to be as effective as cognitively simple persons do. One reason for this is that the same skill that lets an analytic person abstract the more relevant variables in a communication situation also makes him or her more critical of his or her own ability to effect the desired outcome in a communication event. Thus, what the nonanalytic person accepts as sufficient, the cognitively complex person may not. You may know someone who analyzes every situation to death and, therefore, is never satisfied with the decision he or she made.

A question that you may have been raising as you read this book is, Who has the responsibility to adjust to the other culture's norms? If culture *A* is universalistic, abstractive, and open-minded, and culture *B* is particularistic, associative and open-minded, which one should accept the other's cultural norms and try to fit into them? Ideally, both cultures should negotiate a compromise culture (a combination of the two), but this seldom happens. Culture *A*, being more cognitively complex, should be able to understand the position and behavior of culture *B* better than the inverse. At the same time, the more cognitively complex culture usually is trying to change the less complex culture to be more like it. Once you have learned how to abstract, you cannot live as an associative being. Do you see the dilemma? What are the ethics involved?

COMMUNICATION STYLE

Norton (1983) tells us that in one sense "style is seen as a function that *gives form to content*. In this sense, communicator style is broadly conceived to mean 'the way one verbally, nonverbally, and paraverbally interacts to signal how literal meaning should be taken, interpreted, filtered, or understood.' Style is a message about content" (p. 19). In this sense style acts like a nonverbal code; it acts as meta-communication, or in this case, as a meta-message—telling the communicatee how to perceive the communiqué. If we receive a birthday present, the way it is packaged and/or wrapped gives a psychological set or predisposition to how we will receive/feel about it. Our communication style is analogous in terms of the message we decode from the communiqué; it sets up expectations about the message we are decoding. Interculturally, this is an extremely important part of the communication event. Different cultures have different styles, and one can easily offend another without knowing it.

By giving form to content, communicator style also makes possible the second of its meanings. Norton says that

> Style is seen as a function of *consistently recurring communicative associations*. Here style not only entails the first function, but is the relatively enduring pattern of human interaction associated with the individual. Observed behavior triggers the associations. This does not mean that the pattern is invariant across situation, context, or time. It does mean that the pattern is sufficiently recurring and consistent that at least one person reliably associates it with the individual (pp. 19-20).

Thus, the form we give to our signals is identified with us and becomes a way of knowing who we are. This style has both individual and cultural norms, as when someone says, "That's not like Nancy. She is usually not that aggressive." The style they observed was not Nancy's usual style but was identifiable as an aggressive style in that culture. U.S. style is brusk, objective, and often forces communicatees into a binary decision-making situation with no easy way to "save face."

Concepts such as dominant, dramatic, contentious, relaxed, and open have been associated with communicator style. You may have used such terms as aggressive, wimpy, stubborn, or whiny to refer to people you know. If communication styles are patterned, it stands to reason that they should be categorizable. In his research Norton (1983) discusses three distinct communicator styles.

Open Style

This refers to the accessible and unrestrained communicator. This style carries many problems with it, for the best deceivers are those who appear to be open. We almost always equate honesty and self-disclosure with openness. Neither of these may occur, however, even though the communicator appears to be open. Since communicator style, like beauty, is in the eye of the beholder, one can be perceived as being open when in reality his or her behavior is quite closed, e.g., one gives false information about oneself. In like manner we may be open and appear to be self-disclosing but achieve this appearance by deceptive means.

Self-disclosure and honesty are two important components of the open style. When one engages in self-disclosure, she or he makes the self vulnerable to the other because the other receives meaningful information about the self. This is risky business because an unethical other may use this information to harm you. An open style says that the information transmitted is personal, private, and honest. It is to be accepted as representative of the self and as such says that more information is available. It invites one to question but also to reciprocate in kind. Norton says,

> At minimum, the person with an open style seems to grant permission to explore specified aspects of the personal domain. At maximum, the person with an open style invites radically intense and reciprocal interaction that may entail the boundaries of one's identity, value system, beliefs, idiosyncracies, and core commitments (p. 107).

Thus, this style should lead to deeper, more meaningful interpersonal relationships. But the differences among cultures often interfere with one's perception of the intimacy of the relationship (Barnlund, 1989).

Dramatic Style

This refers to the communicative spotlight. When we want to emphasize a point, the stress and intonation patterns of our speech indicate this. When we want to say one thing and mean another, our facial expression usually makes the difference. We all use the dramatic style at times to highlight some aspect of our communicative behavior. We dramatize for a reason—to draw attention to some part of the message. It may emphasize the truthfulness of the statement or its falseness. Because we are playing with the meaning of our communiqué, the dramatic style is inherently ambiguous, and we must know the communicator to have any assurance that we understand what she or he said.

The ability to play communication games, make a play on words, puns, jokes, etc., is a skill that some covet and others detest. If you use this style constantly, you appear to be superficial and uncaring. (You may be the life of the party, but you may never be taken seriously!) At the same time, we all use it to get out of tight situations, for with it we can both relieve or build tensions. We use it to elicit information by playing dumb, to attract attention by playing coy, and to command respect by playing the strong, silent type. All of this is done through deviations in our verbal and nonverbal behaviors.

Norton indicates that this is one of the most complex and exciting communicator styles. He postulates that,

> Because dramatic style creates the extraordinary, it not only is one of the most noticeable form-giving components, but it also serves a profound, complex, sometimes unconscious, communicative function. In general, the dramatic communicator manipulates messages through exaggerations, fantasies, stories, metaphors, rhythm, voice, and other stylistic devices to highlight, understate, or alter literal meaning (p. 129).

As a communicator style the dramatic style can be highly useful, but it should be used with care as its purpose is easily misunderstood.

Attentive Style

This refers to the communicative coordinator. If you are really involved in a conversation, you are displaying the attentive style. This can be from the speaker perspective or the listener perspective but is usually thought of in terms of the listener. Because the attentive style signals involvement, one who displays this style tends toward leadership and is more conversational and effective. An attentive listener affects the speaker and may modify the signals he or she is transmitting. When two people are involved in a conversation, the attentive style reinforces the communicative behavior of each person. Without this reinforcement, a dialogue may end up as a monologue.

The attentive style is closely related to listening, feedback, and empathy. Although it is more than listening, one has to listen to be attentive. You may give feedback without being attentive, but you cannot be attentive without giving feedback. Empathy is the ability to put yourself in someone else's shoes. You must be attentive to that person to be able to do this, but you do not have to do this to be attentive. Attentiveness is an active process in which one's involvement in the communication process compels him or her to not only react to the speaker's signals but to help carry the process through his or her own actions.

The heightened awareness of speaker and listener when both are attentive communicators leads to a strong bonding of these two components in the HCS. Norton says,

> In short, manifesting an attentive style through responsive feedback gives form to the other's messages because it acts as a governor that signals the degree of understanding. With attentiveness, conversations tend to be more structured, coherent, accurate, efficient, and dialectic. Accordingly, the attentive style is not

merely a matter of showing the other person that listening is done, but it actively entails an influential, participant process (p. 156).

Active participation in the communication process signals an involvement with the other person in some form of relationship. It may enhance or dissolve it, but it is certain to affect it.

Although these three communication styles are all found in U.S. culture, other cultures may display them more and make it appear as though the United States has only one style—cold, objective, and business oriented. In most other cultures the style of communication is less direct and more involved in relationship building. If you can be trusted as a person, then you get the work, and signing a contract takes little time. Initial encounters begin with finding out about your immediate and extended family, and its health will be a constant in all of the encounters you have from that time on. For many, nothing is communicated head-on. Your conversation covers all kinds of things, including your business, but only in what we would call a passing fancy. One can usually tell something about a culture's style of communicating by the way it handles time. The more punctual in keeping time, the more direct in communication style.

COMMUNICATION STRATEGIES

Although we have been talking about intercultural communication as though it were one culture communicating with another, we must remember that all communication is basically one person communicating with another interpersonally. This means that an interpersonal relationship is developing (an HCS is being formed) and the communication that occurs creates the bonds of the system. Although we may start with the position of a culture on the cultural orientation model and know something about its communication style, this information is used to approximate the cognitive style and communication style of the person with whom we are communicating. In every intercultural communication event, we are communicating with another person and, therefore, we must be aware of the fact that the personal characteristics of the communicatee may differ radically from those of her or his cultural norm. In developing friendships across cultures, we must search for the basic belief systems that activate the other's behavior and develop a joint understanding of the underlying schemas for the concepts being used.

In developing communication strategies one should use the orientation of a culture on the three dimensions of the cultural orientation model only as a *first approximation* of the cognitive style of a person from that culture. Heavy emphasis is placed on "first approximation" because of the danger of the negative or permanent use of this stereotype. In using this stereotype as a starting point, one must employ the five key constructs of General Semantics to assist in the development of a more accurate cognitive representation of the one with whom you are communicating. Thus, the attentive style of communication with some openness is the most appropriate.

The primary construct is that of awareness, and it should be practiced continuously. Trying to understand the cultural schemas of the other person while making your own schemas visible will enhance the probability for understanding. Checking your own with the other person's perspective taking may also be beneficial. Knowing that your decision making is constrained by the interaction of your personal, situational, and cultural orientation may help you understand why you cannot accept some of the behaviors of persons from other cultures. Understanding that your self-concept, like his or hers, is the regulator (cybernetic) of your behavior may also help you understand why the two of you differ on what you are able to accomplish. The fact that all communication is intentional on the part of both communicators (while intention on the part of one allows us to collect or disseminate information) makes us realize that we must be extremely careful in our interpretation of what we think are nonverbal cues. Much of the time we are merely gathering information that is erroneously interpreted from our own cultural constructs.

Segall (1986) says that "At the very heart of the concept culture is the expectation that different peoples will possess different values, beliefs, and motives reflected in numerous behaviors. Travelers to foreign lands detect them quickly, sensing that they are viewing not only different lifestyles but also different attitudes toward life itself" (p. 541). We have seen that cultures can be characterized by their values on the dimensions of power distance, uncertainty avoidance, individualism/collectivism, and masculine/feminine. Hart (1984) says that "If one accepts the extant research, communication and values appear to be interdependent phenomena that produce cultural profiles. That cultural profiles differ from one another becomes, then, as much a communicative fact as an axiological reality" (p. 752). That the four value dimensions mentioned above (Hofstede, 1984) can be used to position cultures has been shown by Gudykunst, Chua, and Gray (1987). Thus, we can use a culture's position on these four value dimensions as the normative values of that culture.

Besides the values themselves, each of these four value dimensions has a construct that is of particular importance to the understanding of a person in that culture. Power distance does not only let us see where the culture is positioned on the value of equality, it may also give us an idea of a person's style of conflict management. Uncertainty avoidance gives us the orientation of a culture on reducing the unknown through communication and the development of the components of a person's self-concept. The individualism/collectivism dimension positions a culture on individual freedom and a person's locus of control. The masculine/feminine dimension shows us a culture's achievement orientation and a person's concern for the changing sex-role and sex-trait stereotypes. Each of these should help us understand the intercultural communication process.

When you become involved in an intercultural communication event, you will find out how little you know about yourself and your culture. It may be a frightening experience, but there is no better way to understand yourself. Your growth and communication effectiveness will depend on how open, unassuming, and committed you are to the experience. I hope you have inculcated sufficient information to get you started on a most fascinating adventure of life. *Buena Suerte* (Good Luck)!

INDEPENDENT STUDY

1. For a group project, try to rank the seven constructs in the order of their importance to competency in intercultural communication.

2. When visiting another culture, who is obliged to change their cultural orientation? What are the implications of your answer? Is it ethical?

3. Go to your informants from another culture and see if you can find differences in their communication style from yours. You may find that there are some more global differences than just individual styles. The following questions may help you get started:

   A. What are the uses and importance of the mass media?
   B. Are there communication differences within the culture?
   C. What are the major types of communication networks: family, friends, colleagues, etc.?
   D. Are there differences in public and private communication: courtship, showing emotions, etc.?
   E. What are the communication rituals: greetings, leavings, etc.?
   F. Are there problems in translating from your language to your informant's language?
   G. How do they use colloquialisms, slang, jargon, etc.?
   H. Are there nonverbal cues that have different meanings in the two cultures?
   I. What are the most obvious nonverbal differences between the two cultures?

References

Adler, N. J., and Jelinek, M. (1986). Is 'organization culture' culture bound? *Human Resource Management, 25*, 73–90.

Ajzen, I. and Fishbein, M. (1980). *Understanding attitudes and predicting social behavior.* Englewood Cliffs, NJ: Prentice-Hall, Inc.

Asimov, I. (1983, May/June). Write, write, write. *Communicator's Journal, 1*, 40–45.

Atwood, R. (1984). Critical perspectives on the state of intercultural communication research. In B. Dervin and M. J. Voigt (Eds.), *Progress in communication sciences, 4* (pp. 63–90). Norwood, NJ: ABLEX Publishing Corp.

Barnlund, D. C. (1989). *Communicative styles of Japanese and Americans.* Belmont, CA: Wadsworth Publishing Company.

Bem, D. (1970). *Beliefs, attitudes, and human affairs.* Monterey, CA: Brooks/Cole Publishing Co.

Benedict, R. (1934). *Patterns of culture.* New York: Houghton Mifflin.

Berger, C. R. (1987). Communicating under uncertainty. In M. E. Roloff and G. R. Miller (Eds.), *Interpersonal processes: New directions in communication research* (pp. 39–62). Beverly Hills, CA: Sage Publications.

Berger, C. R. and Bradac, J. J. (1982). *Language and social knowledge: Uncertainty in interpersonal relations.* London: Edward Arnold (Publishers) Ltd.

Bernard, J. (1968, January). The status of women in modern patterns of culture. In A. K. Hottel (Ed.), Women around the world (special issue). *The Annals of the American Academy of Political and Social Science, 375*, 3-14.

Berne, E. (1961). *Transactional analysis in psychotherapy.* New York: Grove Press, Inc.

Berne, E. (1964). *Games people play: The psychology of human relationships.* New York: Grove Press, Inc.

Bernstein, B. (1966). Elaborated and restricted codes: Their social origins and some consequences. In A. G. Smith (Ed.), *Communication and culture* (pp. 427–441). New York: Holt, Rinehart and Winston.

Biesanz, R., Biesanz, K. Z., and Biesanz, M. H. (1988). *The Costa Ricans*. Prospect Heights, IL: Waveland Press, Inc.

Birdwhistell, R. (1952). *Introduction of kinesics*. Louisville, KY: University of Louisville Press.

Bitzer, B. (1968). The rhetorical situation. *Journal of Philosophy and Rhetoric, 1–14*.

Bochner, S. (1982). *Cultures in contact*. Oxford: Pergamon Press.

Borden, G. A. (1963). Mathematical transformations and communication theory. *Human Communication Research, 13*, 87–93.

Borden, G. A. (1982, December). *The effect of Machiavellianism on intercultural communication*. Paper presented at the Speech Communication Association of Puerto Rico, San Juan, Puerto Rico.

Borden, G. A. (1983, December). *A comparison of subjectivity/objectivity and Machiavellianism in three American cultures*. Paper presented at the North/South Communication Conference, Cholula, Mexico.

Borden, G. A. (1985a). *Human communication systems*. Boston: American Press.

Borden, G. A. (1985b, May). *Cultural awareness and perspective-taking in north/south communication*. Paper presented at the International Communication Association Conference, Honolulu, HI.

Borden, G. A. (1985c, November). *Particularism vs. universalism: The interaction of culture and sex*. Paper presented at the Speech Communication Association Conference, Denver, CO.

Borden, G. A. (1986). Values and ethics: The communicator's dilemma. In D. A. Miller & B. A. Hines (Eds.), *Ethical trends and issues in public relations education (pp. 45–48)*. *Proceedings from the 1984 and 1985 Educators Workshops sponsored by the International Association of Business Communicators (IABC), U.S. District 3*.

Borden, G. A. (1989). Communication discriminators in male/female relationships in four American cultures, *Puerto Rican Communication Studies*. (In press.)

Borden, G. A., and Stone, J. D. (1976). *Human communication: The process of relating*. Menlo Park, CA: Cummings Publishing Co.

Borden, G. A., and Tanner, J. M. (1980). *La universidad estatal a distancia: An impact study*. Report for USAID in Costa Rica.

Boski, P. (1988, September). Cross-cultural studies of person perception: Effects of ingroup/outgroup membership and ethnic schemata. *Journal of Cross-Cultural Psychology, 19*, 287–328.

Buck, R. (1983). Nonverbal receiving ability. In J. Wiemann & R. Harrison (Eds.), *Nonverbal interaction* (pp. 209–242). Beverly Hills, CA: Sage Publications.

Bugental, J. F. T. (1976). *The search for existential identity*. San Francisco: Jossey-Bass Publishers.

Burgoon, J. K., and Hale, J. L. (1988, March). Nonverbal expectancy violations: Model elaboration and application to immediacy behaviors. *Communication Monographs, 55*, 58–79.

Burgoon, J., and Saine, T. (1978). *The Unspoken Dialogue*. Boston: Houghton Mifflin Co.

Buriel, R. (1975). Cognitive styles among three generations of Mexican American children. *Journal of Cross-Cultural Psychology, 6*, 417–429.

Burk, J. (1974). An explication and evaluation of cognitive anthropology. In F. L. Casmir (Ed.), *The international and intercultural communication annual* (pp. 24–38). Annandale, VA: Speech Communication Association.

Burleson, B. R. (1982). The affective perspective-taking process: A test of Turiel's role-taking model. In M. Burgoon (Ed.), *Communication yearbook 6* (pp. 473–488). Beverly Hills, CA: Sage Publications, Inc.

Burleson, B. R., and Waltman, M. S. (1988). Cognitive complexity: Using the role category questionnaire measure. In C. H. Tardy (Ed.), *A handbook for the study of human communication*. Norwood, NJ: ABLEX Publishing Corp.

Carroll, J. (1963). The linguistic *weltanschauung* problem. In J. A. Rycenga & J. Schwartz (Eds.), *Perspectives on language* (pp. 286–292). New York: The Ronald Press Co.

Casse, P. (1979). *Training for the cross-cultural mind* (2nd ed.). Washington, DC: The Society for Intercultural Education, Training and Research.

Chaiken, S., and Stangor, C. (1987). Attitudes and attitude change. In M. R. Rosenzweig & L. W. Porter (Eds.), *Annual review of psychology, 38*, (pp. 575–630). Palo Alto, CA: Annual Reviews Inc.

Chomsky, N. (1959). Review of B. F. Skinner's *Verbal Behavior*. *Language, 35*, 26–58.

Chomsky, N. (1965). *Aspects of the theory of syntax*. Cambridge, MA: The MIT Press.

Christie, R., and Geis, F. L. (1970). *Studies in Machiavellianism*. New York: Academic Press.

Collier, M. J. (1986). Culture and gender: Effects on assertive behavior and communication competence. In M. L. McLaughlin (Ed.), *Communication yearbook 9* (pp. 576–592). Beverly Hills, CA: Sage Publications.

Copeland, L., and Griggs, L. (1985). *Going international*. New York: Random House.

Cushman, D. P., Valentinsen, B., and Dietrich, D. (1982). A rules theory of interpersonal relationships. In F. E. X. Dance (Ed.), *Human communication theory* (pp. 90–119). New York: Harper & Row, Publishers.

D'Andrade, R. (1987). A folk model of the mind. In D. Holland, & N. Quinn (Eds.), *Cultural models in language and thought* (pp. 112–148). New York: Cambridge University Press.

Datan, N., Rodeheaver, D., and Hughes, F. (1987). Adult development and aging. In M. R. Rosenzweig & L. W. Porter (Eds.), *Annual review of psychology, 38* (pp. 153–180). Palo Alto, CA: Annual Review Inc.

Deal, R. E., and Kennedy, A. A. (1982). *Corporate cultures*. Reading, MA: Addison-Wesley Publishing Co.

Deese, J. (1970). *Psycholinguistics*. Boston: Allyn and Bacon, Inc.

Delia, J. G., O'Keefe, B. J., and O'Keefe, D. J. (1982). The constructivist approach to communication. In F. E. X. Dance (Ed.), *Human communication theory* (pp. 147–191). New York: Harper & Row, Publishers.

Diez, M. E. (1984). Communicative competence: An interactive approach. In R. N. Bostrom (Ed.), *Communication yearbook 8* (pp. 56–79). Beverly Hills, CA: Sage Publications.

Dizard, W. P. (1982). *The coming information age*. New York: Longman.

Downs, J. F. (1971). *Cultures in crisis*. Beverly Hills, CA: Glencoe Press.

Duncan, H. D. (1968). *Symbols in society*. New York: Oxford University Press.

Durbin, M. (1973). Cognitive anthropology. In J.J. Honigmann (Ed.), *Handbook of social and cultural anthropology* (pp. 447–478). Chicago: Rand McNally and Co.

Eco, U. (1979). *A theory of semiotics*. Bloomington, IN: Indiana University Press.

Ehrenhaus, P. (1982). Attribution theory: Implications for intercultural communication. In M. Burgoon (Ed.), *Communication yearbook 6* (pp. 721–734). Beverly Hills, CA: Sage Publications, Inc.

Ekman, P., and Friesen, W. (1975). *Unmasking the face*. Englewood Cliffs, NJ: Prentice-Hall, Inc.

Estevanovich, E. (1981). *Tico lingo*. Private publication.

Fairhurst, G. T. (1986). Male-female communication on the job: Literature review and commentary. In M. L. McLaughlin (Ed.), *Communication yearbook 9* (pp. 83–116). Beverly Hills, CA: Sage Publications, Inc.

Farb, P. (1968). *Man's rise to civilization as shown by the Indians of North America from primeval times to the coming of the industrial state.* New York: E. P. Dutton & Co., Inc.

Fast, J. (1971). *Body language.* New York: Pocket Books.

Faules, D. F., and Alexander, D. C. (1978). *Communication and social behavior: A symbolic interaction perspective.* Reading, MA: Addison-Wesley Publishing Co.

Feibleman, J. and Friend, J. W. (1969). The structure and function of organizations. In F. E. Emery (Ed.), *Systems Thinking* (pp. 30–55). Baltimore, MD: Penguin Books Inc.

Festinger, L. A. (1957). *A theory of cognitive dissonance.* Evanston, IL: Row, Peterson.

Foglesang, A. (1982). *About understanding.* Uppsala, Sweden: Dag Hammarskjold Foundation.

Frake, C. (1964). A structural description of Subanum "religious behavior." In W. Goodenough (Ed.), *Explorations in Cultural Anthropology* (pp. 111–129). New York: McGraw-Hill.

Frankl, V. (1963). *Man's search for meaning: An introduction to logotherapy.* New York: Washington Square Press.

Furnham, A., and Bochner, S. (1986). *Culture shock.* New York: Methuen.

Furth, H. G. (1969). *Piaget and knowledge.* Englewood Cliffs, NJ: Prentice-Hall, Inc.

Geertz, C. (1973). *The interpretation of cultures.* New York: Basic Books, Inc., Publishers.

Gilligan, C. (1982). *In a different voice.* Cambridge, MA: Harvard University Press.

Glenn, E. S. (1981). *Man and mankind.* Norwood, N.J.: ABLEX Publishing Corporation.

Goldstein, K. M., and Blackman, S. (1978). *Cognitive style: Five approaches and relevant research.* New York: John Wiley & Sons.

Granberg, D. (1982). Social judgment theory. In M. Burgoon (Ed.), *Communication yearbook 6* (pp. 304–329). Beverly Hills, CA: Sage Publications, Inc.

Gudykunst, W. B., Chua E., and Gray, A. J. (1987). Cultural dissimilarities and uncertainty reduction processes. In M. L. McLaughlin (Ed.), *Communication yearbook 10* (pp. 456–469). Beverly Hills, CA: Sage Publications.

Hall, E. P. (1986). The etic-emic distinction: Its observational foundation. In B. Dervin & M. J. Voigt (Eds.), *Progress in communication sciences, 7* (pp. 123–151). Norwood, NJ: ABLEX Publishing Corporation.

Hall, E. T. (1959). *The silent language.* Garden City, NY: Anchor Books.

Hall, E. T. (1969). *The hidden dimension.* Garden City, NY: Anchor Books.

Hall, E. T. (1988). Context and meaning. In L. A. Samovar & R. E. Porter (Eds.), *Intercultural communication: A reader* (5th ed.) (pp. 44–54). Belmont, CA: Wadsworth Publishing Co.

Hamilton, D. L. (1978). Cognitive biases in the perception of social groups. In J. S. Carroll & J. W. Payne (Eds.), *Cognition and social behavior* (pp. 81–93). Hillsdale, NJ: Lawrence Erlbaum Associates, Publishers.

Harari, H., Jones, C. A., and Sek, H. (1988). Stress syndromes and stress predictors in American and Polish college students. *Journal of Cross-Cultural Psychology, 19,* 243–255.

Harris, M. (1979). *Cultural materialism.* New York: Random House.

Harris, P. R., and Moran, R. T. (1979). *Managing cultural differences.* Houston, TX: Gulf Publishing Company.

Hart, R. P. (1984). The functions of human communication in the maintenance of public values. In C. C. Arnold & J. W. Bowers (Eds.), *Handbook of rhetorical and communication theory* (pp. 749-791). Boston: Allyn and Bacon, Inc.

Haslett, B. J. (1987). *Communication: Strategic action in context*. Hillsdale, NJ: Lawrence Erlbaum Associates, Publishers.

Hayakawa, S. I. (1939). *Language in thought and action*. New York: Harcourt, Brace & World, Inc.

Heath, D. H. (1965). *Explorations of maturity*. New York: Appleton-Century-Crofts.

Heider, F. (1958). *The psychology of interpersonal relations*. New York: John Wiley & Sons.

Heider, F. (1963). Perceiving the other person. In E. P. Hollander & R. G. Hunt (Eds.), *Current perspectives in social psychology* (pp. 311–324). New York: Oxford University Press.

Henley, N. M. (1977). *Body politics: Power, sex and nonverbal communication*. Englewood Cliffs, NJ: Prentice-Hall, Inc.

Hertzler, J. O. (1965). *A sociology of language*. New York: Random House.

Hess, E. (1975). *The tell-tale eye*. New York: Van Nostrand Reinhold.

Higgins, E. T., and Bargh, J. A. (1987). Social cognition and social perception. In M. R. Rosenzweig & L. W. Porter (Eds.), *Annual review of psychology, 38* (pp. 369–425). Palo Alto, CA: Annual Reviews Inc.

Hirsch, E. D., Jr. (1988). *Cultural literacy: What every American needs to know*. New York: Vintage Books.

Hocker, J. L., and Wilmot, W. W. (1985). *Interpersonal conflict* (2nd ed.). Dubuque, IA: Wm. C. Brown Publishers.

Hofstede, G. (1980). *Culture's consequences: International differences in work-related values*. Beverly Hills, CA: Sage Publications.

Hofstede, G. (1984). *Culture's consequences: International differences in work-related values* (Abridged ed.). Beverly Hills, CA: Sage Publications.

Hofstede, G., and Bond, M. H. (1984, December). Hofstede's culture dimensions: An independent validation using Rokeach's value survey. *Journal of Cross-Cultural Psychology, 15*, 417–433.

Hoijer, H. (1954). The Sapir-Whorf hypothesis. In H. Hoijer (Ed.), *Language in culture* (pp. 92–105). Chicago: The University of Chicago Press.

Holloman, R. (1982). Conclusion. In C. A. Loveland & F. O. Loveland (Eds.), *Sex roles and social change in native lower Central American societies* (pp. 166–173). Urbana, IL: University of Illinois Press.

Hopson, J. (1979). *Scent signals*. New York: William Morrow and Co., Inc.

Ishii, S., and Bruneau, T. (1988). Silence and silences in cross-cultural perspective: Japan and the United States. In L. A. Samovar & R. E. Porter (Eds.), *Intercultural communication: A reader* (5th ed.) (pp. 310–315). Belmont, CA: Wadsworth Publishing Co.

Jacobs, S. (1985). Language. In M. L. Knapp & G. R. Miller (Eds.), *Handbook of interpersonal communication* (pp. 313–343). Beverly Hills, CA: Sage Publications.

Jensen, J. V. (1973, Sept.). Communicative functions of silence. *ETC: A Review of General Semantics, 30*, 249–257.

Johnson, W. (1946). *People in Quandaries: The semantics of personal adjustment*. New York: Harper & Brothers Publishers.

Jones, S. (1979). Integrating etic and emic approaches in the study of intercultural communication. In M. Asante, E. Newmark, & C. Blake (Eds.), *Handbook of intercultural communication* (pp. 57–74). Beverly Hills, CA: Sage Publications, Inc.

Kash, M. M., and Borich, G. D. (1978). *Teacher behavior and pupil self-concept.* Reading, MA: Addison-Wesley Publishing Co.

Kelly, G. A. (1963). *A theory of personality: The psychology of personal constructs.* New York: W. W. Norton & Co., Inc.

Kelly, G. A. (1970). A brief introduction to personal construct theory. In D. Bannister (Ed.), *Perspectives in personal construct theory* (pp. 1–29). New York: Academic Press.

Kim, H. S. (1986). Coorientation and communication. In B. Dervin & M. J. Voigt (Eds.), *Progress in communication sciences, 7* (pp. 31–54). Norwood, NJ: ABLEX Publishing Corporation.

Kim, Y. Y. (1979). Toward an interactive theory of communication-acculturation. In Nimmo, D. (Ed.), *Communication yearbook 3* (pp. 435–453). Austin, TX: International Communication Association.

Kim, Y. Y., and Gudykunst, W. B. (1987). *Cross-cultural adaption: Current approaches.* Newbury Park, CA: Sage Publications.

King, A. (1987). *Power and communication.* Prospect Heights, IL: Waveland Press, Inc.

Knapp, M., Hart, R., Friedrich, G., and Schulman, G. (1973). The rhetoric of goodbye: Verbal and nonverbal correlates of human leave-taking. *Speech Monographs, 40,* 182–198.

Kohls, L. R. (1979). *Survival kit for overseas living.* Chicago: Intercultural Press, Inc.

Korten, F. F. (1976). The influence of culture on the perception of persons. In L. A. Samovar & R. E. Porter (Eds.), *Intercultural communication: A reader* (2nd ed.) (pp. 124–134). Belmont, CA: Wadsworth Publishing Company, Inc.

Korzybski, A. (1948). *Selections from science and sanity.* Lakeville, CT: Institute of General Semantics.

Krivonos, P., and Knapp, M. (1975). Initiating communication: What do you say when you say hello? *Central States Speech Journal, 26,* 115–125.

Kroeber, A. L., and Kluckhohn, C. (1952). Culture: A critical review of concepts and definitions, *Harvard University papers of the Peabody Museum of American Archaeology and Ethnology, 47.*

LaFeber, W. (1983). *Inevitable revolutions.* New York: W. W. Norton & Co.

Laing, R. D., Phillipson, H., and Lee, A. R. (1966). *Interpersonal perception.* New York: Springer Publishing Co.

Landar, H. (1966). *Language and culture.* New York: Oxford University Press.

Lande, N. (1976). *Mindstyles/lifestyles.* Los Angeles: Price/Stern/Sloan Publishers, Inc.

Lanier, A. R. (1968, January). Women in the rural areas. In A. K. Hottel (Ed.), Women around the world (special issue). *The Annals of the American Academy of Political and Social Science, 375,* 115–123.

Lee, Y., and Larwood, L. (1983). The socialization of expatriate managers in multinational firms. *Academy of Management Journal, 26,* 657–665.

Lefcourt, H. M. (1976). *Locus of control: Current trends in theory and research.* Hillsdale, NJ: Lawrence Erlbaum Associates, Publishers.

Levine, D. R., Baxter, J., and McNulty, P. (1987). *The culture puzzle: Cross-cultural communication for English as a second language.* Englewood Cliffs, NJ: Prentice-Hall, Inc.

Lewis, O. (1961). *The children of Sanchez.* New York: Vintage Books.

Lidz, T. (1976). *The person* (rev. ed.). New York: Basic Books, Inc., Publishers.

Littlejohn, S. W. (1983). *Theories of human communication* (2nd ed.). Belmont, CA: Wadsworth Publishing Co.

Lustig, M. W. (1988). Value differences in intercultural communication. In L. A. Samovar

& R. E. Porter (Eds.), *Intercultural communication: A reader* (5th ed.) (pp. 55–61). Belmont, CA: Wadsworth Publishing Company.

Maines, D. R. (1984). Suggestions for a symbolic interactionist conception of culture. *Communication and Cognition, 17*, 205–217.

Malandro, L., and Barker, L. (1983). *Nonverbal communication.* Reading, MA: Addison-Wesley Publishing Co.

Markus, H., and Wurf, E. (1987). The dynamic self-concept: A social psychological perspective. In M. R. Rosenzweig & L. W. Porter (Eds.), *Annual review of psychology, 38*, (pp. 299–337). Palo Alto, CA: Annual Reviews Inc.

Maslow, A. H. (1970). *Motivation and personality* (rev. ed.). New York: Harper & Row, Publishers.

May, R. (1969). *Love and will.* New York: W. W. Norton & Company, Inc.

May, R. (1972). *Power and innocence* (A Delta Book). New York: Dell Publishing Co., Inc.

McCall, G. J. (1987). The self-concept and interpersonal communication. In M. E. Roloff & G. R. Miller (Eds.), *Interpersonal processes: New directions in communication research* (pp. 63–76). Beverly Hills, CA: Sage Publications.

Mehrabian, A. (1971). *Silent messages.* Belmont, CA: Wadsworth Publishing Co., Inc.

Miller, J. G. (1978). *Living systems.* New York: McGraw-Hill Book Co.

Mitchell, A. (1984, August). Nine American lifestyles. *The Futurist*, 4–14.

Morris, D., Collett, P., Marsh, P., and O'Shaughnessy, M. (1979). *Gestures.* New York: Stein and Day, Publishers.

Motley, M. T. (1986). Consciousness and intentionality in communication: A preliminary model and methodological approaches. *Western Journal of Speech Communication, 50*, 3–23.

Motley, M. T., and Borden, G. A. (1974, November). Cloze procedure: What does it really mean? Paper presented at the Speech Communication Conference, San Francisco, CA.

Motley, M. T., and Camden, C. T. (1988). Facial expression of emotion: A comparison of intentional and unintentional displays. Unpublished paper. Dept. of Rhetoric and Communication, The University of California at Davis.

National data book and guide to sources. *Statistical abstract of the United States 1987* (107th ed.). Washington, DC: U.S. Department of Commerce, Bureau of the Census.

Newmark, E., and Asante, M. K. (1974). Perception of self and others: An approach to intercultural communication. In F. L. Casmir (Ed.), *The international and intercultural communication annual, II* (pp. 54–61). Falls Church, VA: Speech Communication Association.

Norton, R. (1983). *Communicator style.* Beverly Hills, CA: Sage Publications.

Oden, G. C. (1987). Concept, knowledge, and thought. In M. R. Rosenzweig & L. W. Porter (Eds.), *Annual review of psychology, 38* (pp. 203–227). Palo Alto, CA: Annual Reviews Inc.

Osgood, C. E., May, W. H., and Miron, M. S. (1975). *Cross-cultural universals of affective meaning.* Urbana, IL: University of Illinois Press.

Osgood, C. E., Suci, G. J., and Tannenbaum, P. H. (1957). *The measurement of meaning.* Urbana, IL: University of Illinois Press.

Parsons, T. (1951). *The social system.* Glencoe, IL: Free Press.

Parsons, T., and Shils, E. (Eds.). (1951). *Toward a general theory of action.* Cambridge, MA: Harvard University Press.

Pearce, W. B., and Cronen, V. E. (1980). *Communication, action, and meaning.* New York: Praeger.

Pike, Kenneth L. (1966). Etic and emic standpoints for the description of behavior. In A. G. Smith (Ed.), *Communication and culture* (pp. 152–163). New York: Holt, Rinehart and Winston.

Polanyi, M. (1969). *Knowing and being: Essays by Michael Polanyi* (M. Grene, Ed.). Chicago: University of Chicago Press.

Quinn, N., and Holland, D. (1987). Culture and cognition. In D. Holland & N. Quinn (Eds.), *Cultural models in language and thought* (pp. 3–40). New York: Cambridge University Press.

Rapoport, A. (1982). *The meaning of the built environment.* Beverly Hills, CA: Sage Publications.

Reardon, R. (1981). *Persuasion: Theory and context.* Beverly Hills, CA: Sage Publications.

Riesman, D. (1961). *The lonely crowd* (abridged ed.). New Haven, CT: Yale University Press.

Rogers, C. R. (1971). Toward a modern approach to values: The valuing process in the mature person. In C. R. Rogers & B. Stevens (Eds.), *Person to person: The problem of being human* (pp. 4–21). New York: Pocket Books.

Rokeach, M. (1960). *The open and closed mind.* New York: Basic Books.

Rokeach, M. (1968). *Beliefs, attitudes and values.* San Francisco: Jossey-Bass Inc., Publishers.

Rokeach, M. (1973). *The nature of human values.* New York: The Free Press.

Rokeach, M. (1979). Value theory and communication research: Review and commentary. In D. Nimmo (Ed.), *Communication yearbook 3* (pp. 7–28). New Brunswick, NJ: Transaction Books for the Intercultural Communication Association.

Roloff, M. E. (1987). Communication and conflict. In C. R. Berger & S. H. Chaffee (Eds.), *Handbook of communication science* (pp. 484–534). Beverly Hills, CA: Sage Publications.

Rosengren, K. E., (1986). Media linkages between culture and other societal systems. In M. L. McLaughlin (Ed.), *Communication yearbook 9* (pp. 19–56). Beverly Hills, CA: Sage Publications.

Ruhly, S. (1976). The major triad revisited: A potential guide for intercultural research. In F. L. Casmir (Ed.), *The international and intercultural communication annual, 3*, 11–19.

Sapir, E. (1921). *Language.* New York: Harcourt, Brace & World, Inc.

Saral, T. B. (1979). The consciousness theory of intercultural communication. In M. K. Asante, E. Newmark, & C. A. Blake (Eds.), *Handbook of intercultural communication* (pp. 77–84). Beverly Hills, CA: Sage Publications.

Schmidt, C. F. (1976). Understanding human action: Recognizing the plans and motives of other persons. In J. S. Carroll & J. W. Payne (Eds.), *Cognition and social behavior* (pp. 47–67). Hillsdale, NJ: Lawrence Erlbaum Associates, Publishers.

Schrodinger, E. (1968). Order, disorder, and entropy. In W. Buckley (Ed.), *Modern systems research for the behavioral scientist* (pp. 143–146). Chicago: Aldine.

Scott, W. A., Osgood, D. W., and Peterson, C. (1979). *Cognitive structure: Theory and measurement of individual differences.* New York: Wiley.

Segall, M. H. (1986). Culture and behavior: Psychology in global perspective. In M. R. Rosenzweig & L. W. Porter (Eds.), *Annual review of psychology, 37*, (pp. 523–564). Palo Alto, CA: Annual Reviews Inc.

Shannon C. E., and Weaver, W. (1949). *The mathematical theory of communication.* Urbana, IL: University of Illinois Press.

Shimanoff, S. (1980). *Communication rules: Theory and research.* Beverly Hills, CA: Sage Publications.

Singer, M. R. (1987). *Intercultural communication: A perceptual approach.* Englewood Cliffs, NJ: Prentice-Hall, Inc.

Sitaram, K. S., and Haapanen, L. W. (1979). The role of values in intercultural communication. In M. K. Asante, E. Newmark, & C. A. Blake (Eds.), *Handbook of intercultural communication* (pp. 147–160). Beverly Hills, CA: Sage Publications.

Smith, A. G. (1979). Taxonomies for planning intercultural communication. In N. C. Jain (Ed.), *International and intercultural communication annual, 5,* 1–10.

Smith, E. C., and Luce, L. F. (1979). *Toward internationalism.* Rowley, MA: Newbury House Publishers, Inc.

Stewart, E. C. (1972). *American cultural patterns: A cross-cultural perspective.* Yarmouth, ME: Intercultural Press.

Stouffer, S., and Toby, J. (1951). Role conflict and personality. *The American Journal of Sociology, 56,* 395–406.

Sunday News Journal. (July 18, 1982, p. A5). Wilmington, DE.

Tetlock, P. E. (1983). Cognitive style and political ideology. *Journal of Personality and Social Psychology, 45,* 118–126.

Tetlock, P. E. (1984). Cognitive style and political belief systems in the British House of Commons. *Journal of Personality and Social Psychology, 46,* 365–375.

Triandis, H. C. (1972). *The analysis of subjective culture.* New York: John Wiley & Sons, Inc.

Triandis, H. C. (1974). Subjective culture and interpersonal communication and action. In F. L. Casmir (Ed.), *International and Intercultural Communication Annual, 1,* 17–23.

Triandis, H. C., and Albert, R. D. (1987). Cross-cultural perspectives. In F. M. Jablin, L. L. Putnam, K. H. Roberts, & L. W. Porter (Eds.), *Handbook of organizational communication* (pp. 264–295). Beverly Hills, CA: Sage Publications.

Tyler, L. E. (1978). *Individuality.* San Francisco: Jossey-Bass Publishers.

van Dijk, T. A. (1986). When majorities talk about minorities. In M. L. McLaughlin (Ed.), *Communication yearbook 9* (pp. 57–82). Beverly Hills, CA: Sage Publications.

von Bertalanffy, L. (1968). *General systems theory* (rev. ed.). New York: George Braziller.

Vygotsky, L. S. (1962). *Thought and language.* E. Honfmann & G. Vakar (Eds. & Trans.). Cambridge, MA: The MIT Press.

Wagner, R. (1981). *The invention of culture.* Chicago: University of Chicago Press.

Wedge, B. (1972). Nationality and social perception. In L. A. Samovar & R. E. Porter (Eds.), *Intercultural communication: A reader* (pp. 69–75). Belmont, CA: Wadsworth Publishing Company, Inc.

Weinberg, H. L. (1959). *Levels of knowing and existence.* New York: Harper & Brothers Publishers.

Whorf, B. J. (1956a). The relation of habitual thought and behavior to language. In J. B. Carroll (Ed.), *Language, thought and reality: Selected writings of Benjamin Lee Whorf* (pp. 134–159). New York: John Wiley & Sons, Inc. and the MIT Press.

Whorf, B. J. (1956b). Science and linguistics. In J. B. Carroll (Ed.), *Language, thought and reality: Selected writings of Benjamin Lee Whorf* (pp. 207–219). New York: John Wiley & Sons, Inc. and the MIT Press.

Wiemann, J., and Knapp, M. (1975) Turn-taking in conversations. *Journal of Communication, 25,* 75–92.

Wiener, N. (1961). *Cybernetics.* Cambridge, MA: The MIT Press.

Williams, J. E., and Best, D. L. (1982). *Measuring sex stereotypes: A thirty-nation study.* Beverly Hills, CA: Sage Publications.

Wilson, E. O. (1975). *Sociobiology: The new synthesis*. Cambridge, MA: Harvard University Press.

Wiseman, R. L., and Abe, H. (1986). Cognitive complexity and intercultural effectiveness: Perceptions in American-Japanese dyads. In M. L. McLaughlin (Ed.), *Communication yearbook 9* (pp. 611–622). Beverly Hills, CA: Sage Publications.

Zurcher, L. (1968). Particularism and organizational position: A cross-cultural analysis. *Journal of Applied Psychology, 52*, 139–144.

Author Index

Adler and Jelinek, 84
Ajzen and Fishbein, 55
Anderson, Lustig, and Andersen, 173
Asimov, 196
Atwood, 206

Barnlund, 217
Bem, 40, 69, 96, 98, 159
Berger, 125
Berger and Bradac, 125–127
Bernard, 151
Berne, 148
Bernstein, 176
Biesanz, Biesanz, and Biesanz, 95
Birdwhistell, 174
Bitzer, 39
Bochner, 48
Borden, 2, 5, 6, 32, 51, 61, 91, 92, 101, 102,
    149, 150, 160, 163
Borden and Stone, 135
Borden and Tanner, 108
Boski, 63
Buck, 36
Bugental, 135
Burgoon and Saine, 32, 34
Burgoon and Hale, 174
Buriel, 74
Burk, 200, 203
Burleson, 59, 71
Burleson and Waltman, 68

Carroll, 203
Casse, 186
Chaiken and Stangor, 55
Chomsky, 160, 173

Christie and Geis, 51
Collier, 214
Copeland and Griggs, 185
Cushman, Valentinsen and Dietrich, 207

D'Andrade, 181
Datan, Rodeheaver and Hughes, 157
Deal and Kennedy, 113
Deese, 173
Delia, O'Keefe and O'Keefe, 66, 208
Diez, 215
Dizard, 134
Downs, xiii
Duncan, 176
Durbin, 92

Eco, 64
Ehrenhaus, 63
Ekman and Friesen, 30

Fairhurst, 152
Farb, 80
Fast, 36
Faules & Alexander, 182
Festinger, 74
Foglesang, 177
Frake, 93
Frankl, 44, 120, 121
Furnham and Bochner, 186
Furth, 157

Geertz, 81, 82
Gilligan, 92
Glenn, 54, 84–93, 157, 158, 163–168, 192
Goldstein and Blackman, 68–73

Gudykunst, Chua and Gray, 220

Hall, E. T., 32, 175, 183, 195
Hall, E. P., xiv
Hamilton, 53
Harari, Jones, and Sek, 136
Harris, 78, 79, 81, 208
Harris and Moran, 47, 103
Hart, 220
Haslett, 10
Hayakawa, 194
Heath, 125, 138
Heider, 74
Henley, 33, 113
Hertzler, 182
Hess, 30
Higgins and Bargh, 62, 63
Hirsch, 179, 180
Hocker and Wilmot, 111
Hofstede, 68, 81, 104–106, 109, 110, 112–
      117, 121, 122, 128, 129, 133, 136, 138–
      140, 144, 152, 153, 157, 220
Hofstede and Bond, 104
Hoijer, 202
Holloman, 151
Hopson, 33

Ishii and Bruneau, 35

Jacobs, 173
Jensen, 35
Johnson, 194
Jones, xiv

Kash and Borich, 11
Kelly, 40, 66, 67, 74, 78, 126, 157, 186, 204,
      205, 208
Kim, H., 61
Kim, Y., 186
Kim and Gudykunst, 186
King, 113
Knapp, Hart, Friedrich and Schulman, 58
Kohls, 186
Korten, 62
Korzybski, 161
Krivonos and Knapp, 57
Kroeber and Kluckhohn, 171

LaFeber, 60, 83, 112
Laing, Phillipson and Lee, 59, 60
Landar, 201
Lande, 138
Lanier, 152
Lee and Larwood, 61
Lefcourt, 45, 137
Levine, Baxter and McNulty, 187
Lewis, 137
Lidz, 135
Littlejohn, 205
Lustig, 101

Maines, 182
Malandro and Barker, 31
Markus and Wurf, 122
Maslow, 41, 121
May, 114, 136
McCall, 122
Mehrabian, 26
Miller, 4
Mitchell, 139
Morris, Collett, Marsh and O'Shaugh-
      nessy, 31
Motley, 7
Motley and Borden, 173
Motley and Camden, 30

Newmark and Asante, 61
Norton, 216–219

Oden, 58
Osgood, May and Miron, 25, 74, 98, 147,
      205
Osgood, Suci and Tannenbaum, 25, 74, 75,
      98, 160, 205

Parsons and Shils, 92
Pearce and Cronen, 10
Pike, xiv
Polanyi, 180

Quinn and Holland, 180

Rapoport, 28
Reardon, 46
Riesman, 112, 134
Rogers, 45, 124, 138

Rokeach, 40, 70, 98–104, 133, 159
Roloff, 111
Rosengren, 171, 177
Ruhly, 196

Sapir, 200, 201
Saral, 59
Schmidt, 54
Schrodinger, 4
Scott, Osgood and Peterson, 66, 75
Segall, 220
Shannon and Weaver, 4
Shimanoff, 46
Singer, 52, 204
Sitaram and Haapanen, 102
Smith, xiv, 83
Smith and Luce, 103
Stewart, 103
Stouffer and Toby, 92

Tetlock, 70
Triandis, 204
Triandis and Albert, 171
Tyler, 135

van Dijk, 110
von Bertalanffy, 10
Vygotsky, 203

Wagner, 93, 172
Wedge, 63
Weinberg, 194
Whorf, 201, 202
Wiemann and Knapp, 57
Wiener, 10
Williams and Best, 47, 145–148
Wiseman and Abe, 59, 84, 215

Zurcher, 92

Subject Index

Abstract, 43, 62, 72, 105, 130, 163, 166, 177, 199

Abstracting, 20, 23, 25, 43, 62, 72, 89, 91, 98, 126, 156–157, 160–168, 189, 192–194, 212–213
   differentiation, 53, 64, 72–76, 80, 82–85, 88, 106, 127, 143–145, 149, 158–159, 161, 168, 189
   integration, 14, 43, 72–74, 76, 88–90, 125

Abstractive, 69, 94, 99, 105, 112, 117, 130, 138, 140, 154, 156, 158, 162, 166–168, 175, 215
   learning, 89–90, 166, 192, 216
   thinking, 62, 66–67, 72, 86, 88–91, 164, 166, 215

Acculturation, 186–187, 189–190, 192–194, 197, 211

Associative, 62, 88–91, 94, 99, 117, 130, 156–157, 159, 162, 166–168, 174, 189, 191–192, 197, 215
   learning, 66, 89, 160–166, 187, 190
   processes, 51, 53, 62, 66, 75, 166, 189, 193

Attribution Theory, 205–206

Behavioral uncertainty, 125

Behaviorist theory, 6, 79, 110, 171–172

Belief systems, 1, 55, 68, 70, 74, 78, 94–95, 97, 100, 102, 104, 109, 113, 133, 143, 151, 157, 168, 171–172, 200, 213, 219
   attitudinal frame of reference, 40, 42, 47, 68, 99, 125, 135, 159, 193
   disbelief, 55, 70, 74, 101
   first-order, 97, 159
   higher-order, 98, 159
   instrumental values, 100–101

   non-conscious ideologies, 39–40, 47, 144, 159
   primitive, 97, 107, 158
   terminal values, 100–101
   zero-order, 97, 159

Bicultural, 189, 194, 212, 215

Bilingual, 189, 215

Central America, 3, 26, 60, 111

Classification systems, 82

Closed-minded, 63, 66, 70, 87–88, 91, 99, 117, 130, 140, 154

Co-subjectivity dimension, 165–168, 192–193, 211

Cognition, 55, 66, 68–69, 71, 74, 80, 84–85, 111, 117, 127, 157, 211

Cognitive, 10, 51, 54, 81, 84, 99, 125, 139, 146, 168, 172, 192
   behaviors, 36, 85
   constructs, 43, 85, 157, 194, 199–200, 204–205
   content, 66, 74, 172
   energy, 1, 7, 9
   orientation, 66, 85
   processes, 3, 51, 53, 55, 63, 65–66, 74, 85–86, 157–158, 163, 192, 199, 201, 213
   products, 85
   stability, 68
   structure, 6, 8–9, 19, 41–42, 44–45, 51, 58, 62, 64–65, 67–70, 74–76, 83, 85, 93, 125–127, 157–159, 163, 166–167, 173–174, 187, 192, 194, 199, 203, 205
   uncertainty, 125

Cognitive styles, 68–74, 76, 83, 85–88, 94, 211–213, 215, 219

Cognitive styles (cont'd.)
  authoritarianism, 69, 73–76, 87
  cognitive complexity, 71, 73, 76, 93
  dogmatism, 70, 73, 76, 122, 129
  field dependence/independence, 73, 76
  integrative complexity, 72, 76
Cognitively complex persons, 84, 215
Communication (defined), 1–3, 6–7, 10
  as effect, 1,3
  as function, 1, 3, 7
  as process, 1–3
  competence, 24, 42, 127, 154, 164–165, 215
  information gathering (perception), 8,
    19, 37, 41, 211
  information dissemination (expressive
    behavior), 8, 36, 211
  intention, 7–9, 15, 19, 28, 36–37, 48–49,
    81, 208, 211, 213
Communication process, 1, 19, 28, 39, 54,
    158, 204, 206, 211, 221
  codes, 2, 7, 16–19, 21, 27–30, 33, 36, 51,
    56–57, 62, 82, 127, 163, 171–176, 189,
    194, 202–203, 213–215
  communicatee, 2, 7–8, 19, 26, 30, 34, 53,
    98, 162, 175, 179–180, 205, 209, 211,
    213–214, 216, 219
  communicator, 2, 7–8, 19, 36, 39, 41, 45,
    48, 52, 54, 58–60, 64, 84, 86, 94, 176,
    180, 194, 199, 205, 211, 213–218
  communiqué, 2, 8, 15, 20, 22, 30, 199,
    216–217
  decoding, 2, 7, 9, 17, 21, 25, 27, 41, 64, 82,
    171, 173–174, 199, 204, 213, 216
  encoding, 2, 7, 9, 17, 23–27, 62, 81, 171,
    173–177, 186, 199, 202, 204, 213
  meaning, 2, 8, 18, 19–21, 23–28, 61, 74,
    81–82, 86, 98, 125, 127, 147–148, 160–
    161, 164, 172–173, 176, 180, 182–183,
    188, 192, 199, 205, 208, 213–214, 216,
    217–218
  message, 2, 7, 9, 17–19, 21, 25, 27, 30, 34,
    59–60, 81–82, 172–177, 179, 199, 202,
    204, 206, 213, 216–218, 220
  modes, 18–19, 82, 171, 215
  noise, 2, 15, 35–36, 49, 73, 93, 106, 177,
    197, 211
  sign, 6, 20, 31, 149, 189
  signal, 2, 7, 9, 17–22, 27–31, 34, 36, 41, 49,
    56–58, 81, 94, 125, 173–177, 199, 202,

204, 212–214, 216, 218
  symbol, 6–7, 20–21, 24, 30, 71, 73, 165,
    173, 175–177, 179, 182–183, 212
Communication strategies, 14, 36, 45, 69,
    78, 83, 214, 219
  first impressions, 55
  greetings, 18, 32, 36, 57
  initiating, 57, 115, 210
  relating, 32, 56
  self-presentation, 55
  terminating, 57
Communication styles, 57, 216, 219
  attentive, 218–219
  dramatic, 217–218
  open, 216
Communicative behavior, 41–44, 46–47,
    54, 82, 103, 107, 127, 148–149, 151,
    173, 177, 182, 198, 201, 209, 214,
    217–218
Conflict management, 111, 220
Constructive alternativism, 67
Constructivist theory, 66
Contexting, 175, 180, 183, 186, 212
  high-context, 175, 179, 181
  low-context, 175, 180, 209
Cost-benefit analysis, 79
Costa Rica, 1, 3, 11, 18, 21, 24, 31, 34, 47,
    50–51, 59–61, 65, 82, 91–92, 94–96,
    101–102, 105, 108, 112, 114–115, 119,
    122–123, 132, 144, 170, 177, 179, 181,
    185, 189–190, 192, 196, 198, 206–207
Creating culture, 199, 203
Cultural
  complexity, 81, 93
  constructs, 103, 127, 197, 199–200, 204,
    206–209, 213, 220
  development, 80
  inequalities, 104, 106, 110
  literacy, 99, 167–170, 179, 183, 199, 212,
    214
  models, 84, 181
  orientation, 3, 54, 59, 61, 78, 83–88, 90,
    93, 117, 130, 145, 152, 154, 157, 164,
    168, 174, 183, 193, 197, 204, 209, 211,
    213, 220
  symbols, 176, 183
Cultural orientation model, 54, 84, 91, 93,
    107, 140, 154, 164, 172, 175, 208–
    209, 213, 219

Cultural orientation model (cont'd.)
  associative/abstractive dimension, 86–
    91, 93, 130, 162, 164, 167, 213
  open-minded/closed-minded dimension,
    84, 86–87, 91, 93, 197, 209, 213, 215
    (*also* broadening/narrowing, 87)
  particularism/universalism dimension,
    86, 90–91, 93, 168, 197, 208, 213
Culture, theories of
  cognitivists, 81, 171, 200
  cultural interpretation, 81
  cultural materialism, 78–79, 81, 172, 199
  evolutionary models, 80, 104, 117, 166,
    172, 199, 206
Culture shock, 47, 186

Decision-making, 10, 43, 73, 103, 110, 124,
  128, 133, 135–138, 140, 152, 164, 212,
  215–216, 220

El Salvador, 60, 68
Emic, 81, 127, 197
Enculturation, 45, 48, 99, 104, 156, 158–
  160, 163–166, 168, 183, 186, 192, 199,
  208, 211
Environment, 14, 28, 30, 51, 54, 56, 58–59,
  61–62, 68, 71–72, 80, 84–87, 97, 99,
  112, 117, 123, 127–128, 135, 139, 145,
  153, 158–159, 163–165, 167, 172–173,
  177, 182, 186, 199, 204, 212
Equality, 65, 92, 95, 100, 110–111, 114, 116,
  140, 145, 151, 153, 220
Ethics, 52, 101–103, 106, 123, 136, 217
Ethnocentrism, 6, 47, 54, 60, 63, 67, 69, 88,
  102–103, 122, 151, 159, 178
Etic, 79, 81, 89, 123, 127, 151, 171, 197, 211
Experiential knowledge, 55, 86, 89, 127,
  164–166

Freedom, 47, 67, 87, 93, 95, 99–100, 111, 114,
  116, 120, 133, 139–140, 145, 221
Friendship, 32, 43, 50–52, 74–75, 77, 91–92,
  100–101, 104, 120, 140, 149, 152, 167,
  181, 183, 205, 219

General semantics, 23, 36, 82, 93, 194, 220
General systems theory, 2–4
Germany, 105, 181

Group identity, 52
Guatemala, 60

Honduras, 60
Human communication, nature of, 2, 6
Human communication systems, 5–6, 17,
  39–40, 48, 64, 94, 125, 182–183, 212
  bonding, 4, 7–10, 15–17, 22, 34, 36, 76,
    78, 93, 111, 168, 204, 209, 219
  boundaries (constraints) 4, 40, 43, 45,
    48, 182, 211–212
  channels, 3, 17, 87, 195, 213
  cultural dimension, 41, 45, 186, 211, 214
  cybernetic, 4, 6, 10–11, 14, 36, 76, 94, 106,
    122, 124, 130, 136, 138, 163, 168, 186,
    211, 214, 220
  entropy, 4, 14, 36, 49, 93, 111, 113, 125,
    168, 209
  environment, 10, 28, 39–40, 43, 45, 212
  equifinality, 4
  feedback, 2–4, 7, 10, 12, 14, 22, 28, 218
  personal dimension, 40, 43, 45, 66, 211
  situational dimension, 41, 43, 211
  synergy, 4, 14–16, 21, 26, 36, 89, 111, 113,
    168, 209
  teleological behavior, 5, 40, 68, 78

Individualism/collectivism dimension,
  104–105, 132–134, 137–138, 220
  high IDU, 138–139
  low IDU, 138–139
Information management, 22
Information processing, 53, 66, 134

Language, 17, 20–26, 34, 36, 46, 64, 79, 82,
  111, 157, 160, 162, 165–166, 171–174,
  176, 187–189, 196, 200–203, 212
  competence, 173–175, 194, 212, 214
  first, 13, 89, 160–163, 187, 194–195
  grammar, 21, 160–161, 163, 188–190, 202
  performance, 173, 194
  second, 3, 13, 19, 21, 82, 180, 185, 187–
    188, 190, 195
  syntax, 22, 160–161, 163, 176, 188–190,
    202
  vocabulary, 21, 34, 82, 111, 160–161, 163,
    173, 176, 180, 185, 188–189, 201–202
  within a language, 26

Latin America, 3, 18, 26, 30, 32, 34, 74–75, 83, 90, 92, 96, 101, 120, 143, 149, 151, 159, 170, 196
Life styles, 15, 46, 138, 172, 220
Locus of control, 45, 124, 133, 136–139, 213, 221
Locus of evaluation, 45, 124, 133, 135, 138

Masculinity/femininity dimension, 104–105, 142–154, 213, 220
    androgynous, 143–144, 152
    gender, 106, 143, 146, 149, 188
    high mas, 152–153
    low mas, 152–153
    sex, 29, 53, 72, 79, 92, 104, 106, 143–146, 149, 151, 153
Media, 3, 14, 83, 121, 179
Mental processes, 41, 81
    models, 46, 58, 81
    programming, 47, 68, 86, 135, 157
Meta-communication, 28, 173, 216
Metaphors, 21, 24, 34, 177, 179, 183, 200, 218
Mexico, 25, 34, 82, 101, 105, 177
Myths, 44, 110, 177–178, 183

Nicaragua, 60, 112, 123, 151
Nonverbal behavior, 2, 7, 9, 18–19, 29, 32, 36, 46, 78, 149–150, 163, 165, 170, 175, 206, 217
    competence, 173–174
    inference, 28, 36, 48, 58
Nonverbal codes, 7, 17, 19, 28–29, 51, 56, 82, 127, 172–174, 189, 203, 213–214, 216
    acoustics, 34–35, 57
    artifacts, 28–29, 41, 54, 64, 177
    chromatics, 30, 56
    chronemics, 28, 33, 47, 56–57, 194
    facial expressing, 29, 32, 34–35, 56–57
    gustics, 28, 34, 56
    haptics, 32, 56–57, 174
    kinesics, 30–31, 35, 56–57, 163, 174
    oculemics, 30, 56–57, 163
    olfactics, 28, 33, 56
    personal appearance, 29, 56
    proxemics, 28, 32, 56–57, 163, 174
    silence, 35, 56–57
    vocalics, 34, 56–57

Norms, 3, 12, 14, 21, 32–33, 39, 41, 45–48, 55, 66, 78, 82, 84, 91–92, 96, 113, 115, 117, 121–122, 125, 136, 140, 151, 171, 174, 182, 200, 202, 212, 214–215

Objectivity dimension, 91–93, 91, 165, 167, 192, 194
Open-minded, 70, 84, 87–88, 117, 138, 192
Opinion molecules, 99

Panamá, 111, 125
Particularism, 90–93, 101, 117, 127, 140, 168, 174, 183, 215
Perceptual identity, 52
Personal Construct Theory, 40, 67, 70–71, 74, 78, 84, 124, 154, 168, 199, 208, 211–212
Personal orientations, 64–67, 69, 76, 183
    doables, 64, 106
Perspective taking, 58–60, 215, 220
Power, 112–114, 133, 145, 152
    authority, 30, 72, 97, 109, 113, 115, 117, 137, 149, 158
    dominance, 42, 43, 47, 54, 82, 113, 117, 119, 134, 140, 144, 146–149, 151, 158, 187, 190, 216
    status, 28, 32, 39, 41, 46, 69, 103–104, 110, 113, 117, 149, 153
Power distance dimension, 104, 107–109, 111–117, 122, 122, 133, 213, 220
    high PDI, 114–115
    low PDI, 114–115
Pseudo-objectivity dimension, 137
Psycho-logic, 98, 163, 168, 194, 205
Psychological constructs, 66–68, 85, 158, 164–165, 187, 192–193, 196, 211
Psychological set, 8, 23, 41–43, 216
Puerto Rico, 34, 142

Quasi-subjectivity dimension, 193

Regulative rules, 46, 192
Religion, 104, 119–121, 129, 134, 158
Restricted code/elaborated code, 176
Rituals, 18, 21, 36, 48, 56–57, 104, 122, 126, 130, 168, 212, 215
Rules Theory, 207

Sapir-Whorf Hypothesis, 200–202
Schemas, 8, 51, 53, 62–64, 72, 93, 98, 103, 120, 122, 125, 130, 135, 138, 149, 156–157, 159, 163, 167, 180–181, 183, 186–189, 192–193, 197, 212, 219
Self-concept, 12, 14–15, 73, 122, 124, 130, 136, 138, 140, 163, 168, 186, 211, 214, 220
  bodily self, 11, 56, 122
  self-esteem, 12–13, 56, 124
  self-extension, 12, 14, 123
  self-identity, 11–12, 14, 123
  self-image, 13, 124
Self-disclosure, 217
Semantic differential, 25, 205
Semantic space, 23–25, 74–75, 98, 160–163, 188, 190–191, 209, 212
Semantics, 24, 37, 189
Sex-role stereotypes, 143, 145, 151, 154, 213
Sex-trait stereotypes, 146–152, 154, 213, 221
Situational orientation, 39, 41, 43, 49–50, 59, 64, 88, 212
  exigences, 39, 42
Socio-logic, 163, 168
Spanish, 9, 21, 24, 27, 34, 39, 46, 108, 133, 159, 173, 176, 185, 188, 191, 195, 202
Stereotypes, 23, 29, 42, 52–53, 59, 63–64, 69, 75, 78, 82–83, 87, 91, 98, 111, 117, 125–126, 143, 146–148, 151, 156, 194, 214, 220
Subjective culture, 171–172, 181, 204–205, 207, 209

Subjectivity dimension, 91–92, 146, 165
Symbolic action theory, 182
Systems complexity, 5, 10, 15, 36, 94

Tacit knowledge, 125–126, 130, 164, 167, 180–181, 193, 211–213
Taxonomic systems, 82
Transactional analysis, 148

Uncertainty avoidance dimension, 104–105, 119–122, 130, 133, 213, 220
  high UAI, 128–130
  low UAI, 128–130
Uncertainty reduction, 105, 120, 125–127, 130, 144, 213
Universalism, 86, 90–94, 110, 117, 130, 138, 140, 154, 168, 175, 183, 215

Values, 40, 43–46, 61, 74, 79, 83, 95–96, 98–106, 111–112, 117, 121, 125, 128, 133, 145, 152–154, 158–159, 163, 165–166, 171, 188–189, 193, 196, 205, 212, 220
Value dimensions, 104–107, 113, 144, 213, 220
Value systems, 104, 112–113, 127, 138, 140, 145, 153–154, 168, 217
Verbal behavior, 23, 26–27, 46, 78, 163, 217
  competency, 173–174

Words, 19, 22–25, 64, 82, 161, 176, 180, 188–190, 196, 202